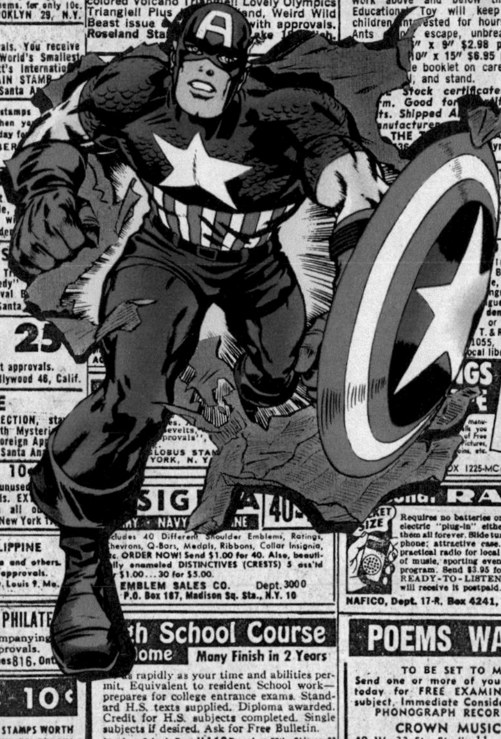

MARVEL

THE LITTLE BOOK OF

CAPTAIN AMERICA

Roy Thomas

TASCHEN

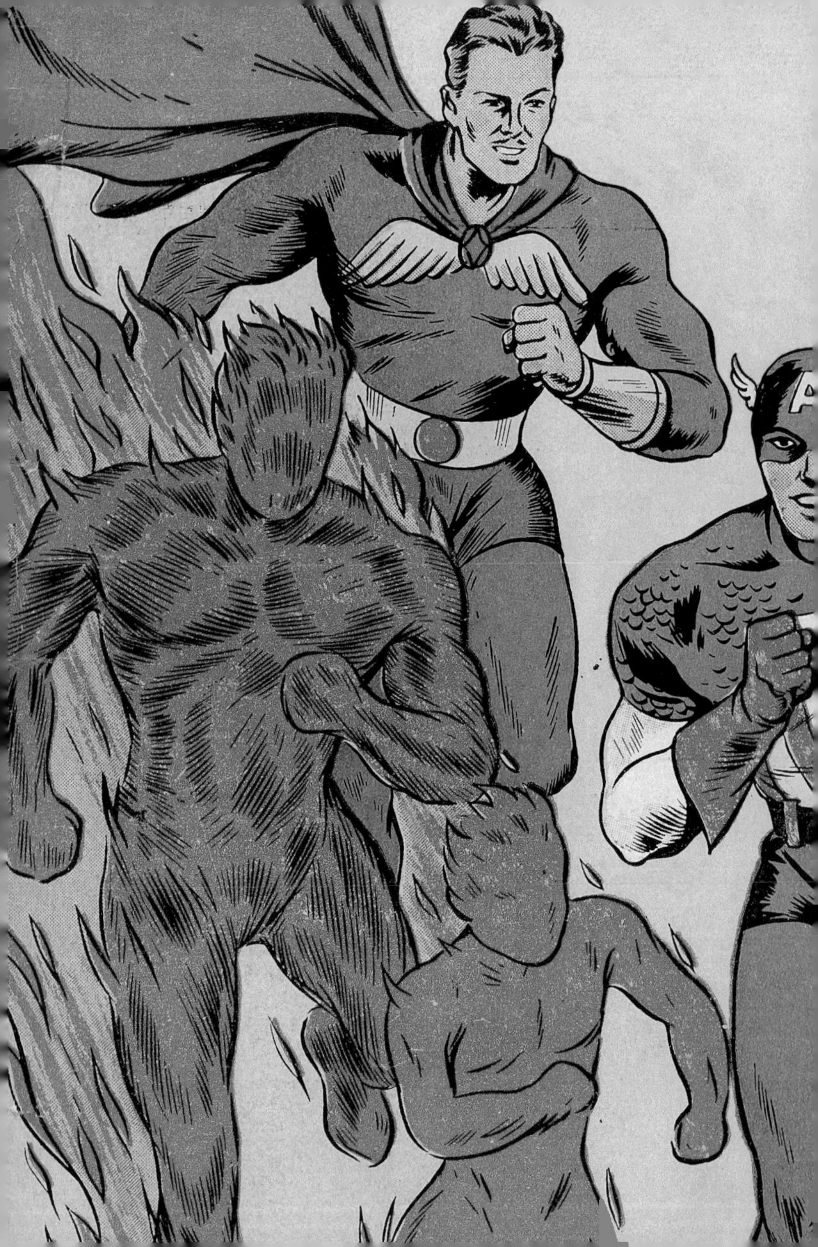

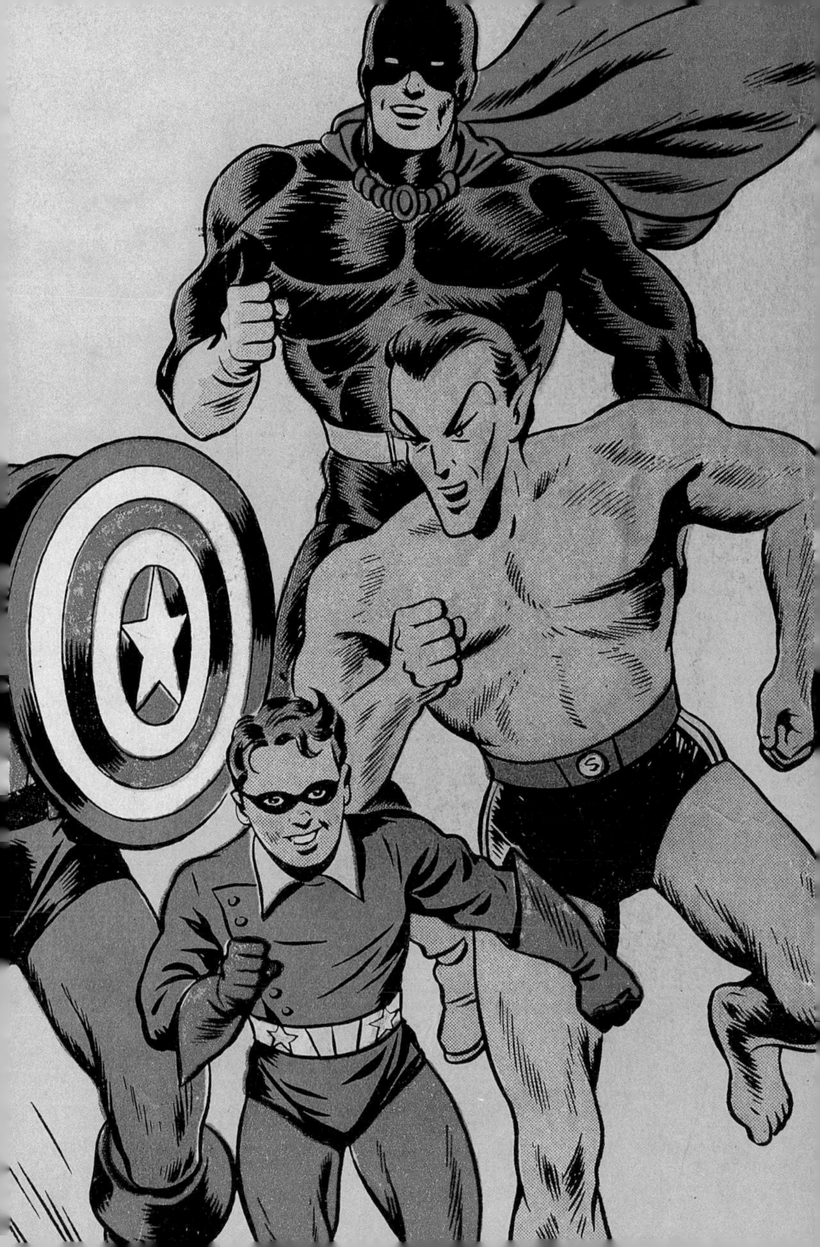

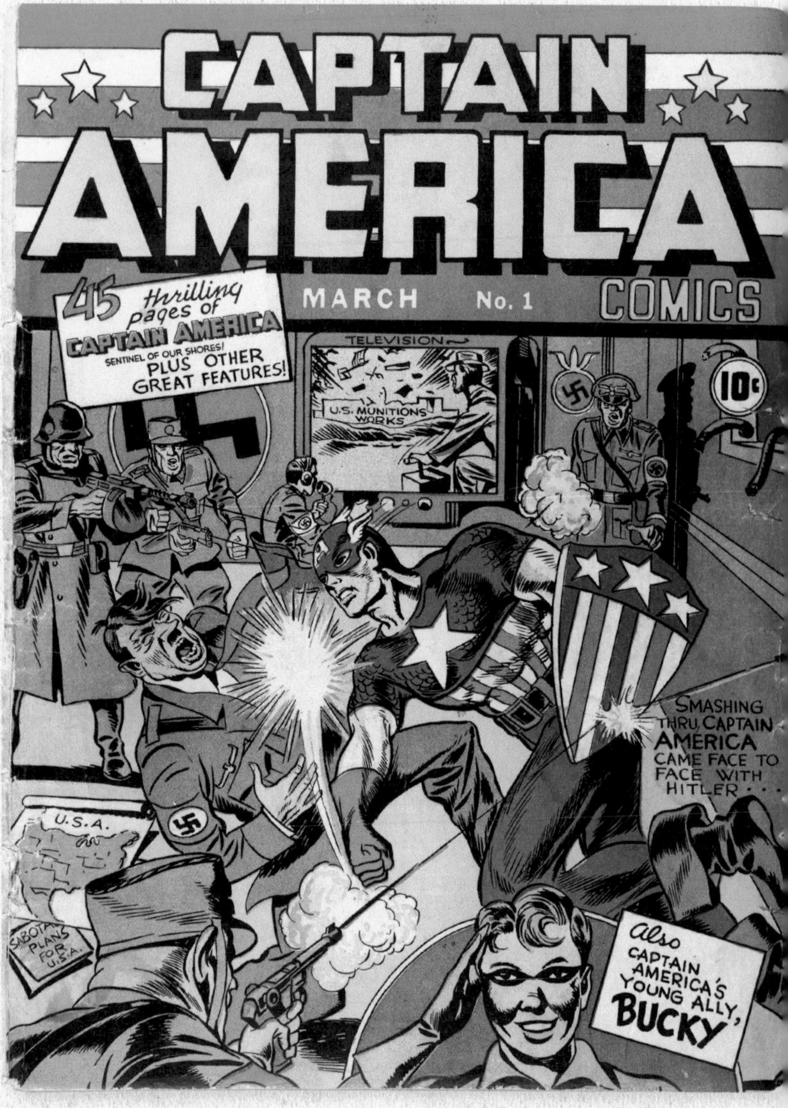
CAPTAIN AMERICA
COMICS
MARCH
No. 1
10¢
45 thrilling pages of CAPTAIN AMERICA
SENTINEL OF OUR SHORES!
PLUS OTHER GREAT FEATURES!
TELEVISION
U.S. MUNITIONS WORKS
SMASHING THRU, CAPTAIN AMERICA CAME FACE TO FACE WITH HITLER . . .
U.S.A.
SABOTAGE PLANS FOR U.S.A.
Also CAPTAIN AMERICA'S YOUNG ALLY, BUCKY

WHAT'S SO GREAT ABOUT CAPTAIN AMERICA?

Right from the start, everybody who encountered Captain America *knew* he was great. All they had to do was *look* at him. He was a walking, talking American flag!

The public's first glimpse of Timely/Marvel's fabled Sentinel of Liberty was the cover of *Captain America Comics* No. 1, on sale in late 1940. It was the product of two supremely talented artists/writers: Joe Simon and Jack Kirby.

Other super heroes of that day had made their debuts tossing automobiles around or swinging from rooftops or burning through steel doors.

Captain America? He slugged Adolf Hitler squarely in the jaw.

Nowadays, artwork like that might cause an international incident. After all, while Nazi Germany had conquered much of Europe in the past year, it wasn't officially at war with the United States. America was giving "all aid short of war" to Great Britain, but surely showing a red-white-and-blue-clad hero who bore his country's name striking the German head of state didn't just cross a line—it *obliterated* it.

From the outset, though, Captain America went his own way.

First, there was that punch, right in *Der Führer*'s face.

Then there was Kirby's artwork. As one comics historian put it, Kirby "brought anatomy to the comics." Captain America leaped

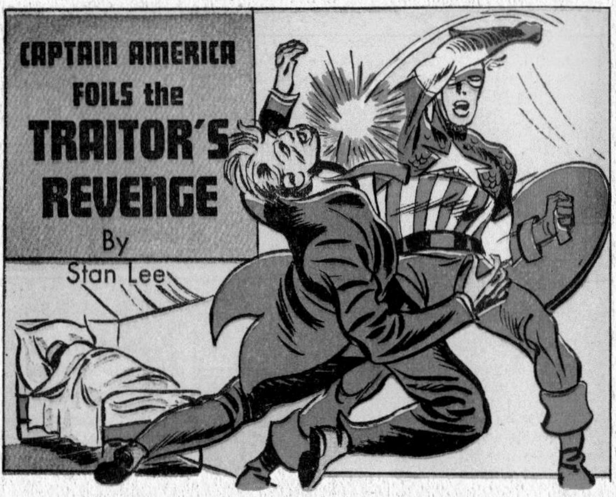
CAPTAIN AMERICA FOILS the TRAITOR'S REVENGE
By
Stan Lee

and smashed and ripped his way through any foe who stood in his path—even though he was, ostensibly, just a human being turned into an extreme athlete by a "super-soldier serum."

When Simon and Kirby were lured away to DC, so powerful was the legacy and look they had created for their star-spangled hero that, even under their former assistants, Cap stayed near the top of the super hero heap for the rest of the war. All the other American-flag-wearing comics characters seemed like pale imitations of him—even the one or two that had come out *before* him! In 1944 he even appeared in a Saturday matinee movie serial.

After the war, Cap's star—like those of other super heroes—faded. His alter ego, Steve Rogers, quit the army and became...a high school teacher. By 1949, he was gone. A mid-1950s attempt to revive him (along with Timely's Human Torch and Sub-Mariner) didn't last long.

Stan Lee's first assignment in comics had been to write a prose story about the hero in *Captain America Comics* No. 3—and the writer/editor who launched *Fantastic Four* and other Marvel titles in

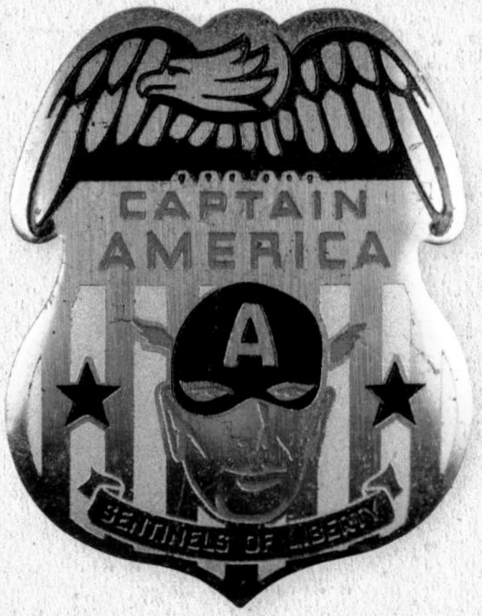
CAPTAIN
AMERICA
A
SENTINELS OF LIBERTY

the 1960s had a soft spot for the character. But how did you handle a hero forged in a World War II that had ended two decades before?

Lee—working with artist/co-plotter Kirby, who'd returned to the company in the late 1950s—reintroduced Cap in *The Avengers* No. 4. There, it was revealed that, near war's end, he'd been frozen in ice—his young sidekick Bucky presumably blown up. Thawed out, Cap found himself a man out of time—uncertain of his role in a world that had moved on. And that's how Marvel played him for the next several years, even in his new solo series.

He became the Avengers' leader, even though he was less powerful than some of its other members. In the 1970s he gained a new partner—the Falcon, the first African-American hero ever featured regularly in the title logo of a super hero comic. He battled a sinister organization called the Secret Empire, whose masked leader, the story's climax seemed to indicate, was none other than the then-President of the United States. Afterward, a disillusioned Cap temporarily discarded his patriotic garb and became the soul-searching Nomad.

CAPTAIN AMERICA COMICS No. 1

Page 6: *Cover; pencils, Jack Kirby; inks, Joe Simon; March 1941.* While it is now considered one of the most iconic covers of the Golden Age of comics, it inflamed tensions surrounding the war in Europe. According to Simon, protesters were "lining up at the building, raging…waving some signs…." The police arrived and Simon received a call from Mayor Fiorello LaGuardia. "You boys over there are doing a good job," he said. "The City of New York will see that no harm comes to you."

CAPTAIN AMERICA COMICS No. 3

Page 8: *Interior, "Captain America Foils the Traitor's Revenge"; script, Stan Lee; art, Jack Kirby; May 1941.* "Nobody read those stories. That's why they let me do one. But you couldn't call a comic a magazine and get the magazine postal rates unless you had two pages of type. One day I was hanging around filling inkwells and erasing pages for the guys, and someone said, 'Hey, Stan, we need a two-page story.' So I wrote one. And that was that." — Stan Lee

BADGE OF HONOR

Page 9: *Captain America fan club badge, 1941.* Members of the Sentinels of Liberty fan club could wear their pride on their sleeve (or, more appropriately, over their heart).

TALES OF SUSPENSE No. 94

Opposite: *Interior, "If This Be MODOK!"; script, Stan Lee; pencils, Jack Kirby; inks, Joe Sinnott; October 1967.* Kirby's explosive action takes center stage in this panel detail.

Eventually it was revealed that Bucky hadn't died at all in 1945, but had been captured and brainwashed into becoming the Winter Soldier—at first Cap's foe, later his friend. In 2007 Cap seemed to have been assassinated; but before long he was back in action. Though several people, over the years, wore the Captain America costume, including Bucky Barnes, there was never much doubt there was only one real Captain America—and his name was Steve Rogers.

There've been a lot of other patriotically garbed, inspiringly named heroes.

But none of those ever rivaled the greatness of Captain America!

— *ROY THOMAS*

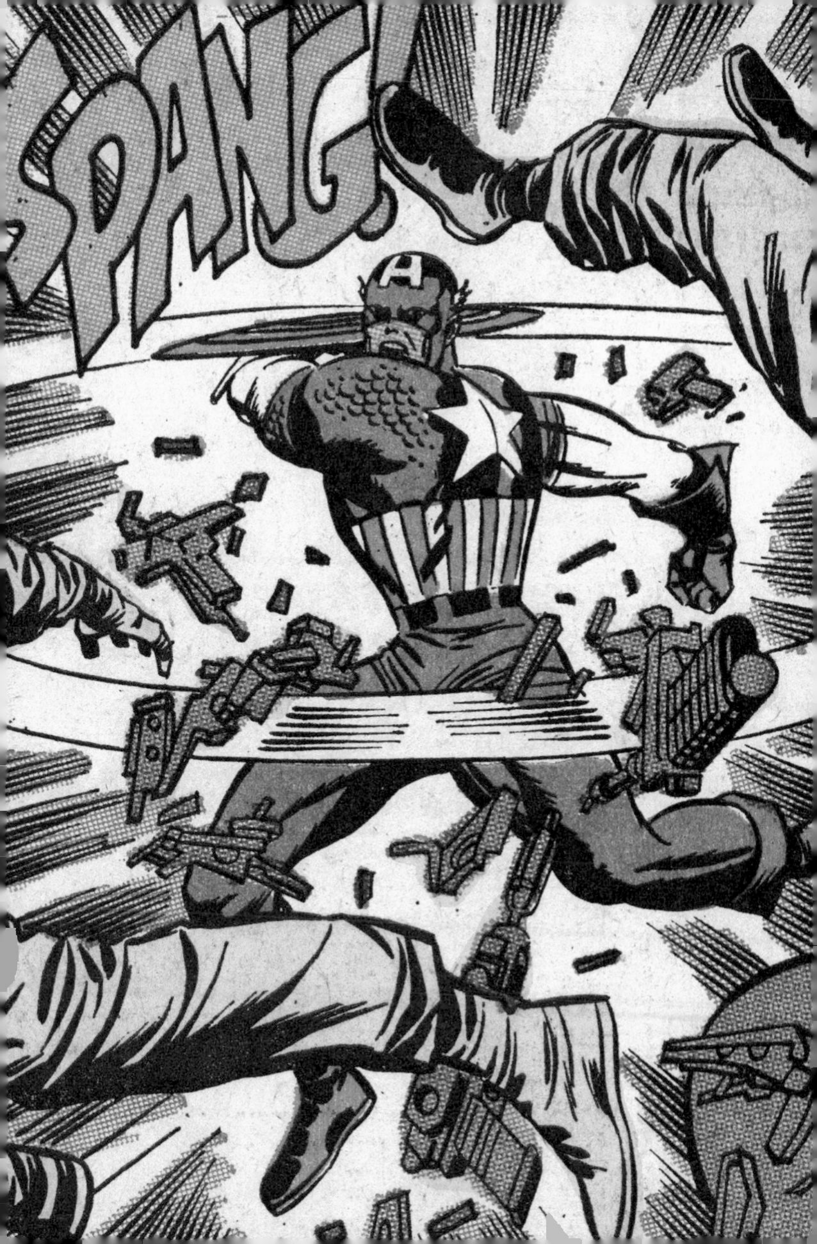
SPANG!

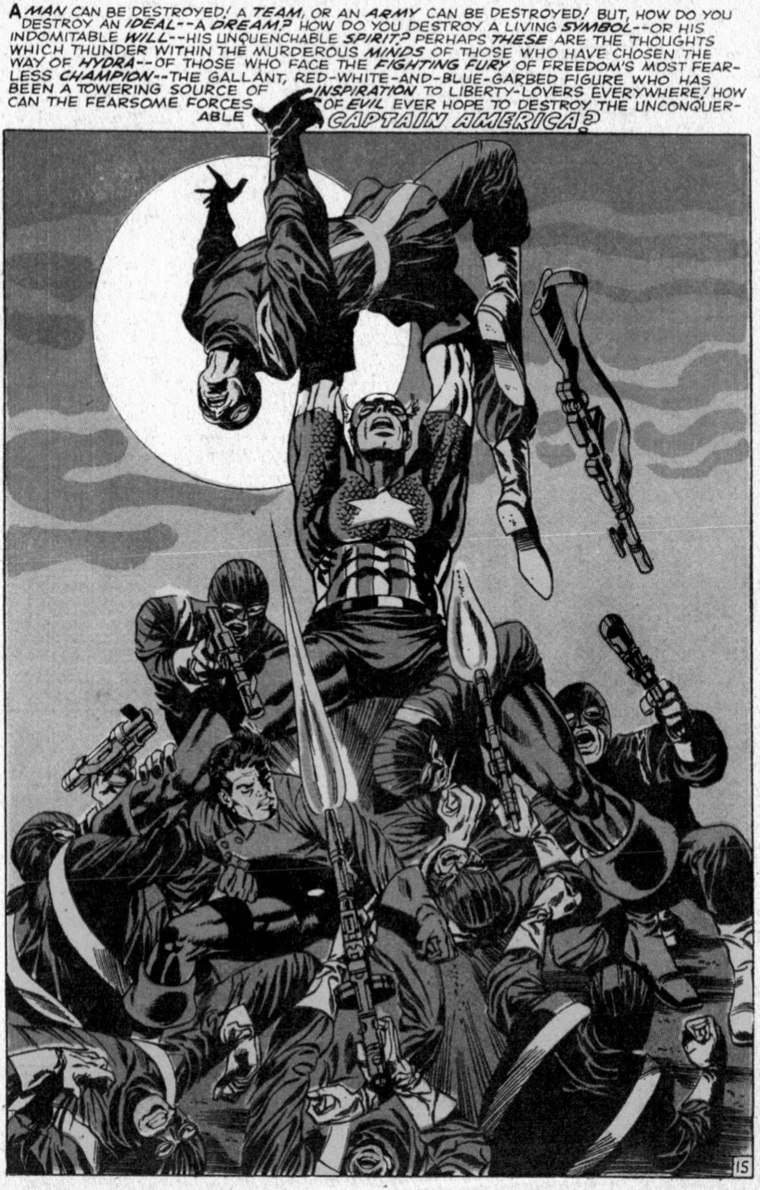
A MAN CAN BE DESTROYED! A TEAM, OR AN ARMY CAN BE DESTROYED! BUT, HOW DO YOU DESTROY AN IDEAL--A DREAM? HOW DO YOU DESTROY A LIVING SYMBOL--OR HIS INDOMITABLE WILL--HIS UNQUENCHABLE SPIRIT? PERHAPS THESE ARE THE THOUGHTS WHICH THUNDER WITHIN THE MURDEROUS MINDS OF THOSE WHO HAVE CHOSEN THE WAY OF HYDRA--OF THOSE WHO FACE THE FIGHTING FURY OF FREEDOM'S MOST FEARLESS CHAMPION--THE GALLANT, RED-WHITE-AND-BLUE-GARBED FIGURE WHO HAS BEEN A TOWERING SOURCE OF INSPIRATION TO LIBERTY-LOVERS EVERYWHERE! HOW CAN THE FEARSOME FORCES OF EVIL EVER HOPE TO DESTROY THE UNCONQUERABLE CAPTAIN AMERICA?
15

WAS IST SO GROSSARTIG AN CAPTAIN AMERICA?

Jeder, der Captain America begegnete, wusste sofort, dass er großartig war. Man musste ihn einfach nur *ansehen*. Er war die lebende amerikanische Flagge!

Zum ersten Mal sah man den berühmten Wächter der Freiheit aus dem Verlag Timely/Marvel auf dem Titelbild von *Captain America Comics* 1, das Ende 1940 an die Kioske kam. Der Comic war das Produkt zweier extrem talentierter Autoren und Zeichner: Joe Simon und Jack Kirby.

Andere Superhelden jener Zeit warfen bei ihrem Debüt Autos durch die Gegend oder schwangen sich von Dächern herunter oder brannten sich durch Stahltüren. Und Captain America? Er verpasste Adolf Hitler einen Kinnhaken.

Heutzutage könnten solche Motive zu internationalen Verstimmungen führen. In jenem Jahr 1940 hatte das nationalsozialistische Deutschland zwar einen großen Teil Europas erobert, doch mit den Vereinigten Staaten befand es sich offiziell nicht im Krieg. Und Amerika unterstützte zwar Großbritannien so gut es konnte, doch einen rot-weiß-blau gekleideten Helden zu zeigen, der den Namen seines Landes trug und den deutschen Staatsführer niederschlug, *überschritt* nicht nur eine Grenze – es *pulverisierte* sie.

Captain America ging schon immer seinen eigenen Weg.

Erst war da dieser Kinnhaken direkt in das Gesicht des „Führers". Dann waren da die Zeichnungen von Kirby. Wie ein Comic-Historiker es ausdrückte: Kirby „brachte Anatomie in die Comics". Captain America sprang und schlug und sprengte sich seinen Weg frei – gleichgültig, welcher Feind sich ihm in den Weg stellte. Und das, obwohl er angeblich nur ein gewöhnlicher Mensch war, den ein „Supersoldatenserum" in einen Modellathleten verwandelt hatte.

Als Simon und Kirby zum Konkurrenzverlag DC gewechselt waren, hinterließen sie ein solch großartiges Erbe, dass Cap in den verbleibenden Kriegsjahren selbst unter ihren vormaligen Assistenten zu den beliebtesten Superhelden zählte. All die anderen Comic-Figuren, die die amerikanische Flagge am Leib trugen, wirkten wie ein billiger Abklatsch – sogar die ein oder zwei Helden, die vor ihm entstanden waren. 1944 erschien Cap außerdem in einer Filmreihe, die samstagmorgens in den Kinos lief.

Nach dem Krieg ging Caps Popularität – ebenso wie die anderer Superhelden – zurück. Sein Alter Ego Steve Rogers quittierte den Armeedienst und wurde ... Lehrer an einer Highschool. 1949 verschwand er ganz. Das Experiment, ihn Mitte der 1950er-Jahre zurückzubringen (zusammen mit seinen Timely-Kollegen Human Torch und Sub-Mariner), währte nicht lange.

Stan Lees erste veröffentlichte Comic-Arbeit war eine Textgeschichte mit dem Wächter der Freiheit in *Captain America Comics* 3. Auch später sollte der Autor und Redakteur, der ab 1961 Serien wie *Fantastic Four* startete, eine besondere Vorliebe für die Figur bewahren. Doch was fing man in den 1960er-Jahren mit einem Helden an, der in einem Krieg entstanden war, der zwei Jahrzehnte zurücklag?

Ende der 1950er-Jahre war Jack Kirby zu Marvel zurückgekehrt. Und zusammen mit Kirby, der die Comics zeichnete und die Handlung mitbestimmte, brachte Lee den patriotischen Helden 1964 in *The Avengers* 4 zurück. Dort wurde enthüllt, dass Cap gegen Ende des Krieges in arktischem Eis tiefgefroren worden war, während sein junger Partner Bucky bei einer Explosion scheinbar sein Leben verloren hatte. Nachdem die Avengers ihn aufgetaut hatten, lebte Cap in einer Zeit, die ihm fremd war. Immer wieder hinterfragte er seine Rolle in einer Welt, die sich weiterentwickelt hatte. Und genau so stellte Marvel ihn in den nächsten Jahren dar, auch in seiner neuen Soloserie.

Cap wurde zum Anführer der Avengers, obwohl er nicht so mächtig war wie einige der anderen Helden. 1970 erhielt er einen neuen Partner. Es war der Falcon, der erste afroamerikanische Held, dessen

Name regelmäßig im Titelschriftzug eines Superheldencomics stand. Cap kämpfte gegen die Geheimorganisation Secret Empire, deren maskierter Anführer – darauf schien der Höhepunkt der Geschichte hinzudeuten – niemand anderer war als der damalige Präsident der Vereinigten Staaten. Desillusioniert legte Cap sein Flaggenkostüm ab und wurde zu Nomad, der seine Rolle und sein Selbstverständnis neu überdachte.

Schließlich stellte sich heraus, dass Bucky 1945 gar nicht gestorben war. Vielmehr hatte man ihn gefangen genommen, ihm eine Gehirnwäsche verpasst und in den Winter Soldier verwandelt – dieser war zunächst Caps Gegner, später sein Freund. 2007 kam Cap bei einem Attentat scheinbar ums Leben, doch bald darauf kehrte er zurück. Obwohl im Lauf der Jahre mehrere Figuren Caps Kostüm getragen hatten, auch Bucky Barnes, stand doch immer fest, dass es nur einen wahren Captain America geben konnte – und dieser hieß Steve Rogers.

Eine Menge anderer Helden trugen patriotische Kostüme und gaben sich inspirierende Namen.

Doch keiner von ihnen hatte je eine Chance gegen den großartigen Captain America!

– ROY THOMAS

CAPTAIN AMERICA No. 113

Page 12: *Cover; pencils and inks, Jim Steranko. Interior, "The Strange Death of Captain America!"; script, Stan Lee; pencils, Jim Steranko; inks, Tom Palmer; May 1969.* Every generation has seen their Captain America die, but death is not always fatal in the Marvel Universe....So maybe Cap wasn't really dead after all—a great relief to the young legions of dismayed Marvelites unused to such dramatic fare. This splash page is one of Steranko's most iconic, recalling some of the most heroic paintings of the French Romantics (Théodore Géricault's ca. 1818 *The Raft of the Medusa* and Eugène Delacroix's 1830 *Liberty Leading the People*). Steranko's return was worth the wait.

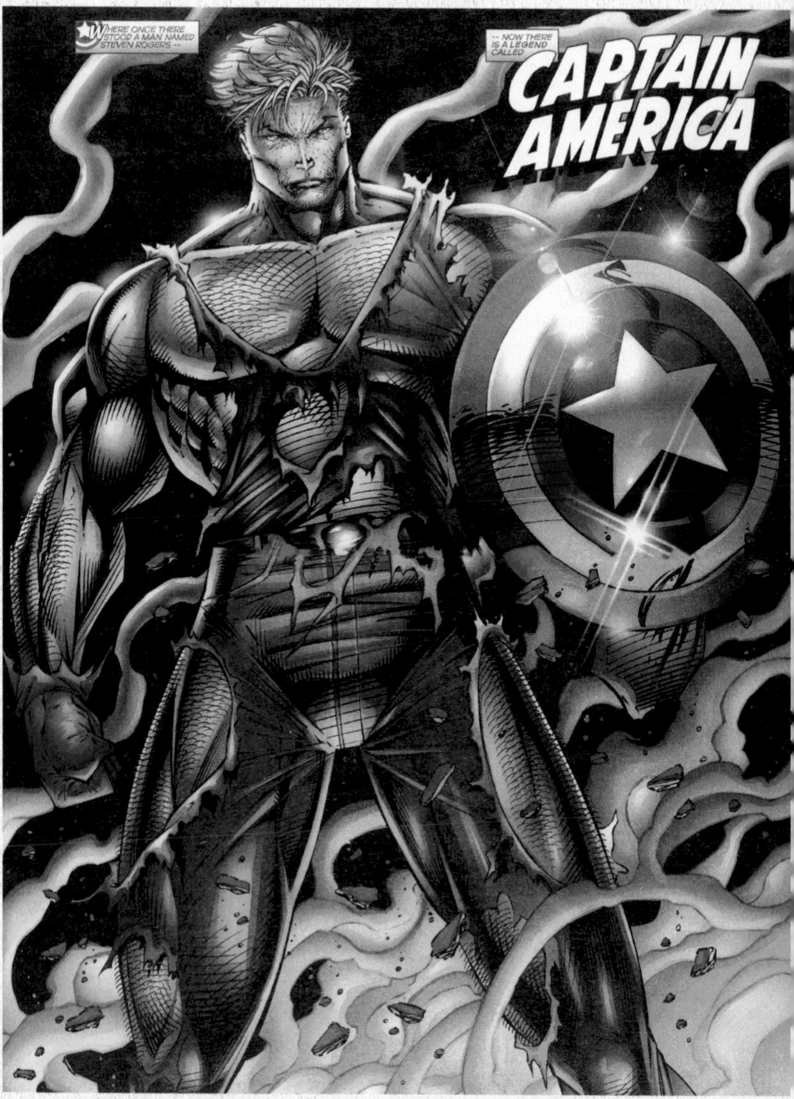
WHERE ONCE THERE STOOD A MAN NAMED STEVEN ROGERS --
-- NOW THERE IS A LEGEND CALLED
CAPTAIN AMERICA

MAIS QU'EST-CE QU'IL A DE SI SPÉCIAL, FINALEMENT, CE CAPTAIN AMERICA ?

Dès le début, il suffisait de croiser la route de Captain America pour *savoir* qu'il était génial. Un seul regard vous disait tout : vous aviez devant vous un drapeau américain sur pattes — doué de la parole, qui plus est. La légendaire Sentinelle de la Liberté de Timely/Marvel a fait sa première apparition en décembre 1940, en couverture du numéro 1 de *Captain America Comics* ; elle jaillissait tout droit de l'imagination d'un tandem créatif au talent prodigieux, composé de Joe Simon et Jack Kirby. Les superhéros, en ce temps-là, se faisaient généralement connaître par leurs embardées automobiles, leur aptitude à bondir de toit en toit ou leur propension à franchir les portes blindées rien qu'en les enflammant. Captain America, lui, commençait par mettre une trempe à Adolf Hitler. Paf ! Dans les dents ! De nos jours, un tel dessin provoquerait un incident diplomatique. Car si l'Allemagne nazie avait envahi un an plus tôt une grande partie de l'Europe, elle n'était pas officiellement en guerre avec les États-Unis. De son côté l'Amérique apportait certes à la Grande-Bretagne «toute l'aide possible sauf la guerre», mais montrer un héros portant le nom et les couleurs de son pays en train de dérouiller de cette façon le chancelier allemand, ça ne dépassait pas seulement les bornes autorisées : ça les pulvérisait.

D'entrée de jeu, Captain America a donc joué les originaux. D'abord avec ce direct du droit expédié au *Führer* puis par la grâce du graphisme de Kirby. Comme l'écrira un historien des comics, celui-ci «a introduit l'anatomie dans la bande dessinée». Avec le Cap ça bondissait, ça fracassait, ça taillait en pièces le moindre ennemi assez sot pour vouloir se placer en travers de son chemin — alors même qu'il n'était, théoriquement, qu'un simple humain changé en athlète d'exception par le «sérum du super-soldat». Lorsque Simon et Kirby seront recrutés par le concurrent DC, leur apport initial et notamment le look qu'ils avaient créé pour leur héros garderont tant de force que même confié à leurs anciens assistants, Captain America ne sera pas loin de conserver la tête du peloton superhéroïque, et ce jusqu'au terme du conflit. Face à lui, tous les autres personnages gratifiés d'une bannière étoilée feront figure de pâles imitations, même ceux arrivés avant lui! En 1944 on pourra même l'admirer au cinéma dans un feuilleton projeté en matinée. Après la guerre, toutefois, l'étoile du Cap perdra de son éclat, à l'exemple des superhéros en général. Son alter ego Steve Rogers, démobilisé, deviendra professeur de lycée et, en 1949, manquera carrément à l'appel. Au milieu des années 1950, une tentative pour le ressusciter aux côtés du Submariner et de la Torche Humaine ne fera pas long feu.

C'est là que va intervenir Stan Lee, dont la carrière d'auteur avait démarré par une nouvelle consacrée au Cap dans le numéro 3 de *Captain America Comics*. Scénariste et désormais directeur éditorial de Marvel, pour lequel il lança *Fantastic Four*, entre autres titres, dans les années 1960, Lee avait gardé un petit faible pour le personnage. Mais que faire d'un héros inventé au cours d'une Seconde Guerre mondiale terminée depuis vingt ans? Avec le soutien, au dessin et au scénario, d'un Kirby revenu chez Marvel à la fin des fifties, Lee restaura le Cap dans le quatrième numéro de *The Avengers*: on y apprenait que vers la fin de la guerre, il avait été congelé dans un bloc de glace et que son jeune acolyte Bucky n'était sans doute pas sorti vivant d'une terrible explosion. Une fois décongelé, Captain America se retrouvait décalé par rapport à son époque et pour le moins perplexe quant au sens de sa vie dans un monde très différent de celui qu'il avait connu. C'est ainsi que Marvel le mettra en scène pendant les quelques années suivantes, y compris dans sa nouvelle série solo. Il deviendra le leader des Vengeurs, malgré son déficit de puissance par rapport à certains de ses partenaires, et s'en verra d'ailleurs assigner un tout neuf dans les années 1970: le Faucon, premier héros afro-américain régulièrement présent dans le logo d'un magazine de superhéros. Face à eux, une sinistre organisation nommée Empire Secret, dont le chef masqué, à en juger par le point d'orgue de l'histoire, ne serait autre que le président des États-Unis. De quoi désenchanter un Cap qui s'allégera temporairement de ses effets patriotiques pour se glisser dans la peau d'un Nomad donnant désormais dans l'introspection. *In fine*, il sera aussi révélé que Bucky n'avait pas du tout trouvé la mort en 1945 mais s'était fait capturer — et endoctriner — par les Soviétiques : devenu le Soldat de l'Hiver, il se dressera contre le Cap avant de redevenir son ami. En 2007, Captain America sera apparemment assassiné puis reprendra rapidement du service.

Ils seront nombreux, au fil des années, à endosser son costume, et parmi eux Bucky Barnes, pourtant le doute ne sera jamais vraiment permis : il ne peut exister qu'un seul Captain America, et il s'appelle Steve Rogers. Des héros au patronyme exaltant et au déguisement patriotique, l'histoire des comics en regorge. Mais pas un seul ne pourra jamais rivaliser avec la grandeur de Captain America !

— ROY THOMAS

CAPTAIN AMERICA Vol. 2 No. 1

Page 16: *Interior, "Courage"; plot and pencils, Rob Liefeld; plot assist, Chuck Dixon; script, Jeph Loeb; inks, Jonathan Sibal; November 1996.* The Avengers and the FF lived out a year's worth of adventures in the side reality illustrated by Jim Lee and Liefeld, Image's prodigal sons returned.

CAPTAIN AMERICA COMICS No. 18

Pages 20–21: *Interior, "The Mikado's Super-Shell"; script, unknown; pencils, Al Avison; inks, Syd Shores; September 1942.* A powerful double-page splash by Al Avison (schooled at the feet of Simon and Kirby) depicts Captain America and Bucky against a seemingly undefeatable horde of Japanese enemies and their fantastic weaponry.

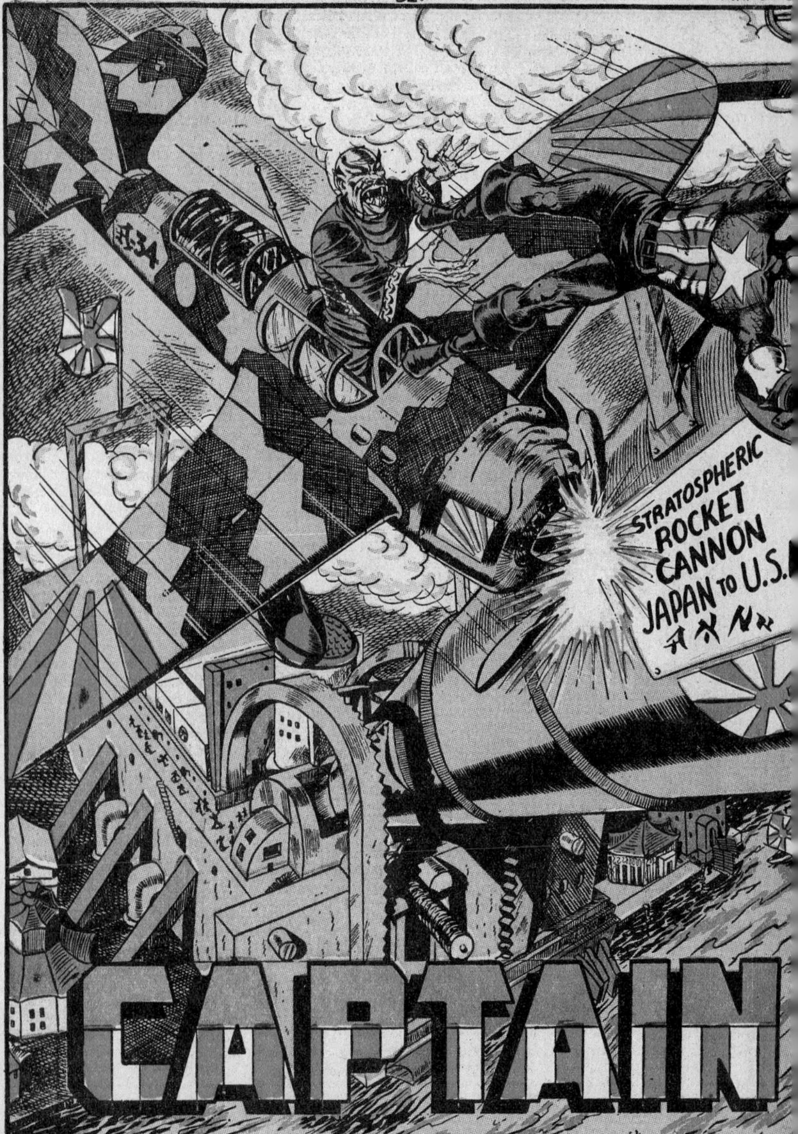
STRATOSPHERIC
ROCKET
CANNON
JAPAN TO U.S.
CAPTAIN

THE
MIKADO'S
SUPER-
SHELL!

AMERICA

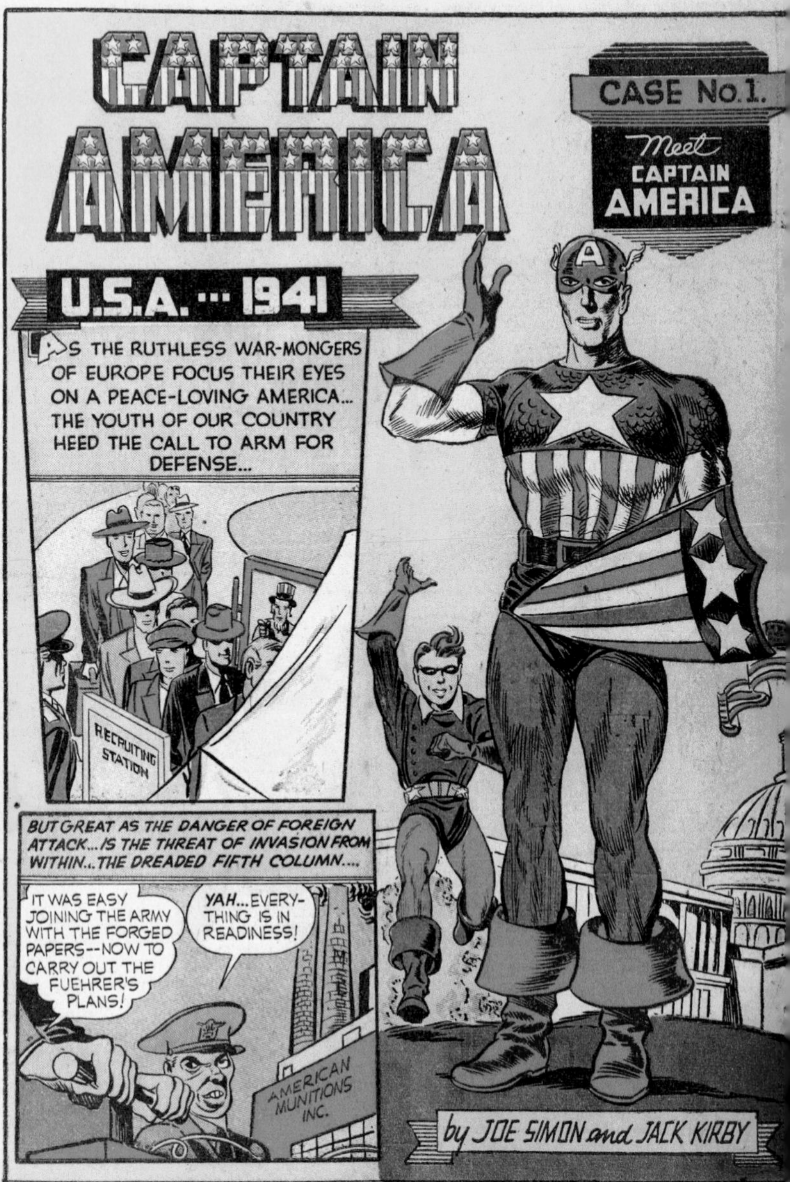
CAPTAIN AMERICA
CASE No.1.
Meet CAPTAIN AMERICA
U.S.A. ... 1941
AS THE RUTHLESS WAR-MONGERS OF EUROPE FOCUS THEIR EYES ON A PEACE-LOVING AMERICA... THE YOUTH OF OUR COUNTRY HEED THE CALL TO ARM FOR DEFENSE...
RECRUITING STATION
BUT GREAT AS THE DANGER OF FOREIGN ATTACK... IS THE THREAT OF INVASION FROM WITHIN... THE DREADED FIFTH COLUMN....
IT WAS EASY JOINING THE ARMY WITH THE FORGED PAPERS--NOW TO CARRY OUT THE FUEHRER'S PLANS!
YAH... EVERY-THING IS IN READINESS!
AMERICAN MUNITIONS INC.
by JOE SIMON and JACK KIRBY

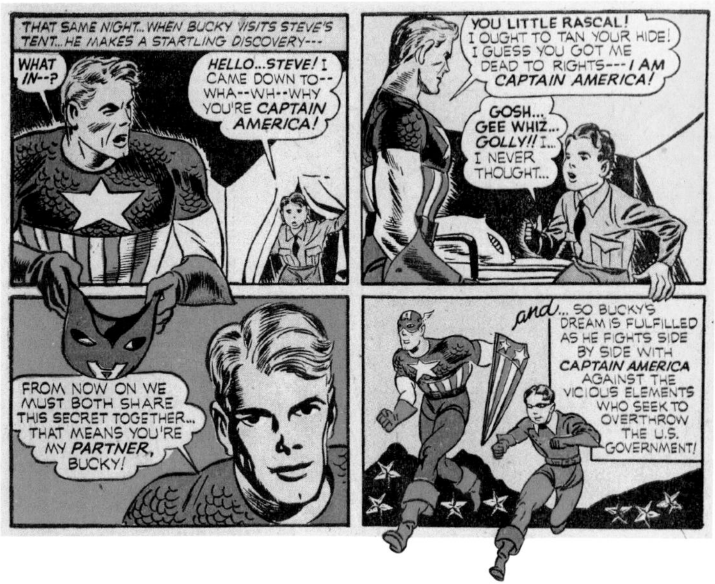
THAT SAME NIGHT...WHEN BUCKY VISITS STEVE'S TENT...HE MAKES A STARTLING DISCOVERY---
WHAT IN--?
HELLO...STEVE! I CAME DOWN TO-- WHA--WH--WHY YOU'RE CAPTAIN AMERICA!
YOU LITTLE RASCAL! I OUGHT TO TAN YOUR HIDE! I GUESS YOU GOT ME DEAD TO RIGHTS---I AM CAPTAIN AMERICA!
GOSH... GEE WHIZ... GOLLY!! I... I NEVER THOUGHT...
FROM NOW ON WE MUST BOTH SHARE THIS SECRET TOGETHER... THAT MEANS YOU'RE MY PARTNER, BUCKY!
and... SO BUCKY'S DREAM IS FULFILLED AS HE FIGHTS SIDE BY SIDE WITH CAPTAIN AMERICA AGAINST THE VICIOUS ELEMENTS WHO SEEK TO OVERTHROW THE U.S. GOVERNMENT!

MEET CAPTAIN AMERICA

Opposite and above: *Interiors,* Captain America Comics *No. 1; script, Joe Simon and Jack Kirby; pencils, Jack Kirby and Joe Simon; inks, Al Liederman, Simon, and Kirby; March 1941.* The classic splash page to the iconic origin story of Captain America. Based on a sketch Joe Simon worked up to show Martin Goodman, the triangular shield was changed to a circular one after ex-business partner Louis Silberkleit, now of MLJ comics, complained it was too similar to their character the Shield, then published in *Pep Comics.*

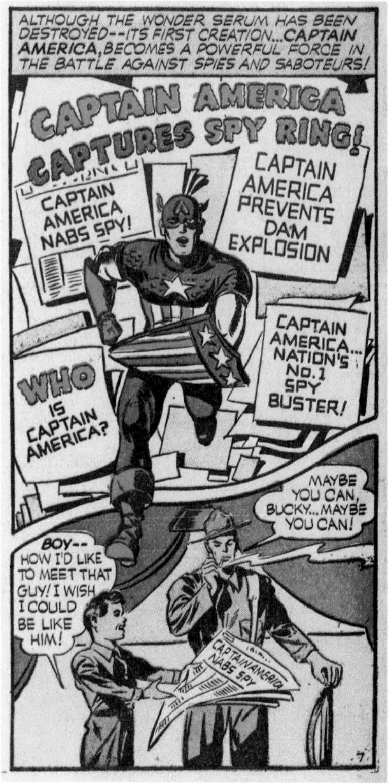
ALTHOUGH THE WONDER SERUM HAS BEEN DESTROYED--ITS FIRST CREATION...CAPTAIN AMERICA, BECOMES A POWERFUL FORCE IN THE BATTLE AGAINST SPIES AND SABOTEURS!
CAPTAIN AMERICA CAPTURES SPY RING!
CAPTAIN AMERICA NABS SPY!
CAPTAIN AMERICA PREVENTS DAM EXPLOSION
CAPTAIN AMERICA... NATION'S No.1 SPY BUSTER!
WHO IS CAPTAIN AMERICA?
MAYBE YOU CAN, BUCKY... MAYBE YOU CAN!
BOY-- HOW I'D LIKE TO MEET THAT GUY! I WISH I COULD BE LIKE HIM!
CAPTAIN AMERICA NABS SPY
7

CAPTAIN AMERICA COMICS No. 1

Above and opposite: *Interiors, "Meet Captain America"; script, Joe Simon and Jack Kirby; pencils, Jack Kirby and Joe Simon; inks, Al Liederman, Simon, and Kirby; March 1941.* Captain America's debut was also his origin story, revealing Private Steve Rogers's physical transformation. As the nation wonders just who Captain America really is, his exploits are plastered in newspapers and newsreels across the country. Camp Lehigh mascot Bucky Barnes tells Steve he'd like to meet Captain America, which he does in the very next panel, in an unexpected way. When he discovers Steve's secret, Cap takes Bucky into his confidence and the duo team up to fight enemies of liberty everywhere.

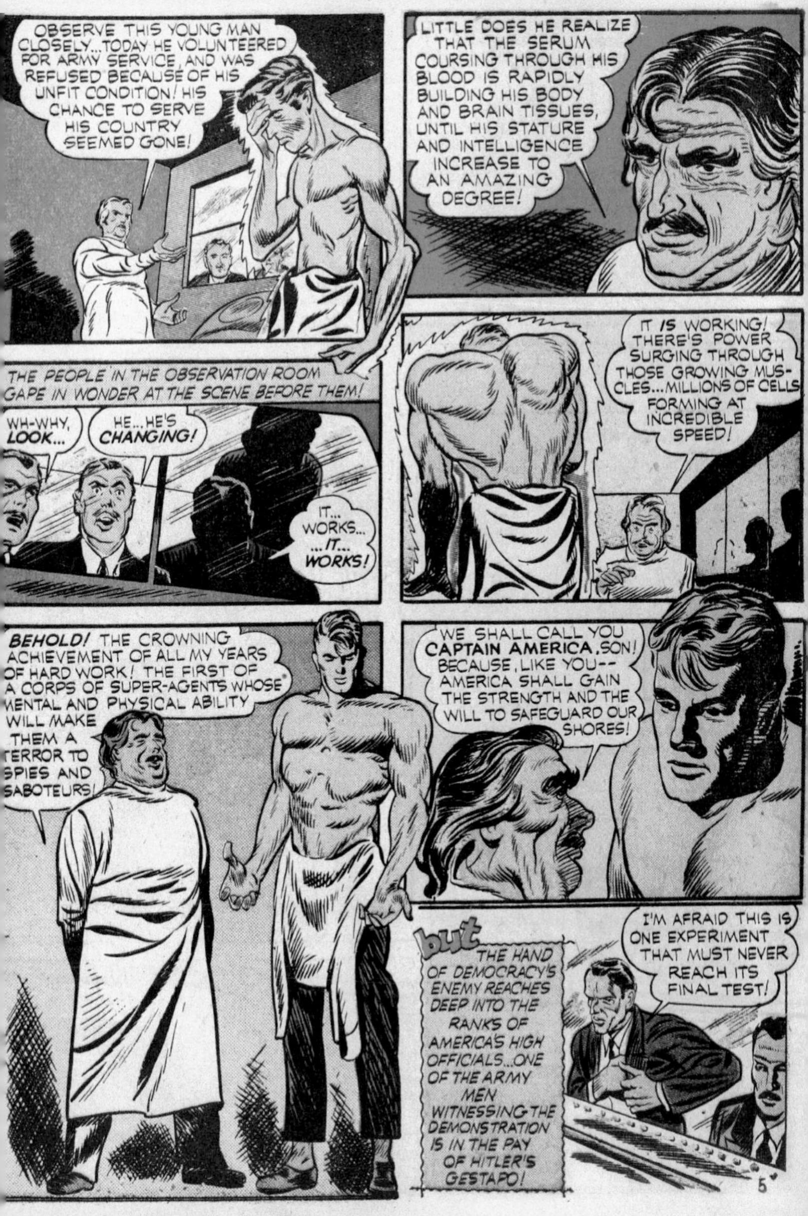

OBSERVE THIS YOUNG MAN CLOSELY...TODAY HE VOLUNTEERED FOR ARMY SERVICE, AND WAS REFUSED BECAUSE OF HIS UNFIT CONDITION! HIS CHANCE TO SERVE HIS COUNTRY SEEMED GONE!
LITTLE DOES HE REALIZE THAT THE SERUM COURSING THROUGH HIS BLOOD IS RAPIDLY BUILDING HIS BODY AND BRAIN TISSUES, UNTIL HIS STATURE AND INTELLIGENCE INCREASE TO AN AMAZING DEGREE!
THE PEOPLE IN THE OBSERVATION ROOM GAPE IN WONDER AT THE SCENE BEFORE THEM!
WH-WHY, LOOK...
HE...HE'S CHANGING!
IT... WORKS... ...IT... WORKS!
IT IS WORKING! THERE'S POWER SURGING THROUGH THOSE GROWING MUSCLES...MILLIONS OF CELLS FORMING AT INCREDIBLE SPEED!
BEHOLD! THE CROWNING ACHIEVEMENT OF ALL MY YEARS OF HARD WORK! THE FIRST OF A CORPS OF SUPER-AGENTS WHOSE MENTAL AND PHYSICAL ABILITY WILL MAKE THEM A TERROR TO SPIES AND SABOTEURS!
WE SHALL CALL YOU CAPTAIN AMERICA, SON! BECAUSE, LIKE YOU-- AMERICA SHALL GAIN THE STRENGTH AND THE WILL TO SAFEGUARD OUR SHORES!
but THE HAND OF DEMOCRACY'S ENEMY REACHES DEEP INTO THE RANKS OF AMERICA'S HIGH OFFICIALS...ONE OF THE ARMY MEN WITNESSING THE DEMONSTRATION IS IN THE PAY OF HITLER'S GESTAPO!
I'M AFRAID THIS IS ONE EXPERIMENT THAT MUST NEVER REACH ITS FINAL TEST!
5

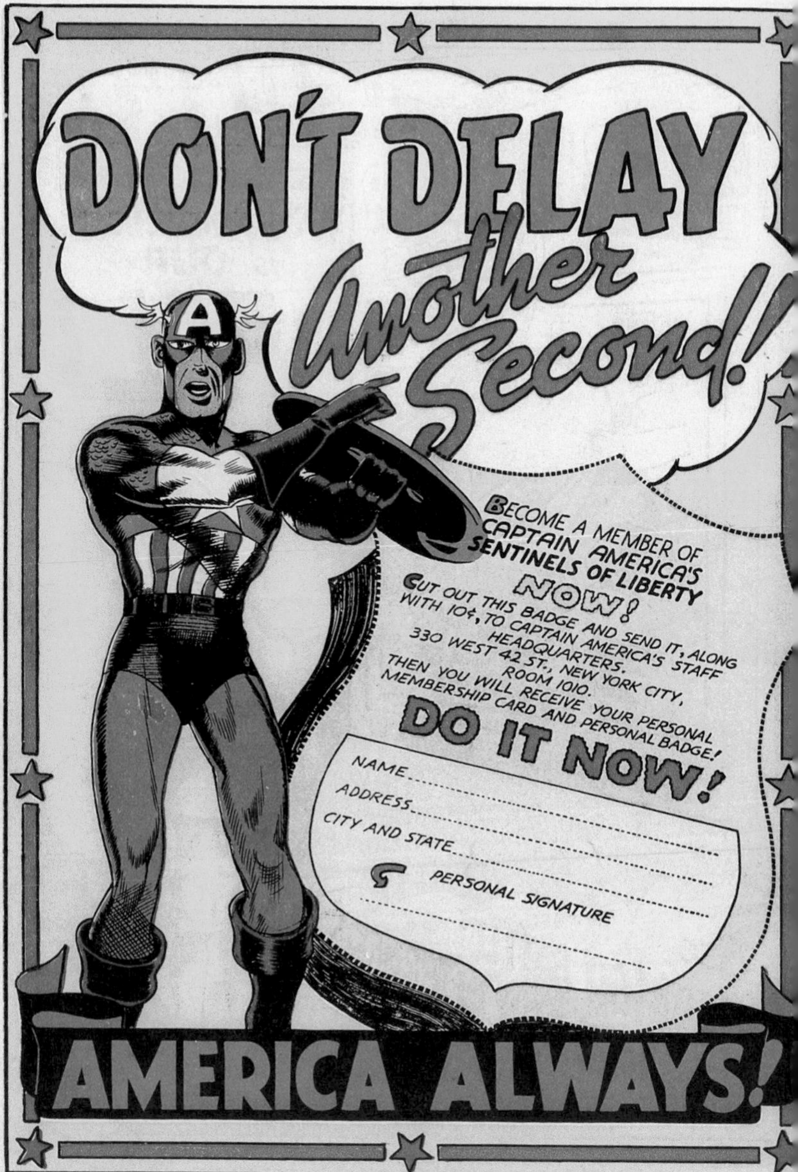

DON'T DELAY Another Second!!
BECOME A MEMBER OF CAPTAIN AMERICA'S SENTINELS OF LIBERTY
NOW!
CUT OUT THIS BADGE AND SEND IT, ALONG WITH 10¢, TO CAPTAIN AMERICA'S STAFF HEADQUARTERS. 330 WEST 42 ST., NEW YORK CITY, ROOM 1010.
THEN YOU WILL RECEIVE YOUR PERSONAL MEMBERSHIP CARD AND PERSONAL BADGE!
DO IT NOW!
NAME
ADDRESS
CITY AND STATE
PERSONAL SIGNATURE
AMERICA ALWAYS!

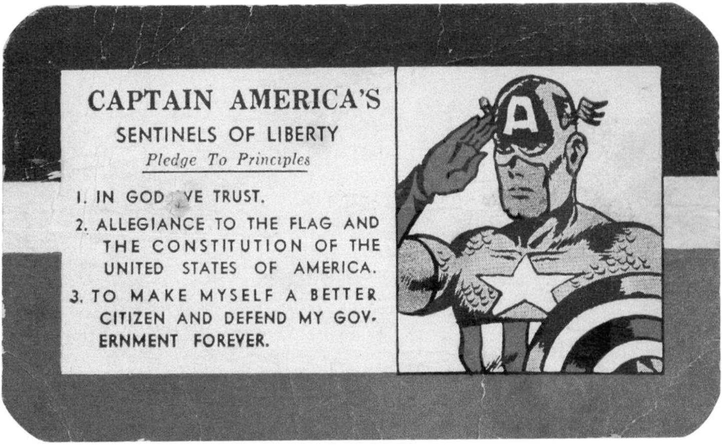
CAPTAIN AMERICA'S
SENTINELS OF LIBERTY
Pledge To Principles
1. IN GOD WE TRUST.
2. ALLEGIANCE TO THE FLAG AND THE CONSTITUTION OF THE UNITED STATES OF AMERICA.
3. TO MAKE MYSELF A BETTER CITIZEN AND DEFEND MY GOVERNMENT FOREVER.

AMERICA ALWAYS!

Opposite: *House ad;* Joker Comics *No. 2, April 1942.*

SENTINELS OF LIBERTY

Above: *Membership card; pencils and inks, Al Avison; 1941.*
In addition to a badge you could wear, enlistment in Captain America's "Sentinels of Liberty" fan club also supplied you with an ID card for your wallet.

SIMON & KIRBY

Below: *Photograph, Jack Kirby (left) and Joe Simon (right), ca. 1950.*

CAPTAIN AMERICA COMICS No. 7

Opposite: *Cover: pencils, Jack Kirby; inks, Joe Simon; October 1941.* A typically dynamic Simon and Kirby cover. Kirby pioneered the visual language for super hero comics in the early 1940s, composing an exaggerated hyper-ballet full of extreme motion that would be copied throughout the industry (but never successfully duplicated). The future King was characteristically blunt when questioned about it years later: "I like to show violence in a graceful way, a dramatic way....But violence, basic raw violence...I won't look at it and I won't tolerate it and I won't put it in my drawings....You'll notice there is no realism in anything I do because they are things as I like to see them. I just like to see them that way; that's my bag and it's my fantasy."

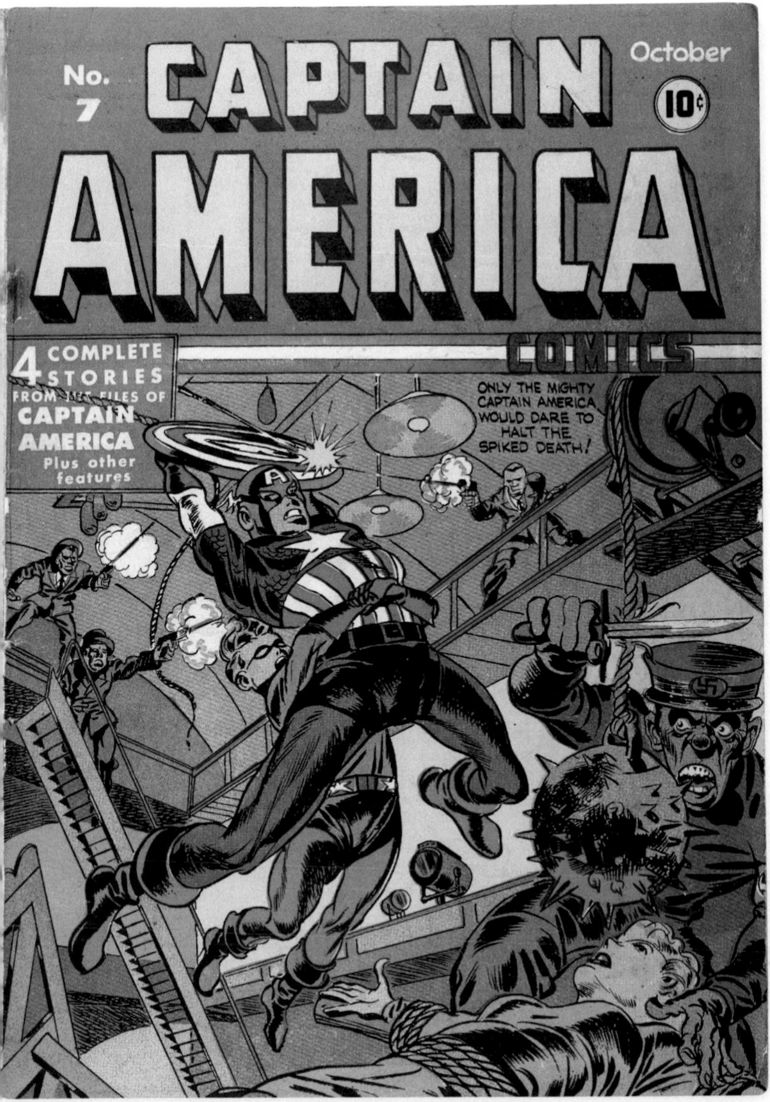
No. 7
CAPTAIN AMERICA
October
10¢
COMICS
4 COMPLETE STORIES FROM THE FILES OF
CAPTAIN AMERICA
Plus other features
ONLY THE MIGHTY CAPTAIN AMERICA WOULD DARE TO HALT THE SPIKED DEATH!

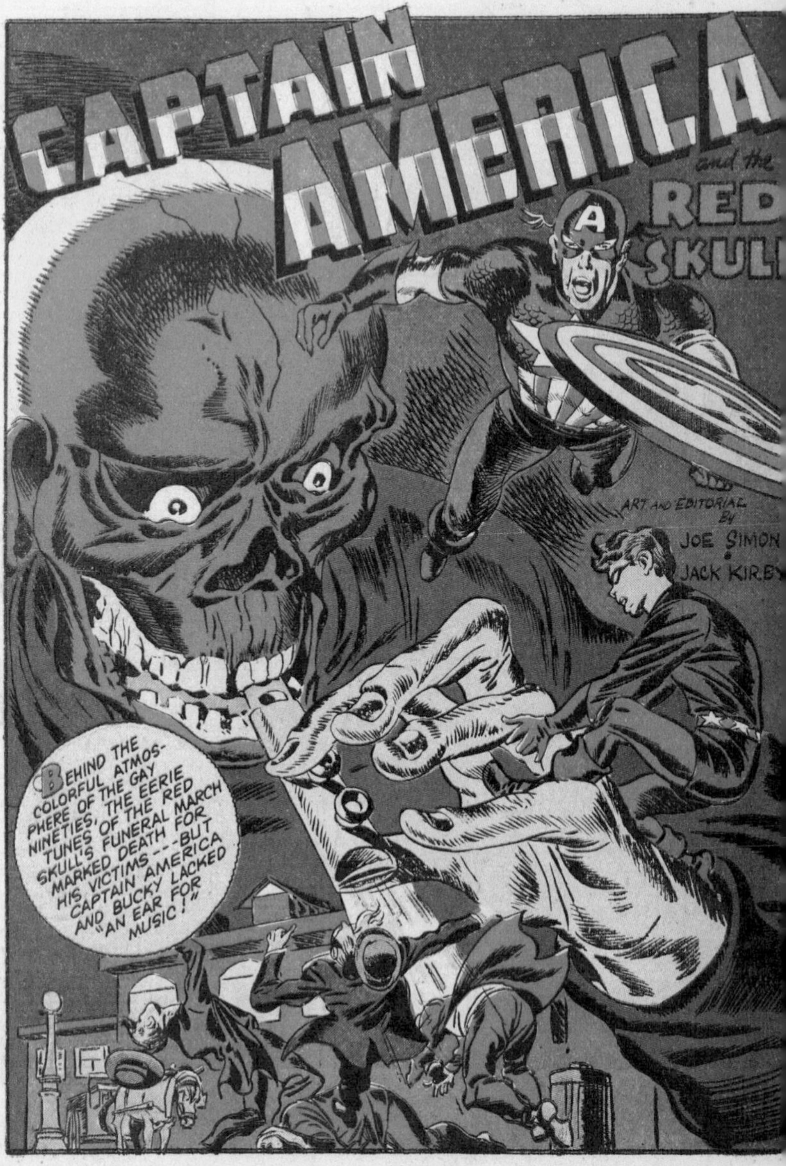

CAPTAIN AMERICA
and the RED SKULL
ART AND EDITORIAL By
JOE SIMON
JACK KIRBY
BEHIND THE COLORFUL ATMOSPHERE OF THE GAY NINETIES, THE EERIE TUNES OF THE RED SKULL'S FUNERAL MARCH MARKED DEATH FOR HIS VICTIMS---BUT CAPTAIN AMERICA AND BUCKY LACKED "AN EAR FOR MUSIC!"

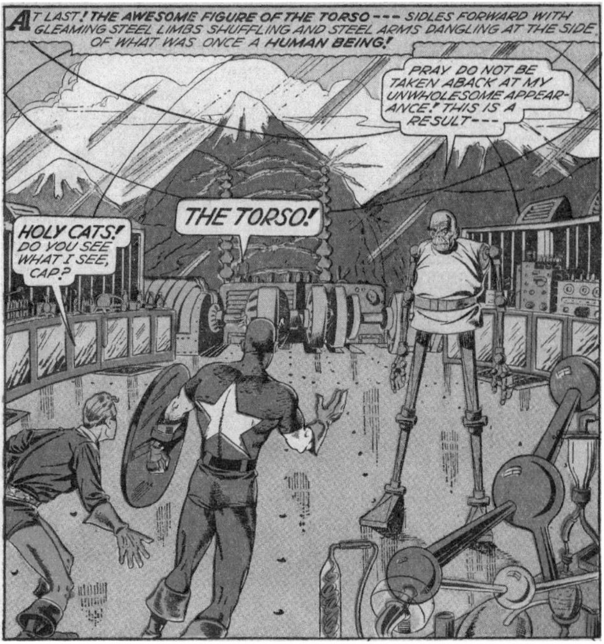
AT LAST! THE AWESOME FIGURE OF THE TORSO --- SIDLES FORWARD WITH GLEAMING STEEL LIMBS SHUFFLING AND STEEL ARMS DANGLING AT THE SIDE OF WHAT WAS ONCE A HUMAN BEING!
PRAY DO NOT BE TAKEN ABACK AT MY UNWHOLESOME APPEAR-ANCE! THIS IS A RESULT---
THE TORSO!
HOLY CATS! DO YOU SEE WHAT I SEE, CAP?

CAPTAIN AMERICA COMICS No. 7

Opposite: *Interior, "Captain America and the Red Skull"; script, Joe Simon and Jack Kirby; pencils, Jack Kirby; inks, Joe Simon; October 1941.* The supreme Nazi villain, the Red Skull, was used to demonstrate unconscionable evil by Simon and Kirby. This dovetailed nicely with publisher Martin Goodman's penchant for an editorial policy that ripped the Axis powers to shreds both on covers and in war-era storylines.

CAPTAIN AMERICA COMICS No. 28

Above: *Interior, "The Challenge of the 'Mad Torso'"; script, unknown; pencils, attributed Syd Shores; inks, attributed Vince Alascia; July 1943.* Every good hero needs a foil, and Cap had plenty of them, many allied with the Axis powers. One of the more bizarre villains was Torso, whose anger over the loss of all his limbs in an explosion stirs a desire to eliminate the human race.

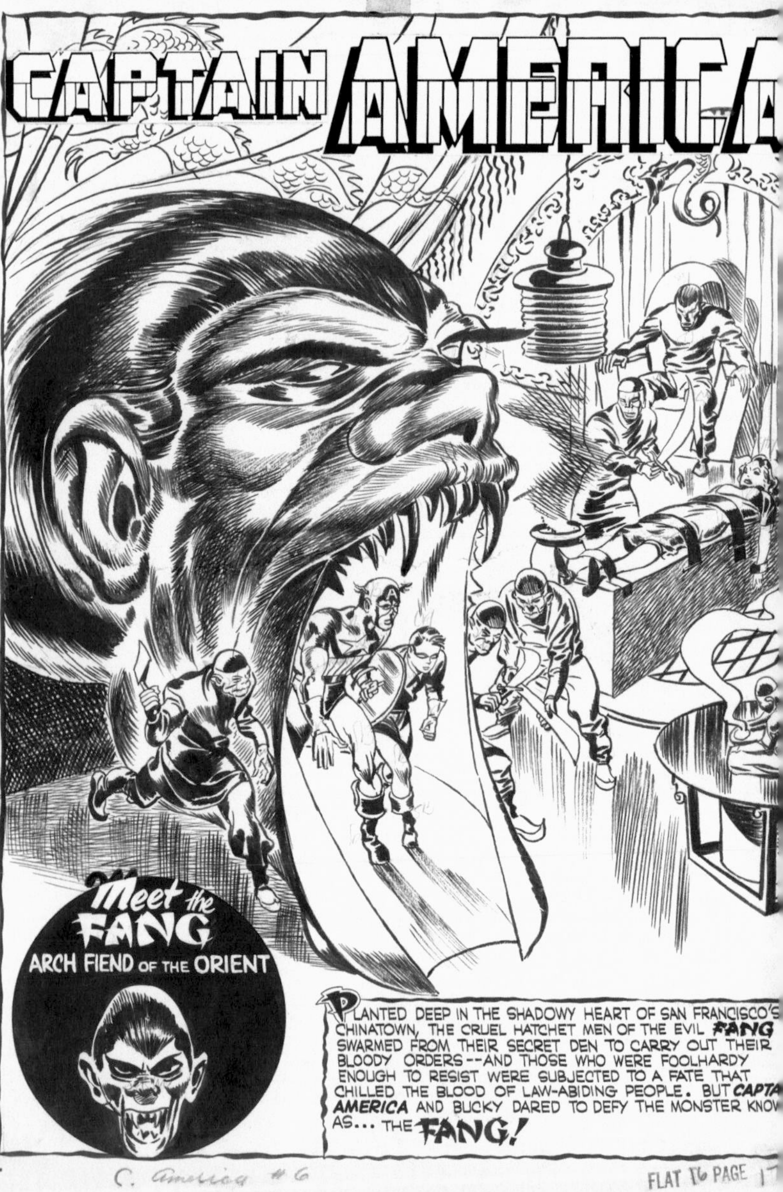
CAPTAIN AMERICA
Meet the FANG
ARCH FIEND OF THE ORIENT
PLANTED DEEP IN THE SHADOWY HEART OF SAN FRANCISCO'S CHINATOWN, THE CRUEL HATCHET MEN OF THE EVIL FANG SWARMED FROM THEIR SECRET DEN TO CARRY OUT THEIR BLOODY ORDERS--AND THOSE WHO WERE FOOLHARDY ENOUGH TO RESIST WERE SUBJECTED TO A FATE THAT CHILLED THE BLOOD OF LAW-ABIDING PEOPLE. BUT CAPTA AMERICA AND BUCKY DARED TO DEFY THE MONSTER KNOW AS... THE FANG!

C. America #6

FLAT 16 PAGE 17

CAPTAIN AMERICA COMICS No. 6

Opposite: *Original interior art, "Meet the Fang, Arch Fiend of the Orient"; script, Joe Simon and Jack Kirby; pencils, Kirby; inks, Simon; September 1941.* One of a tiny handful of Simon and Kirby *Captain America* originals known to exist, this stunning splash page rendered almost nine months before the Pearl Harbor attacks depicts Asian villains in an exaggerated, xenophobic fashion reflecting Sax Rohmer's popular *Fu Manchu* novels.

CAPTAIN AMERICA COMICS No. 23

Page 34: *Interior, "The Idol of Doom"; script, unknown; art, Don Rico, Ernie Hart, Ed Winiarski, George Klein, unknown; February 1943.* A full-page splash leads this artistic jam session of at least five different (four discernible) artists who all pitched in and contributed to this story. Timely's assembly-line process of producing stories on staff, with set pencilers and inkers, promoted these diverse-hands compositions.

CAPTAIN AMERICA COMICS No. 25

Page 35: *Interior, "The Princess of the Atom"; script, Ray Cummings; pencils, Syd Shores; inks, Vince Alascia; April 1943.* On Columbus Day in 1942, 18-year-old Allen Bellman answered an ad in *The New York Times* for the position of inker on the *Captain America* comic book. As Bellman tells it, "Don Rico comes out; he takes my work samples in. I waited a bit and he comes back out and tells me I'm hired. I think they started me off at $25 a week at a time when a married man with a family was making $35 to $45 a week."

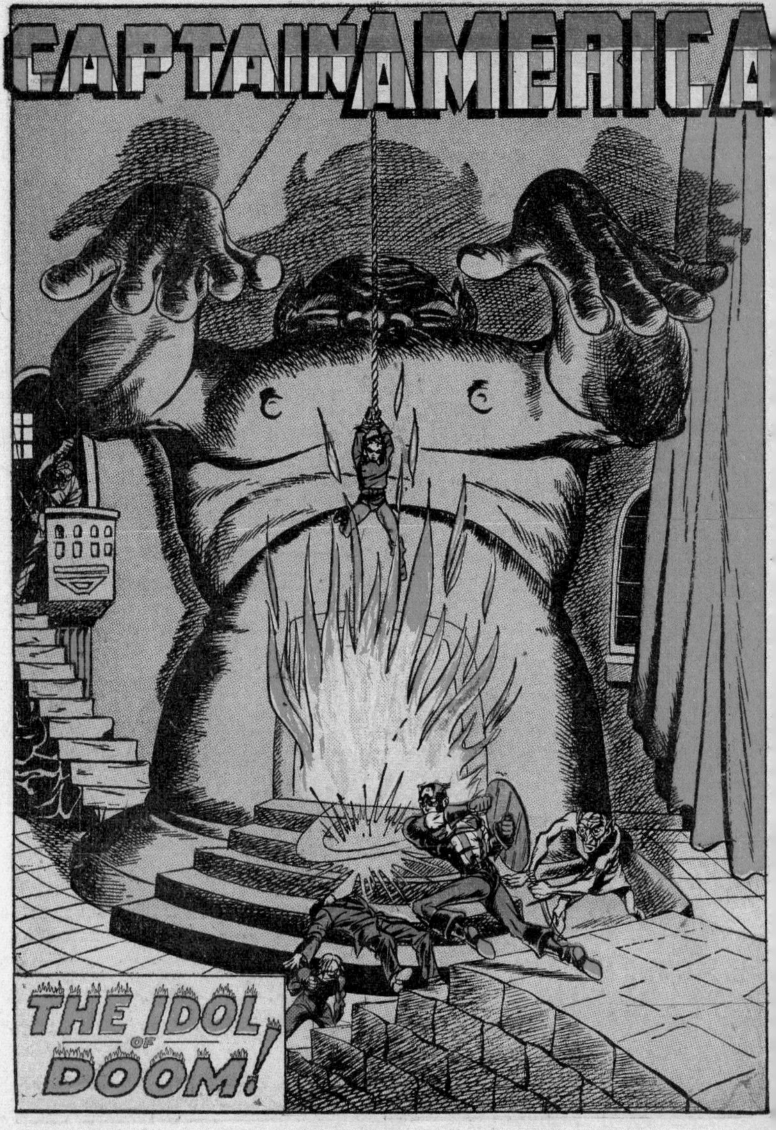
CAPTAIN AMERICA
THE IDOL OF DOOM!

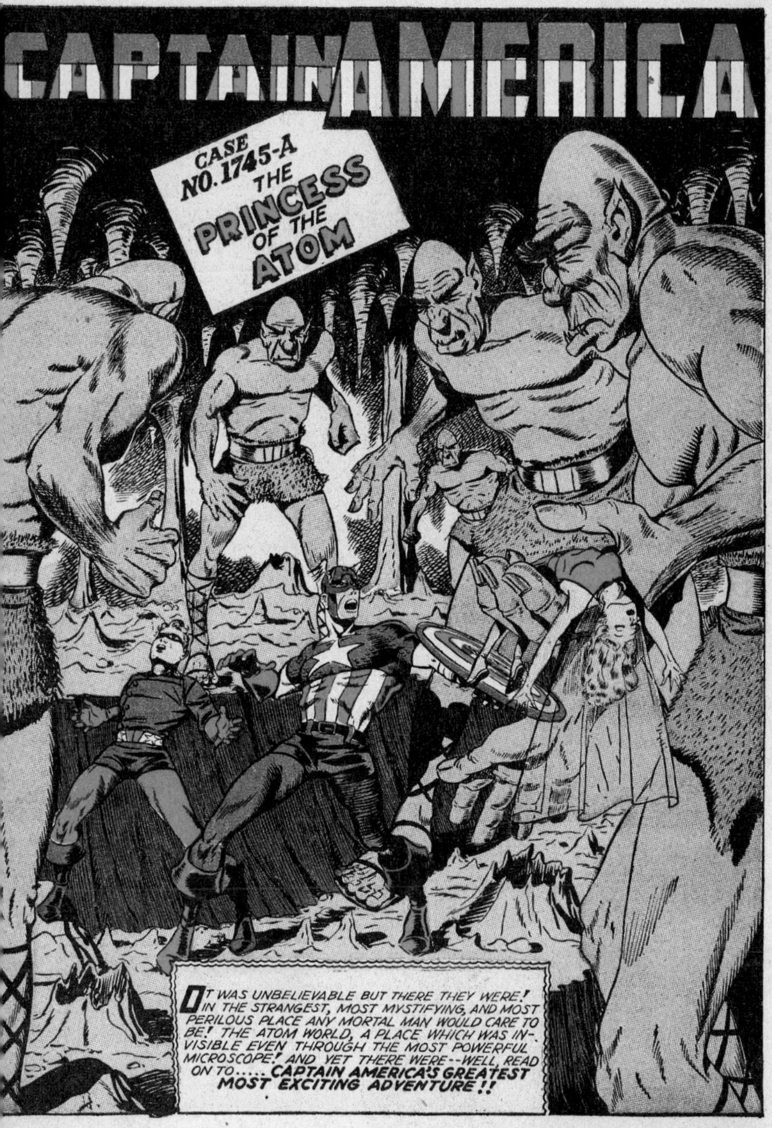
CAPTAIN AMERICA
CASE NO. 1745-A THE PRINCESS OF THE ATOM
IT WAS UNBELIEVABLE BUT THERE THEY WERE! IN THE STRANGEST, MOST MYSTIFYING, AND MOST PERILOUS PLACE ANY MORTAL MAN WOULD CARE TO BE! THE ATOM WORLD, A PLACE WHICH WAS INVISIBLE EVEN THROUGH THE MOST POWERFUL MICROSCOPE! AND YET THERE WERE--WELL, READ ON TO..... CAPTAIN AMERICA'S GREATEST MOST EXCITING ADVENTURE!!

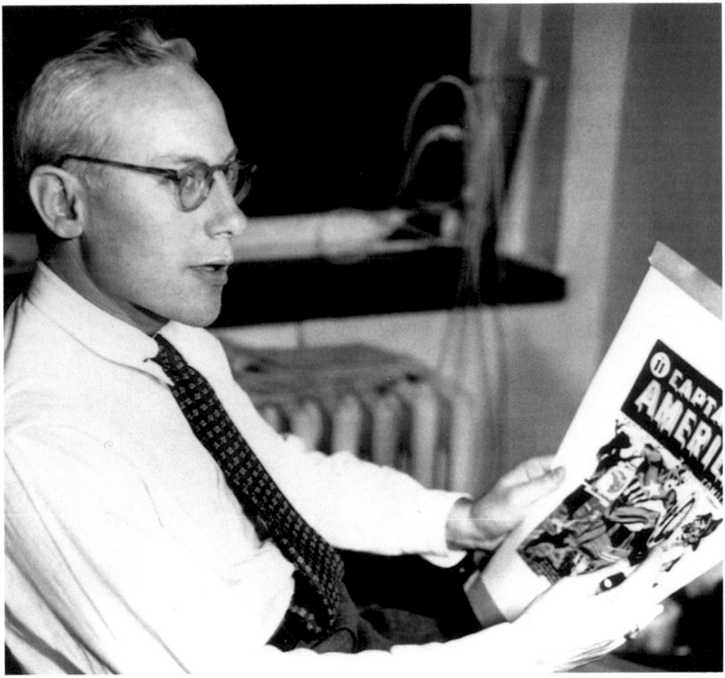
CAPTA
AMERI

I SEE AN EMPIRE IN MY FUTURE!

Above: *Photograph, Martin Goodman, 1941.* Holding in his hands a proof of Al Avison's cover to *Captain America Comics* No. 11, the young publisher (age 33) seems to be contemplating the future of his comic book line (or pondering the recent loss of his top creative team, Simon and Kirby!).

CAPTAIN AMERICA No. 11

Opposite: *Interior, "The Case of the Squad of Mystery"; script, unknown; pencils, Al Avison; inks, Syd Shores and George Klein; February 1942.*

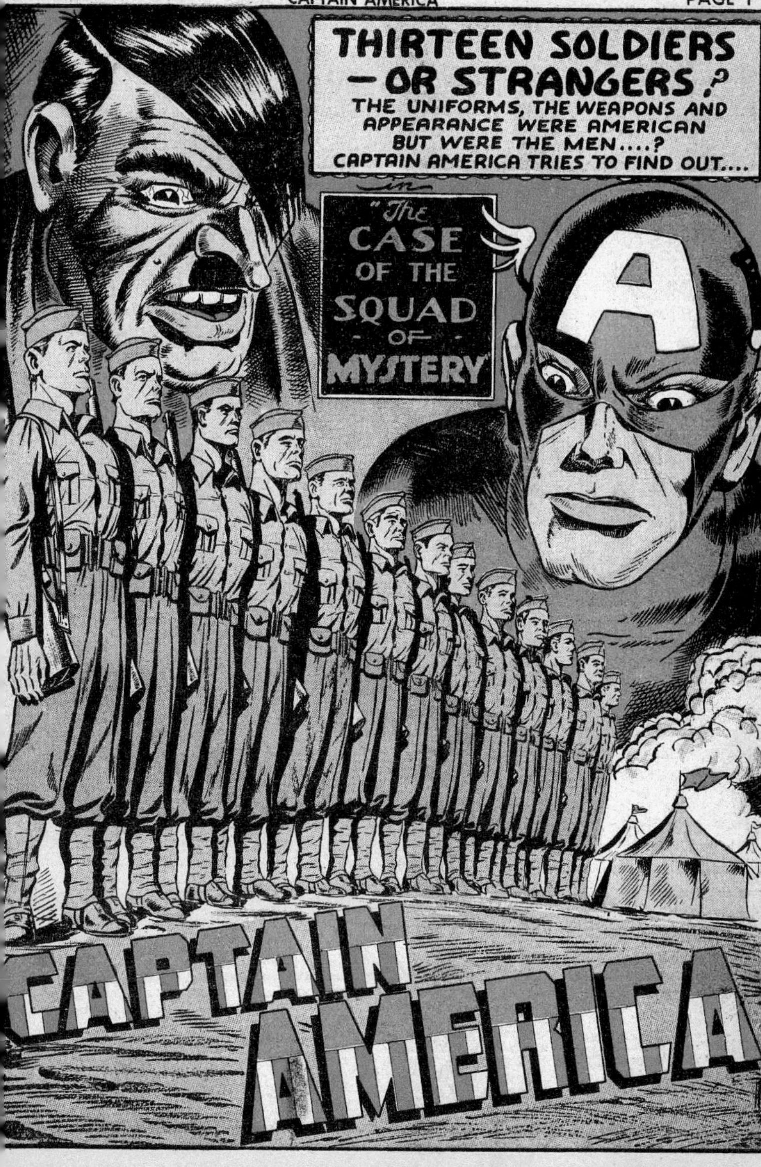
THIRTEEN SOLDIERS
— OR STRANGERS ?
THE UNIFORMS, THE WEAPONS AND
APPEARANCE WERE AMERICAN
BUT WERE THE MEN....?
CAPTAIN AMERICA TRIES TO FIND OUT....
in
"The
CASE
OF THE
SQUAD
- OF -
MYSTERY"
CAPTAIN
AMERICA

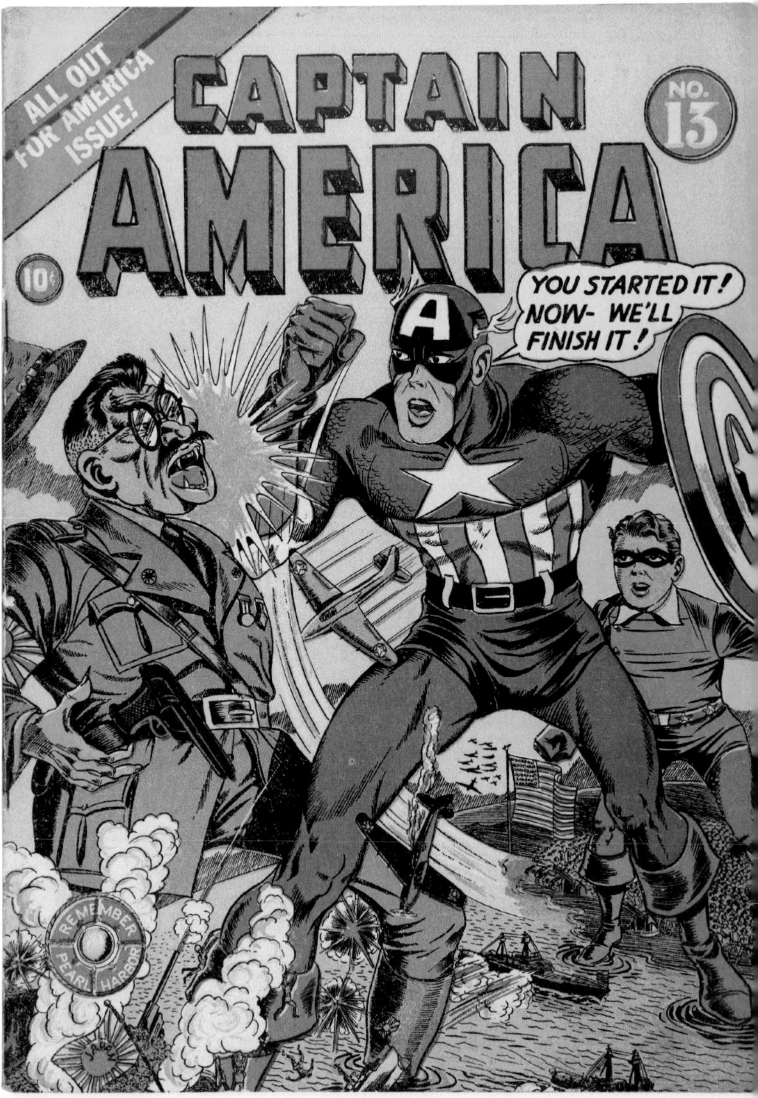
ALL OUT FOR AMERICA ISSUE!
CAPTAIN AMERICA
NO. 13
10¢
YOU STARTED IT! NOW- WE'LL FINISH IT!
REMEMBER PEARL HARBOR

CAPTAIN AMERICA No. 13

Opposite: *Cover; pencils, Al Avison; inks, Syd Shores and George Klein; April 1942.* On sale February 2, 1942, this was the first issue put into production following the attack on Pearl Harbor. Timely reflected the event on this rushed-onto-newsstands war cover.

THE MAN WITH A PLAN!

Above: *Photograph, Stan Lee (right) and friends, ca. 1941.*

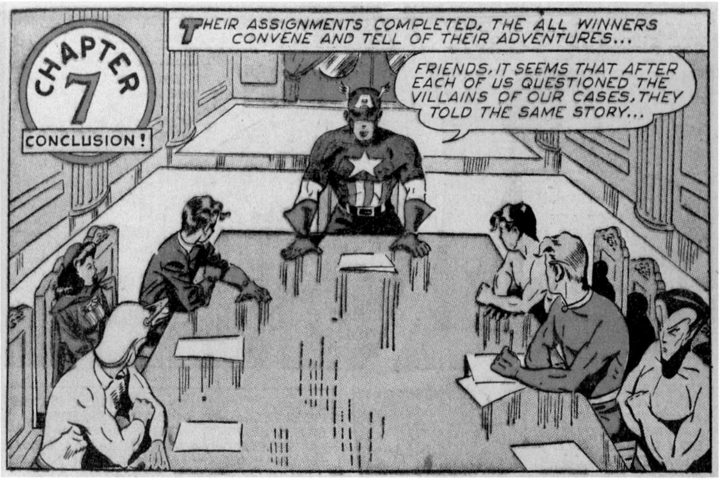
CHAPTER 7
CONCLUSION!
THEIR ASSIGNMENTS COMPLETED, THE ALL WINNERS CONVENE AND TELL OF THEIR ADVENTURES...
FRIENDS, IT SEEMS THAT AFTER EACH OF US QUESTIONED THE VILLAINS OF OUR CASES, THEY TOLD THE SAME STORY...

ALL-WINNERS COMICS No. 19

Above and opposite: *Cover; artist unknown. Interior; script, Bill Finger; pencils, Syd Shores; inks, attributed Vince Alascia; Fall 1946.* After five chapters of solo adventures, the seven heroes convene to compare notes. Finger, the uncredited writer of Bob Kane's Batman feature, makes the first of his rare Timely contributions here.

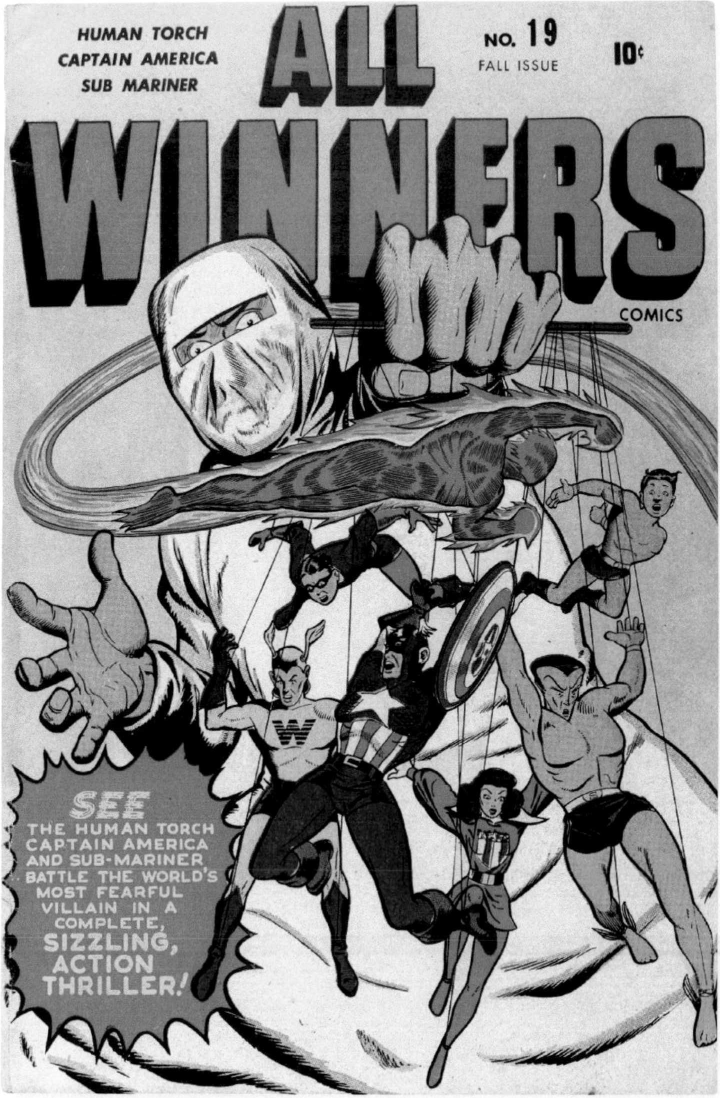
HUMAN TORCH
CAPTAIN AMERICA
SUB MARINER
ALL WINNERS
COMICS
NO. 19
FALL ISSUE
10¢
SEE
THE HUMAN TORCH
CAPTAIN AMERICA
AND SUB-MARINER
BATTLE THE WORLD'S
MOST FEARFUL
VILLAIN IN A
COMPLETE,
SIZZLING,
ACTION
THRILLER!

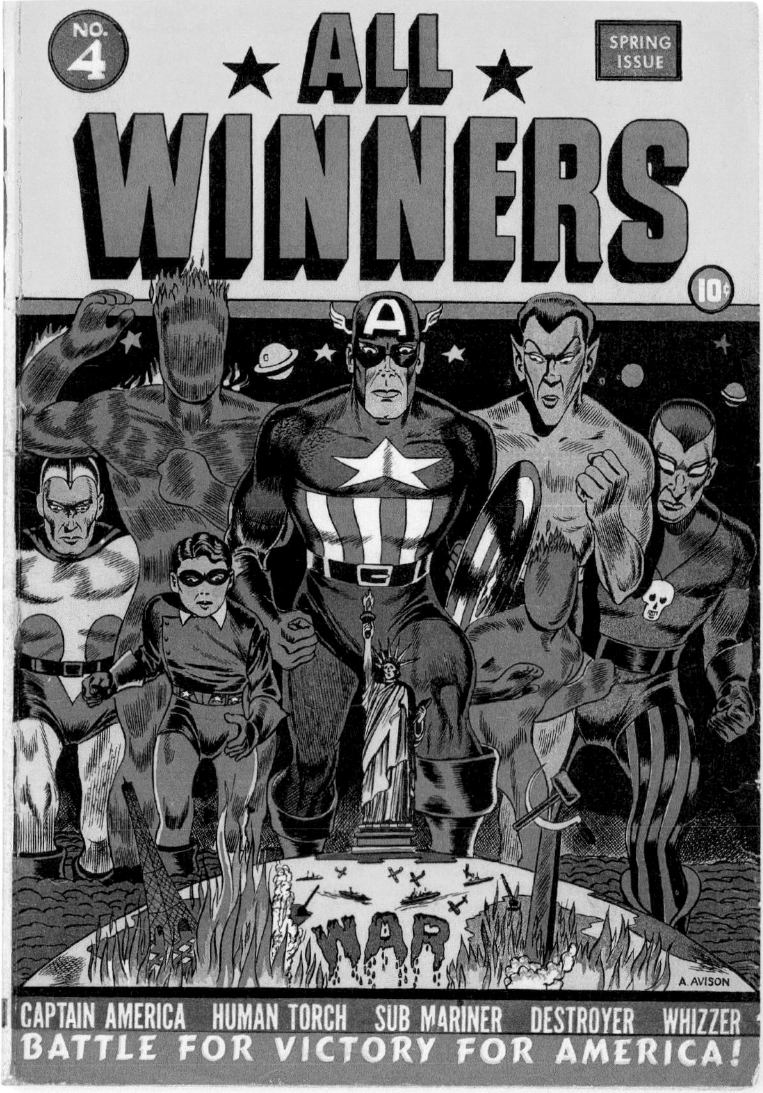
NO. 4
ALL WINNERS
SPRING ISSUE
10¢
WAR
A. AVISON
CAPTAIN AMERICA HUMAN TORCH SUB MARINER DESTROYER WHIZZER
BATTLE FOR VICTORY FOR AMERICA!

ALL-WINNERS COMICS No. 4

Opposite: *Cover; pencils and inks, Al Avison; Spring 1942.* A classic war cover displays all of this title's Timely heroes marching above a blazing image of war-torn Earth.

ALL-SELECT COMICS No. 3

Below: *Cover; pencils and inks, Alex Schomburg; Spring 1944.* An elaborately detailed cover by Timely's master cover artist. Schomburg's blazing action covers usually showcased all of Timely's Big Three cover stars: the Human Torch (and Toro), the Sub-Mariner, and Captain America (with Bucky).

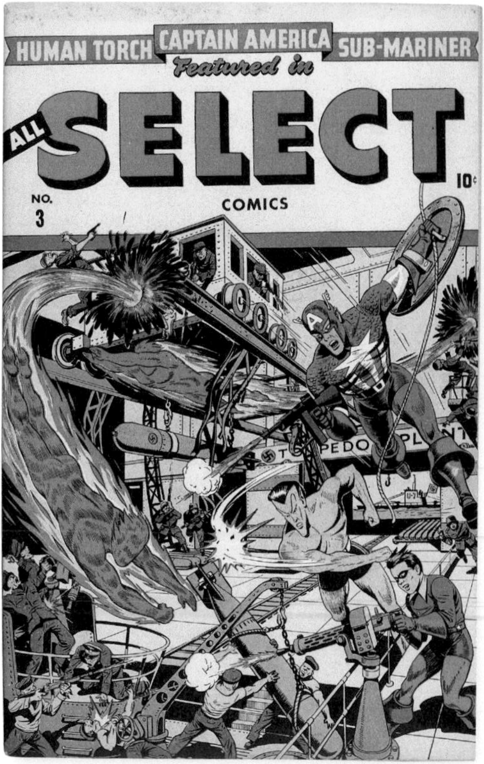

HUMAN TORCH
CAPTAIN AMERICA
SUB-MARINER
Featured in
ALL
SELECT
10¢
NO.
3
COMICS

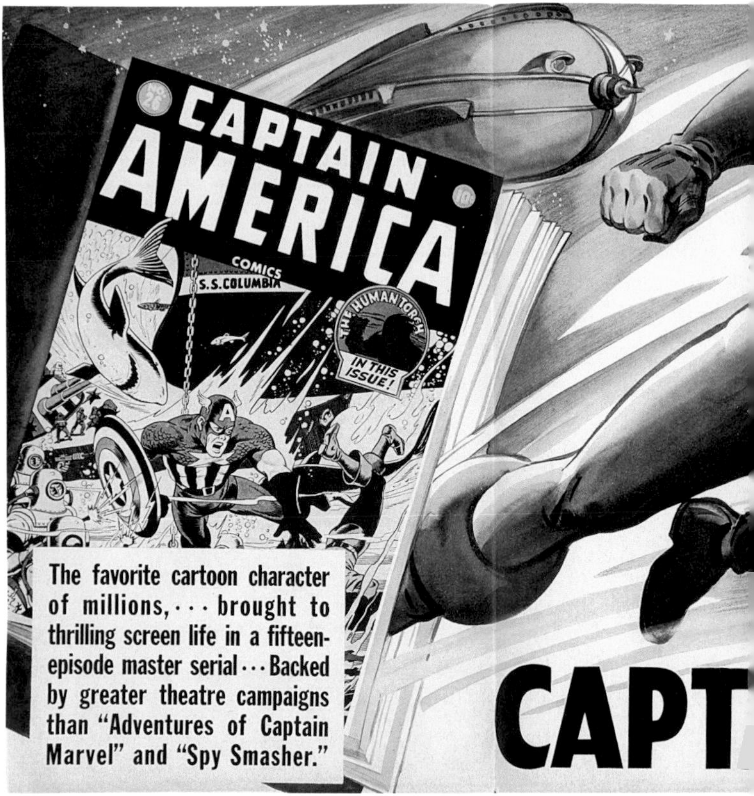
No. 26
CAPTAIN AMERICA
10¢
COMICS
S.S. COLUMBIA
THE HUMAN TORCH
IN THIS ISSUE!
The favorite cartoon character of millions, · · · brought to thrilling screen life in a fifteen-episode master serial · · · Backed by greater theatre campaigns than "Adventures of Captain Marvel" and "Spy Smasher."
CAPT

SELLING THE SERIAL

Above: *Exhibitor's book interior; art, unknown; Republic Pictures; ca. 1944*. Unbelievable by today's blockbuster standards, according to Joe Simon, years later he discovered that Republic "had paid nothing.... Goodman, had given them the rights, gratis, expecting to reap his rewards from publicity." Placement in Republic's lineup of box-office hits introduced "the favorite cartoon character of millions" to an even wider audience, and promoted Timely's best-selling hero alongside the likes of live-action stars John Wayne, Roy Rogers, Gene Autry, and Dorothy Dandridge.

N AMERICA

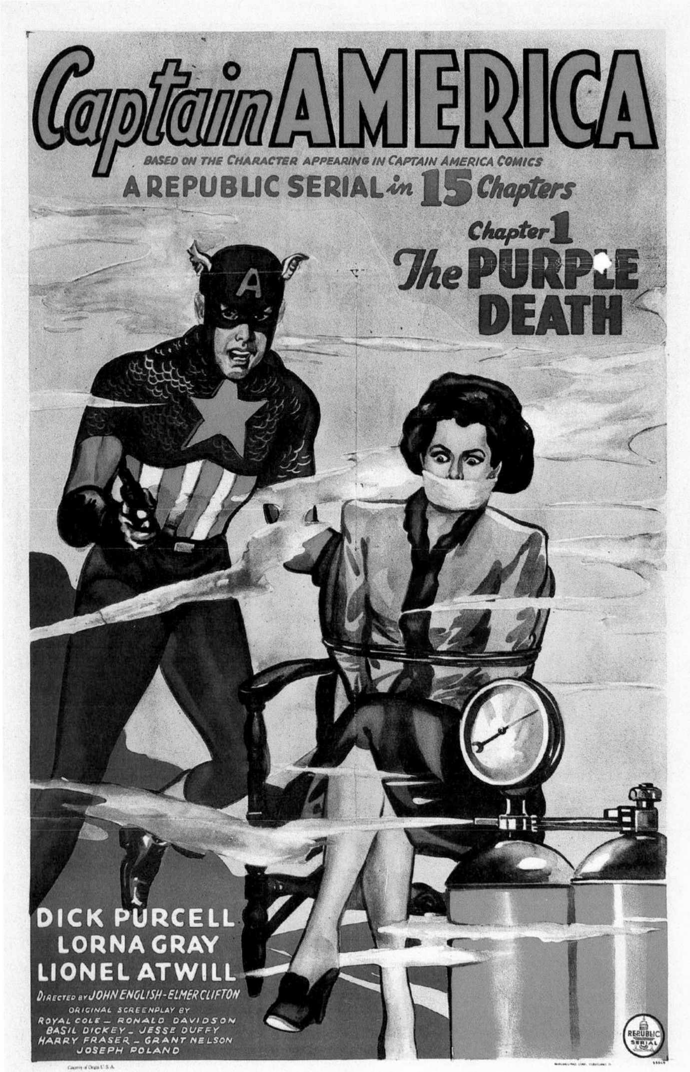
Captain AMERICA
BASED ON THE CHARACTER APPEARING IN CAPTAIN AMERICA COMICS
A REPUBLIC SERIAL in 15 Chapters
Chapter 1
The PURPLE DEATH
DICK PURCELL
LORNA GRAY
LIONEL ATWILL
DIRECTED BY JOHN ENGLISH - ELMER CLIFTON
ORIGINAL SCREENPLAY BY
ROYAL COLE - RONALD DAVIDSON
BASIL DICKEY - JESSE DUFFY
HARRY FRASER - GRANT NELSON
JOSEPH POLAND
REPUBLIC SERIAL

CAPTAIN OF THE BIG SCREEN

Opposite and above: Captain America *serial poster and lobby card detail, "The Purple Death," Republic Pictures, 1944.* The first chapter of 15, starring Dick Purcell as Captain America. Republic's adaptation of Simon & Kirby's super hero bore little resemblance to the character in the comics. Gone was Cap's shield (he now had a gun to fend off foes) and his elaborate costume (which would have been too clunky for the stunts).

CAPTAIN AMERICA LIVES!

Pages 48–49: *Poster; promotional still, Dick Purcell, Republic Pictures. 1944.* Jam-packed with slugfests that could have been choreographed by Simon and Kirby, *Captain America* signaled the end of the wartime super hero serials.

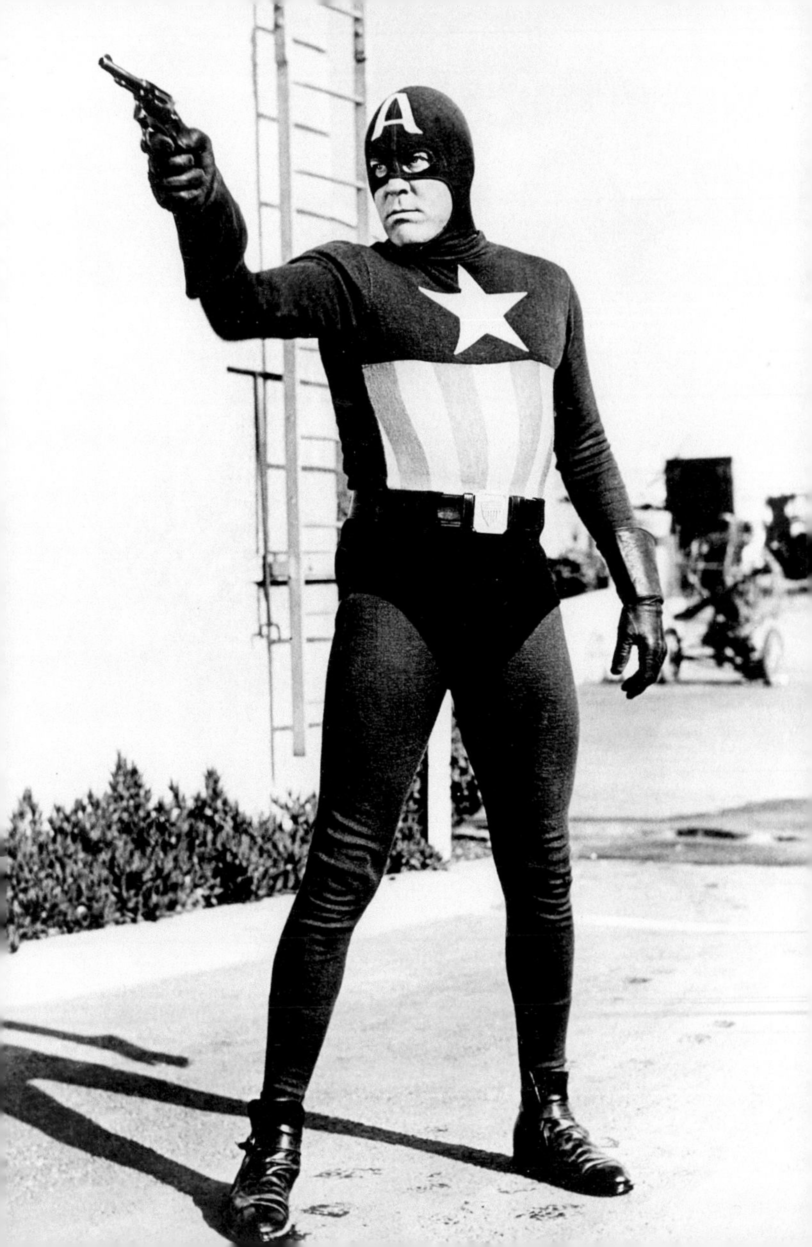

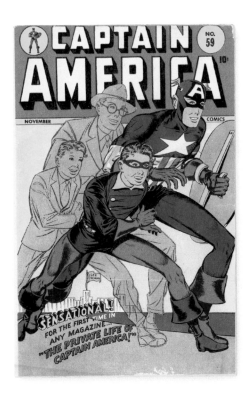

CAPTAIN AMERICA
NO. 59
10¢
NOVEMBER
COMICS
SENSATIONAL!
FOR THE FIRST TIME IN ANY MAGAZINE...
"THE PRIVATE LIFE OF CAPTAIN AMERICA!"

CAPTAIN AMERICA COMICS No. 59

Above: *Cover; pencils and inks, Syd Shores; November 1946.*

CAPTAIN AMERICA COMICS No. 68

Opposite and pages 52–53: *Interiors; script, unknown; pencils, attributed Gene Colan; inks, unknown; September 1948.* "Captain America became more than a character in a comic book. Month by month, he was being woven into the fabric of American folklore. He symbolized our strength and resolve. He became our male, action hero version of the Statue of Liberty. He inspired servicemen, rallied the home front, and encouraged the children of 'The Greatest Generation' during their darkest hour. Comic books were reflecting our times, and as we can clearly see from the hindsight of nearly 70 years, those times cried out for Captain America." —Michael Uslan

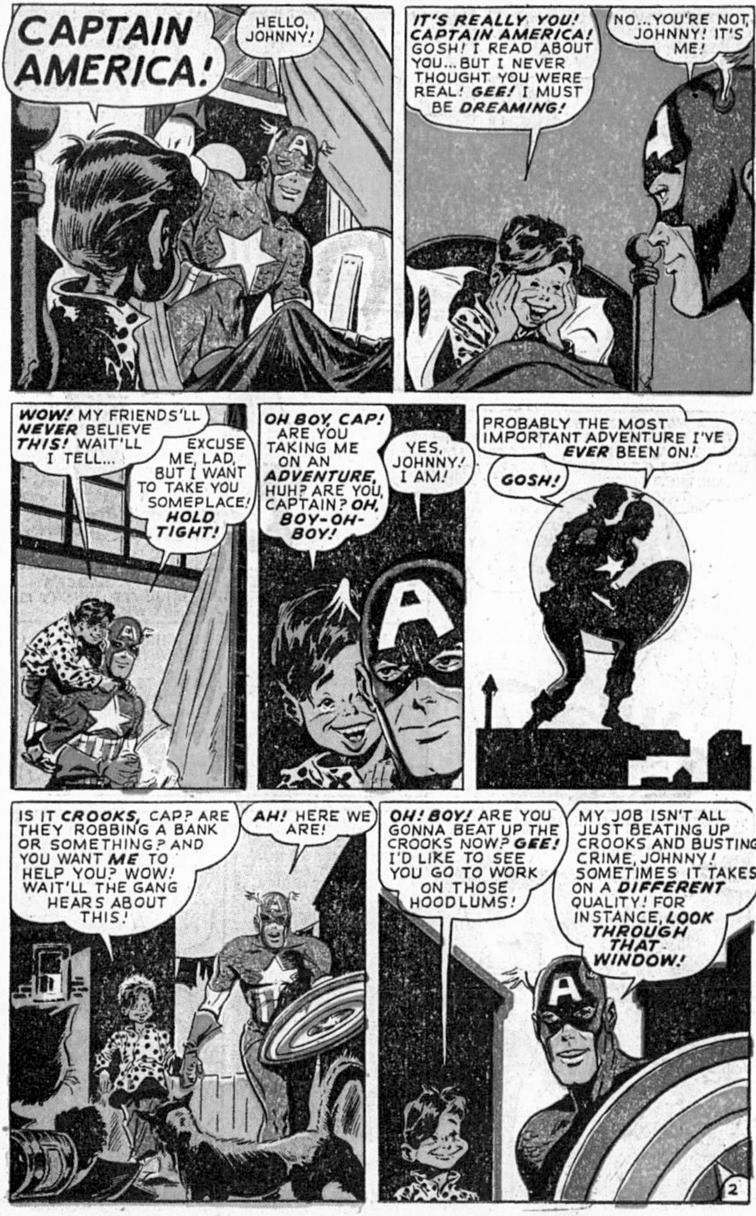
CAPTAIN AMERICA!
HELLO, JOHNNY!
IT'S REALLY YOU! CAPTAIN AMERICA! GOSH! I READ ABOUT YOU... BUT I NEVER THOUGHT YOU WERE REAL! GEE! I MUST BE DREAMING!
NO... YOU'RE NOT, JOHNNY! IT'S ME!
WOW! MY FRIENDS'LL NEVER BELIEVE THIS! WAIT'LL I TELL...
EXCUSE ME, LAD, BUT I WANT TO TAKE YOU SOMEPLACE! HOLD TIGHT!
OH BOY, CAP! ARE YOU TAKING ME ON AN ADVENTURE, HUH? ARE YOU, CAPTAIN? OH, BOY-OH-BOY!
YES, JOHNNY! I AM!
PROBABLY THE MOST IMPORTANT ADVENTURE I'VE EVER BEEN ON!
GOSH!
IS IT CROOKS, CAP? ARE THEY ROBBING A BANK OR SOMETHING? AND YOU WANT ME TO HELP YOU? WOW! WAIT'LL THE GANG HEARS ABOUT THIS!
AH! HERE WE ARE!
OH! BOY! ARE YOU GONNA BEAT UP THE CROOKS NOW? GEE! I'D LIKE TO SEE YOU GO TO WORK ON THOSE HOODLUMS!
MY JOB ISN'T ALL JUST BEATING UP CROOKS AND BUSTING CRIME, JOHNNY! SOMETIMES IT TAKES ON A DIFFERENT QUALITY! FOR INSTANCE, LOOK THROUGH THAT WINDOW!
2

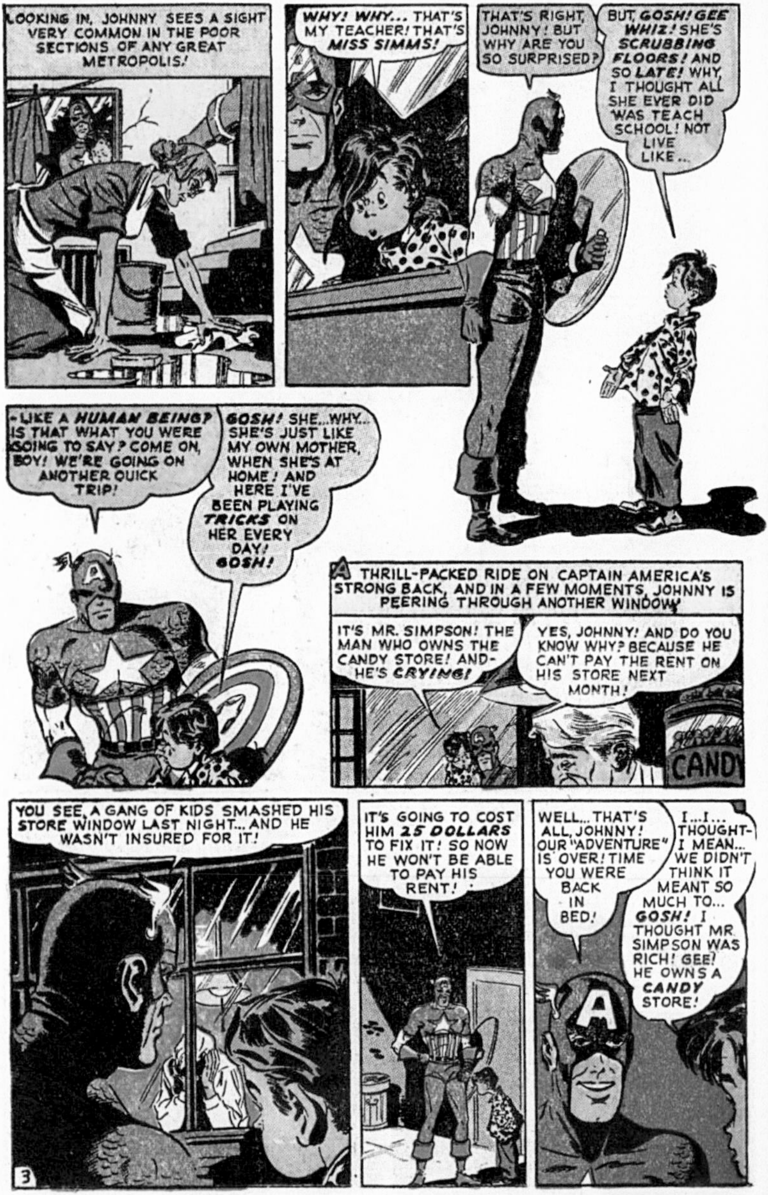
LOOKING IN, JOHNNY SEES A SIGHT VERY COMMON IN THE POOR SECTIONS OF ANY GREAT METROPOLIS!
WHY! WHY... THAT'S MY TEACHER! THAT'S MISS SIMMS!
THAT'S RIGHT, JOHNNY! BUT WHY ARE YOU SO SURPRISED?
BUT, GOSH! GEE WHIZ! SHE'S SCRUBBING FLOORS! AND SO LATE! WHY, I THOUGHT ALL SHE EVER DID WAS TEACH SCHOOL! NOT LIVE LIKE...
-LIKE A HUMAN BEING? IS THAT WHAT YOU WERE GOING TO SAY? COME ON, BOY! WE'RE GOING ON ANOTHER QUICK TRIP!
GOSH! SHE...WHY... SHE'S JUST LIKE MY OWN MOTHER, WHEN SHE'S AT HOME! AND HERE I'VE BEEN PLAYING TRICKS ON HER EVERY DAY! GOSH!
A THRILL-PACKED RIDE ON CAPTAIN AMERICA'S STRONG BACK, AND IN A FEW MOMENTS, JOHNNY IS PEERING THROUGH ANOTHER WINDOW!
IT'S MR. SIMPSON! THE MAN WHO OWNS THE CANDY STORE! AND- HE'S CRYING!
YES, JOHNNY! AND DO YOU KNOW WHY? BECAUSE HE CAN'T PAY THE RENT ON HIS STORE NEXT MONTH!
CANDY
YOU SEE, A GANG OF KIDS SMASHED HIS STORE WINDOW LAST NIGHT... AND HE WASN'T INSURED FOR IT!
IT'S GOING TO COST HIM 25 DOLLARS TO FIX IT! SO NOW HE WON'T BE ABLE TO PAY HIS RENT!
WELL... THAT'S ALL, JOHNNY! OUR "ADVENTURE" IS OVER! TIME YOU WERE BACK IN BED!
I...I... THOUGHT- I MEAN... WE DIDN'T THINK IT MEANT SO MUCH TO... GOSH! I THOUGHT MR. SIMPSON WAS RICH! GEE! HE OWNS A CANDY STORE!
3

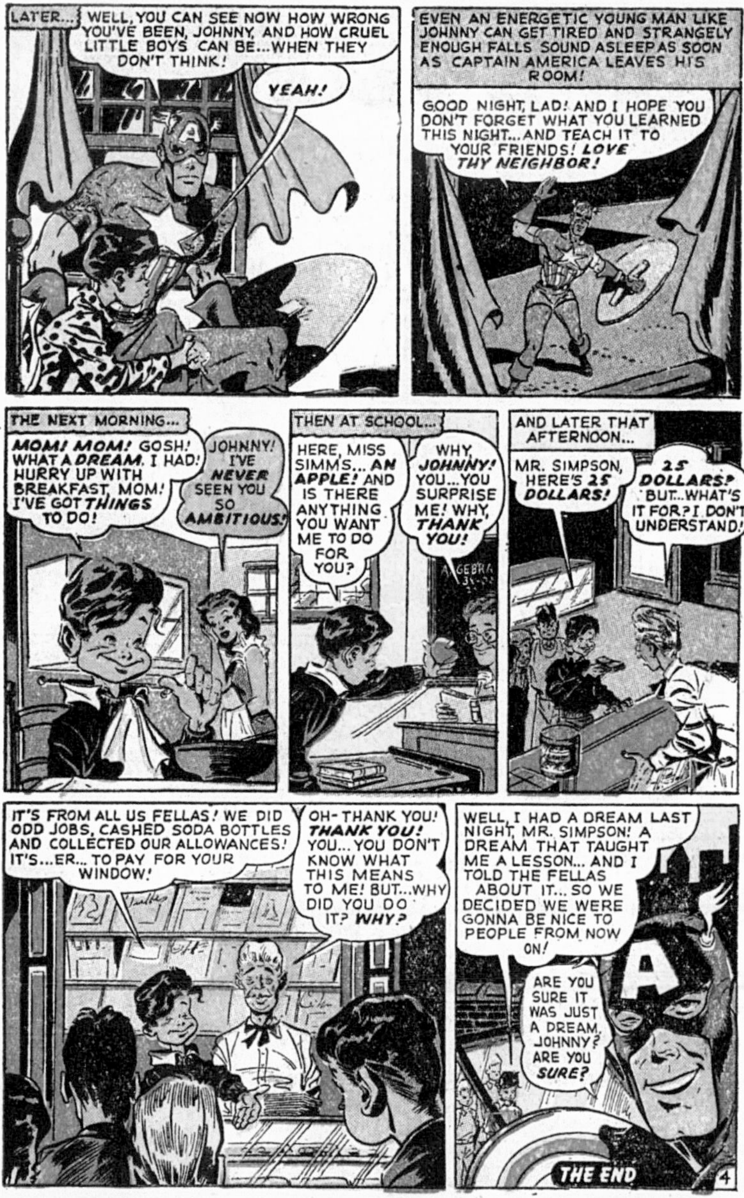
LATER...
WELL, YOU CAN SEE NOW HOW WRONG YOU'VE BEEN, JOHNNY, AND HOW CRUEL LITTLE BOYS CAN BE...WHEN THEY DON'T THINK!
YEAH!
EVEN AN ENERGETIC YOUNG MAN LIKE JOHNNY CAN GET TIRED AND STRANGELY ENOUGH FALLS SOUND ASLEEP AS SOON AS CAPTAIN AMERICA LEAVES HIS ROOM!
GOOD NIGHT, LAD! AND I HOPE YOU DON'T FORGET WHAT YOU LEARNED THIS NIGHT...AND TEACH IT TO YOUR FRIENDS! LOVE THY NEIGHBOR!
THE NEXT MORNING...
MOM! MOM! GOSH! WHAT A DREAM I HAD! HURRY UP WITH BREAKFAST, MOM! I'VE GOT THINGS TO DO!
JOHNNY! I'VE NEVER SEEN YOU SO AMBITIOUS!
THEN AT SCHOOL...
HERE, MISS SIMMS... AN APPLE! AND IS THERE ANYTHING YOU WANT ME TO DO FOR YOU?
WHY, JOHNNY! YOU...YOU SURPRISE ME! WHY, THANK YOU!
AND LATER THAT AFTERNOON...
MR. SIMPSON, HERE'S 25 DOLLARS!
25 DOLLARS? BUT...WHAT'S IT FOR? I DON'T UNDERSTAND!
IT'S FROM ALL US FELLAS! WE DID ODD JOBS, CASHED SODA BOTTLES AND COLLECTED OUR ALLOWANCES! IT'S...ER... TO PAY FOR YOUR WINDOW!
OH- THANK YOU! THANK YOU! YOU... YOU DON'T KNOW WHAT THIS MEANS TO ME! BUT...WHY DID YOU DO IT? WHY?
WELL, I HAD A DREAM LAST NIGHT, MR. SIMPSON! A DREAM THAT TAUGHT ME A LESSON... AND I TOLD THE FELLAS ABOUT IT... SO WE DECIDED WE WERE GONNA BE NICE TO PEOPLE FROM NOW ON!
ARE YOU SURE IT WAS JUST A DREAM, JOHNNY? ARE YOU SURE?
THE END
4

CAPTAIN AMERICA

THE MOST TERRIFYING CRIMINAL IN THE ANNALS OF LAW-LESSNESS...THE HUMAN FLY! SCALING SHEER WALLS, AT-TRACTED BY THE SWEETS OF FRUITFUL CRIME! NEEDING MORE THAN JUST A FLY-SWATTER, NEEDING ALL THE DARING COURAGE AND ATHLETIC SKILL AT THEIR DISPOSAL, **CAPTAIN AMERICA** AND **BUCKY** UNDERTAKE THE HAZARDOUS TASK OF SQUASHING **THE HUMAN FLY!**

"The **HUMAN FLY!**"

CAPTAIN AMERICA'S
WEIRD TALES
OCT.
NO. 74
10¢
MARVEL COMIC
THE RED SKULL STRIKES AGAIN!

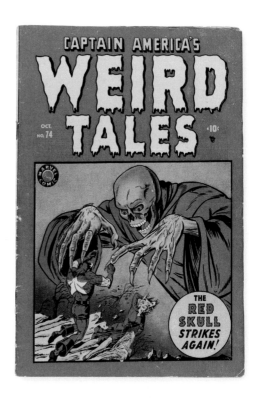

CAPTAIN AMERICA COMICS No. 60

Opposite: *Interior, "The Human Fly"; script, pencils, and inks, unknown; January 1947.* An early permutation of a man in an insect suit who can walk on walls. Simon and Kirby would use this concept in 1960 in *Adventures of the Fly* for Archie Comics.

CAPTAIN AMERICA'S WEIRD TALES No. 74

Above: *Cover; pencils, attributed Mart Nodell; inks, unknown; October 1949.* The penultimate issue of the Golden Age run of *Captain America Comics* showed a title change to reflect the increasing newsstand presence of horror and mystery titles. The lead Captain America story pitted our hero against his arch nemesis, the Red Skull, battling for his life within the gates of hell itself!

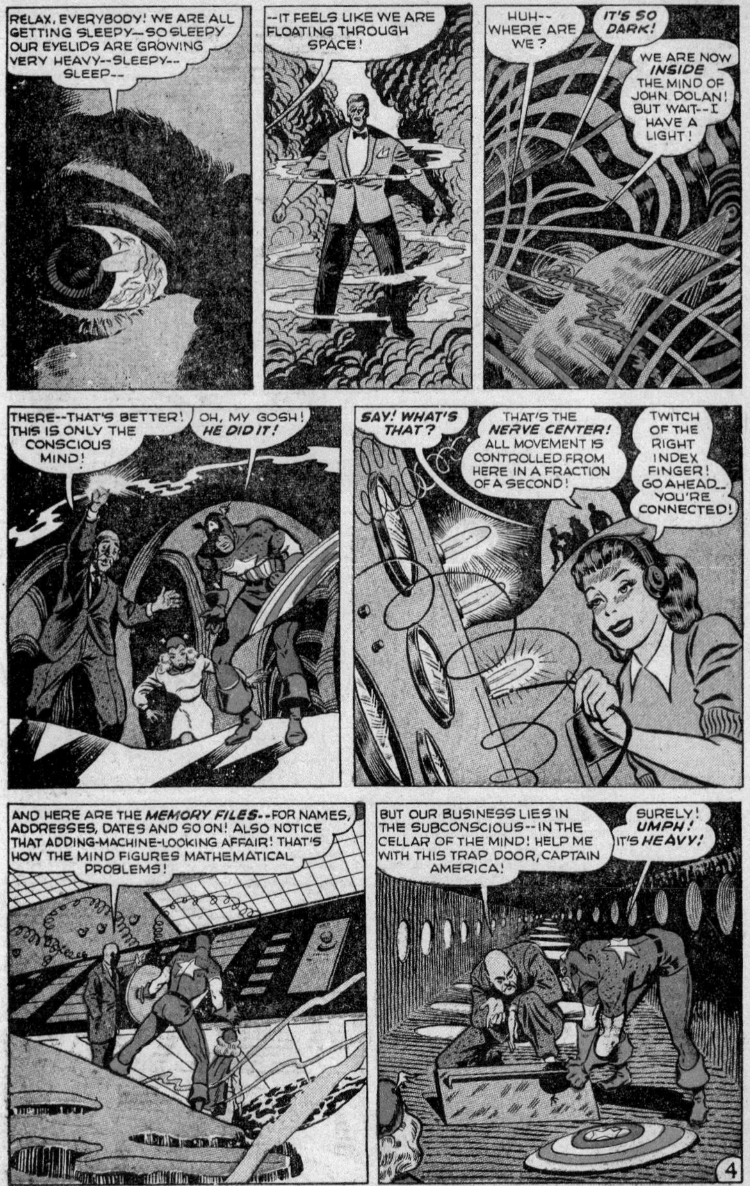
RELAX, EVERYBODY! WE ARE ALL GETTING SLEEPY--SO SLEEPY OUR EYELIDS ARE GROWING VERY HEAVY--SLEEPY--SLEEP--
--IT FEELS LIKE WE ARE FLOATING THROUGH SPACE!
HUH--WHERE ARE WE?
IT'S SO DARK!
WE ARE NOW INSIDE THE MIND OF JOHN DOLAN! BUT WAIT--I HAVE A LIGHT!
THERE--THAT'S BETTER! THIS IS ONLY THE CONSCIOUS MIND!
OH, MY GOSH! HE DID IT!
SAY! WHAT'S THAT?
THAT'S THE NERVE CENTER! ALL MOVEMENT IS CONTROLLED FROM HERE IN A FRACTION OF A SECOND!
TWITCH OF THE RIGHT INDEX FINGER! GO AHEAD-- YOU'RE CONNECTED!
AND HERE ARE THE MEMORY FILES--FOR NAMES, ADDRESSES, DATES AND SO ON! ALSO NOTICE THAT ADDING-MACHINE-LOOKING AFFAIR! THAT'S HOW THE MIND FIGURES MATHEMATICAL PROBLEMS!
BUT OUR BUSINESS LIES IN THE SUBCONSCIOUS--IN THE CELLAR OF THE MIND! HELP ME WITH THIS TRAP DOOR, CAPTAIN AMERICA!
SURELY! UMPH! IT'S HEAVY!
4

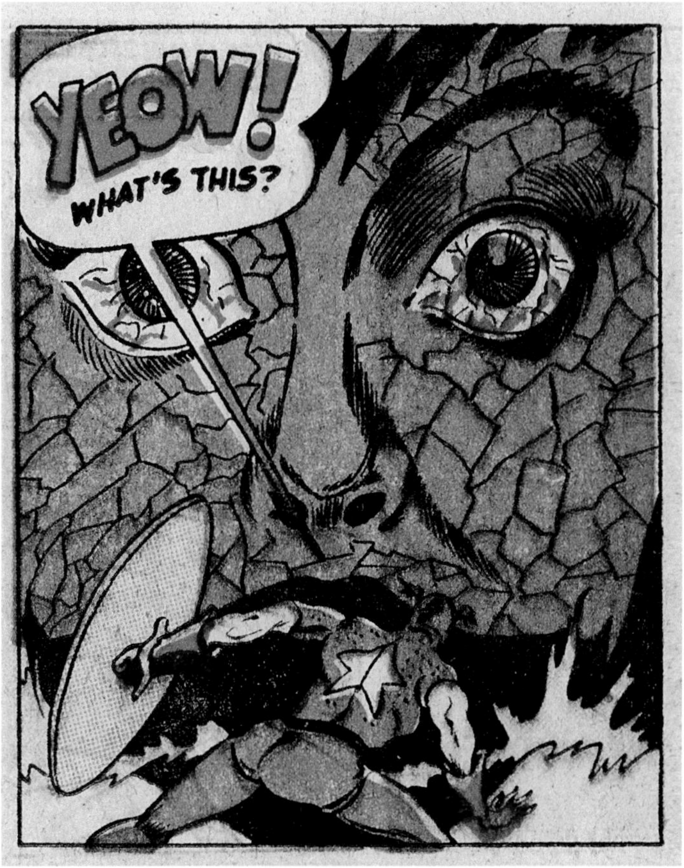
YEOW!
WHAT'S THIS?

CAPTAIN AMERICA COMICS No. 72

Opposite and above: *Interiors, "Murder in the Mind!"; script, unknown; pencils, Gene Colan; inks, George Klein; May 1949.* Gene Colan sharpens the skills he will one day bring to *Doctor Strange* and *Tomb of Dracula* in this 12-page tour de force, in which Captain America explores the myriad psychedelic vistas of the subconscious mind. This is one of at least four Timely super hero stories penciled by Colan in 1948–49.

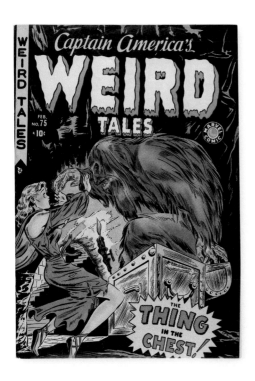

Captain America's
WEIRD
TALES
WEIRD TALES
FEB.
NO. 75
10¢
MARVEL COMIC
THE THING IN THE CHEST!

CAPTAIN AMERICA'S WEIRD TALES No. 75

Above: *Cover; pencils, Gene Colan; inks, unknown; February 1950.* Captain America doesn't even appear anywhere in this, the last issue of Timely's foremost Golden Age super hero title. The book had been slanting toward weird horror stories—still starring Captain America—for about six months before No. 74's hybrid retitling. With this final release, the conversion was complete, and Timely's Big Three were—for the moment, at least—all out of print.

CAPTAIN AMERICA COMICS No. 65

Opposite: *Cover; pencils, Syd Shores; inks, unknown; January 1948.* Bill Woolfolk scripted all three Captain America stories in this issue. In the postwar era, Cap's storylines went from crushing Axis powers to much more mundane matters, in this case getting hoodwinked by this glamorous mobbed-up moll.

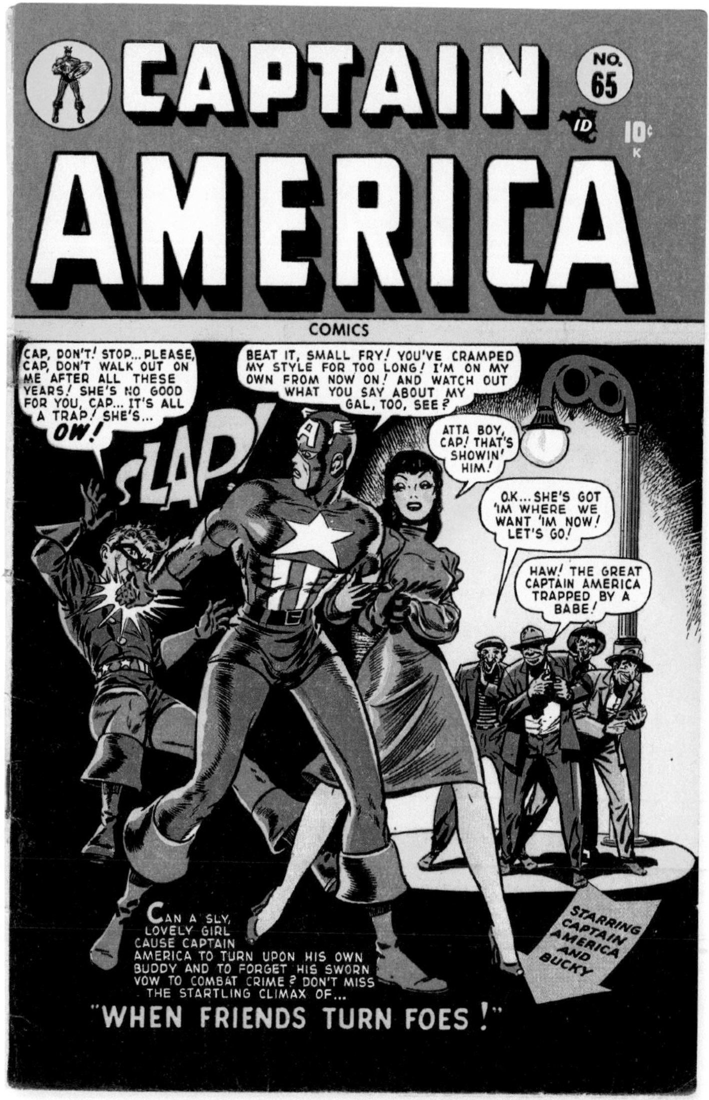
CAPTAIN AMERICA
NO. 65
10¢
COMICS
CAP, DON'T! STOP... PLEASE, CAP, DON'T WALK OUT ON ME AFTER ALL THESE YEARS! SHE'S NO GOOD FOR YOU, CAP... IT'S ALL A TRAP! SHE'S... OW!
BEAT IT, SMALL FRY! YOU'VE CRAMPED MY STYLE FOR TOO LONG! I'M ON MY OWN FROM NOW ON! AND WATCH OUT WHAT YOU SAY ABOUT MY GAL, TOO, SEE?
SLAP!
ATTA BOY, CAP! THAT'S SHOWIN' HIM!
O.K... SHE'S GOT 'IM WHERE WE WANT 'IM NOW! LET'S GO!
HAW! THE GREAT CAPTAIN AMERICA TRAPPED BY A BABE!
CAN A SLY, LOVELY GIRL CAUSE CAPTAIN AMERICA TO TURN UPON HIS OWN BUDDY AND TO FORGET HIS SWORN VOW TO COMBAT CRIME? DON'T MISS THE STARTLING CLIMAX OF...
"WHEN FRIENDS TURN FOES!"
STARRING CAPTAIN AMERICA AND BUCKY

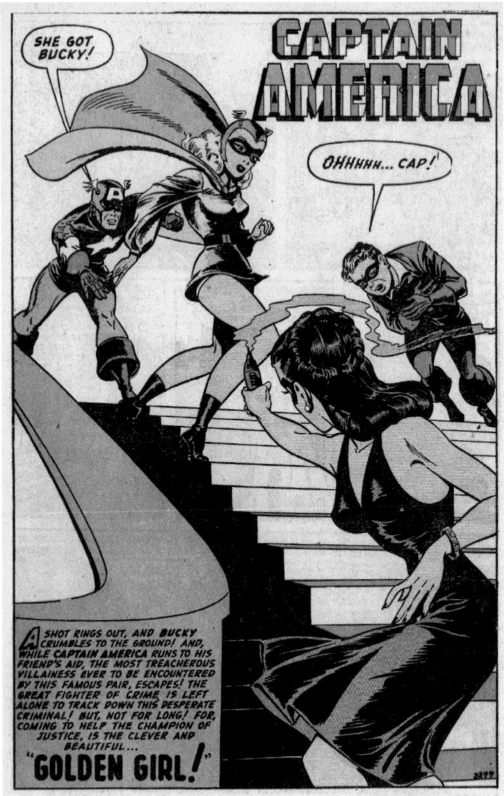
CAPTAIN AMERICA
SHE GOT BUCKY!
OHHHHH... CAP!
A SHOT RINGS OUT, AND BUCKY CRUMBLES TO THE GROUND! AND, WHILE CAPTAIN AMERICA RUNS TO HIS FRIEND'S AID, THE MOST TREACHEROUS VILLAINESS EVER TO BE ENCOUNTERED BY THIS FAMOUS PAIR, ESCAPES! THE GREAT FIGHTER OF CRIME IS LEFT ALONE TO TRACK DOWN THIS DESPERATE CRIMINAL! BUT, NOT FOR LONG! FOR, COMING TO HELP THE CHAMPION OF JUSTICE, IS THE CLEVER AND BEAUTIFUL...
"GOLDEN GIRL!"

CAPTAIN AMERICA COMICS No. 66

Above and opposite: *Interiors, "Golden Girl"; script, Bill Woolfolk; pencils, Syd Shores; inks, unknown; April 1948.* After Bucky was shot and wounded by a ruthless villainess, the long-running supporting character Betty Ross—now wearing a mask and costume and called Golden Girl—was conveniently positioned to replace the teenage sidekick as Cap's new partner, *and* love interest. After being relegated to a hospital bed to recover, Bucky will only see print once more until 1954, while Golden Girl will stick around for seven of the next eight issues.

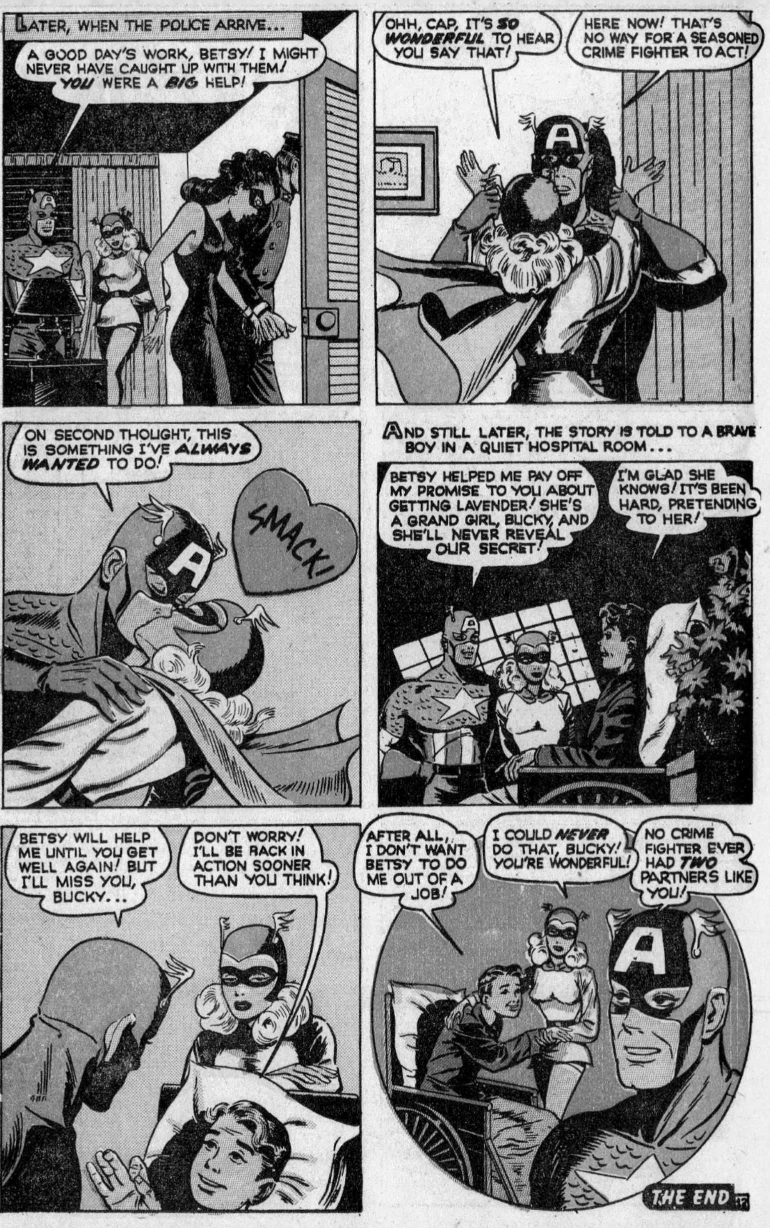
LATER, WHEN THE POLICE ARRIVE...
A GOOD DAY'S WORK, BETSY! I MIGHT NEVER HAVE CAUGHT UP WITH THEM! YOU WERE A BIG HELP!
OHH, CAP, IT'S SO WONDERFUL TO HEAR YOU SAY THAT!
HERE NOW! THAT'S NO WAY FOR A SEASONED CRIME FIGHTER TO ACT!
ON SECOND THOUGHT, THIS IS SOMETHING I'VE ALWAYS WANTED TO DO!
SMACK!
AND STILL LATER, THE STORY IS TOLD TO A BRAVE BOY IN A QUIET HOSPITAL ROOM...
BETSY HELPED ME PAY OFF MY PROMISE TO YOU ABOUT GETTING LAVENDER! SHE'S A GRAND GIRL, BUCKY, AND SHE'LL NEVER REVEAL OUR SECRET!
I'M GLAD SHE KNOWS! IT'S BEEN HARD, PRETENDING TO HER!
BETSY WILL HELP ME UNTIL YOU GET WELL AGAIN! BUT I'LL MISS YOU, BUCKY...
DON'T WORRY! I'LL BE BACK IN ACTION SOONER THAN YOU THINK!
AFTER ALL, I DON'T WANT BETSY TO DO ME OUT OF A JOB!
I COULD NEVER DO THAT, BUCKY! YOU'RE WONDERFUL!
NO CRIME FIGHTER EVER HAD TWO PARTNERS LIKE YOU!
THE END

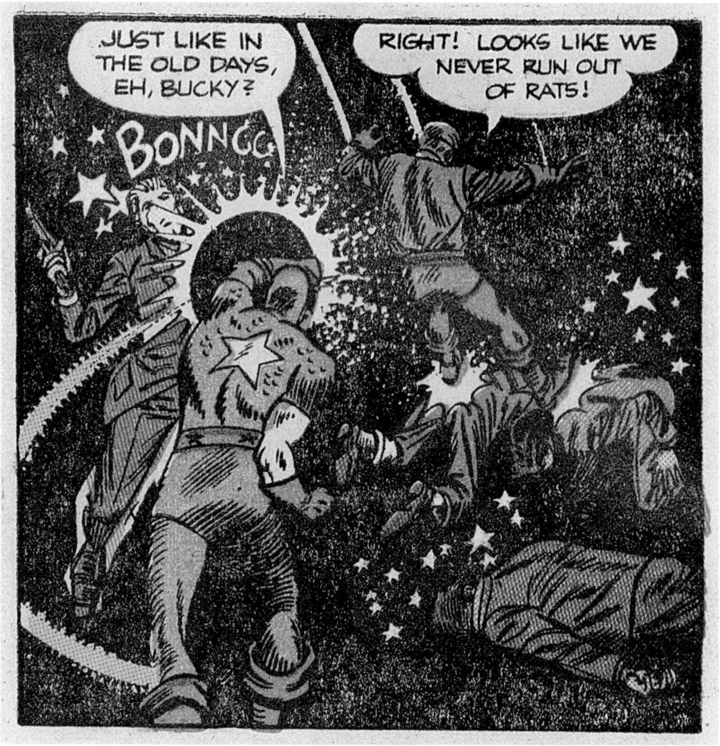
JUST LIKE IN THE OLD DAYS, EH, BUCKY?
RIGHT! LOOKS LIKE WE NEVER RUN OUT OF RATS!
BONNGG

CAPTAIN AMERICA No. 76

Above and opposite: *Cover; pencils, attributed Carl Burgos; inks, Carl Burgos. Interior, "The Betrayers"; script, unknown; pencils and inks, John Romita. May 1954.* Captain America and Bucky…Commie Hunters! With the war long over, the Communists were the next existential threat to Cold War America in the debut of Captain America's hero revival title. Burgos was unofficial cover editor at the time, and had a hand in laying out, penciling, or inking many of them.

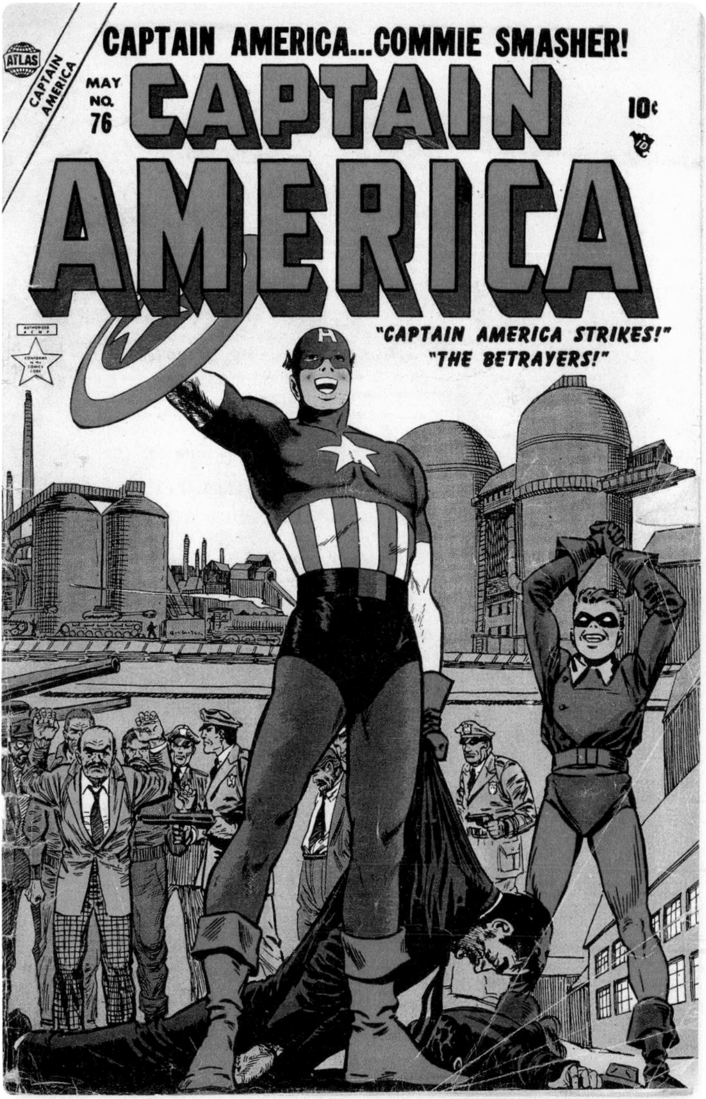
CAPTAIN AMERICA...COMMIE SMASHER!
ATLAS
CAPTAIN AMERICA
MAY
NO. 76
CAPTAIN AMERICA
10¢
"CAPTAIN AMERICA STRIKES!"
"THE BETRAYERS!"

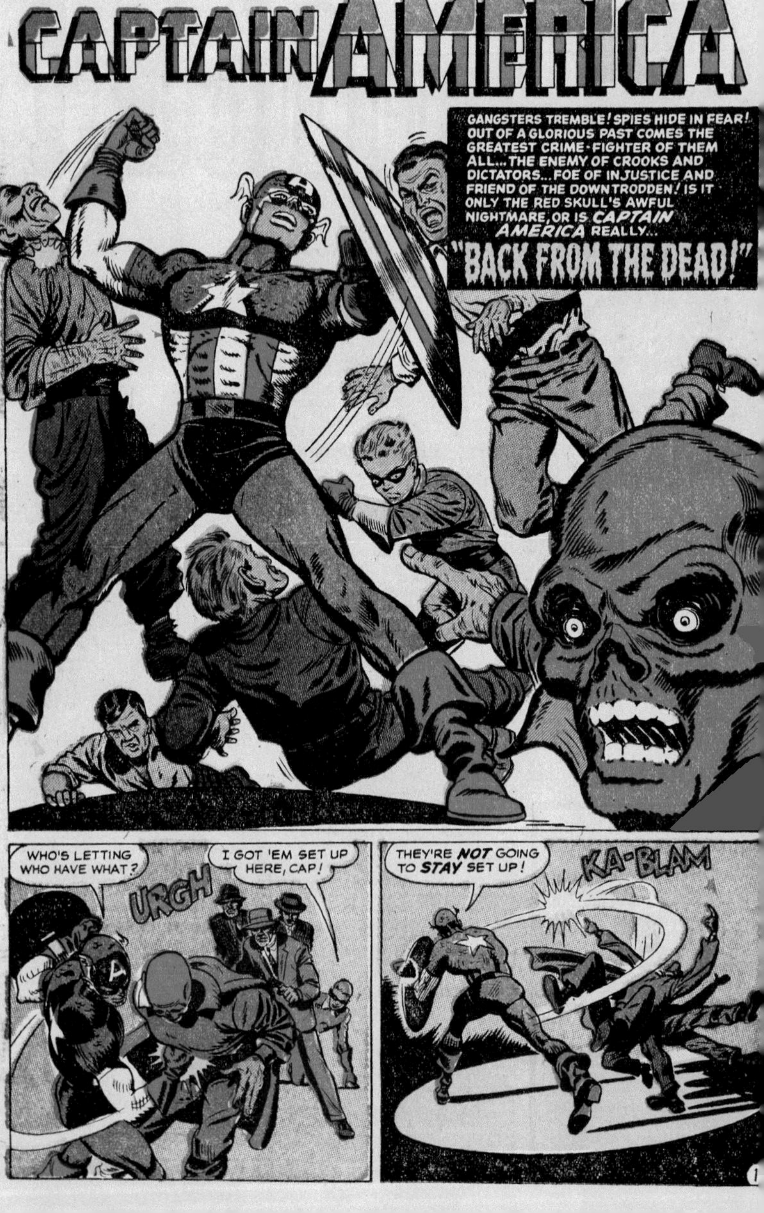
CAPTAIN AMERICA
GANGSTERS TREMBLE! SPIES HIDE IN FEAR! OUT OF A GLORIOUS PAST COMES THE GREATEST CRIME-FIGHTER OF THEM ALL... THE ENEMY OF CROOKS AND DICTATORS... FOE OF INJUSTICE AND FRIEND OF THE DOWNTRODDEN! IS IT ONLY THE RED SKULL'S AWFUL NIGHTMARE, OR IS CAPTAIN AMERICA REALLY...
"BACK FROM THE DEAD!"
WHO'S LETTING WHO HAVE WHAT?
I GOT 'EM SET UP HERE, CAP!
URGH
THEY'RE NOT GOING TO STAY SET UP!
KA-BLAM
1

YOUNG MEN No. 24

Opposite: *Interior, "Back from the Dead!"; script, unknown; pencils, Mort Lawrence and John Romita; inks, John Romita; December 1953.* Captain America returns! The original Romita-drawn splash panel was inexplicably replaced by one by Mort Lawrence. The new splash gives a much larger image of the diabolical Red Skull. While Romita recalls finishing a story that Lawrence had already started, the surviving copies of the art reveal that the original splash is in Romita's hand, and must have been changed after the fact.

CAPTAIN AMERICA No. 77

Below: *Cover concept sketch, John Romita, July 1954.* This was the only Romita *Captain America* cover not laid out by Carl Burgos. Romita's Captain America was wonderfully Caniff-inspired, but the character took a lot of heat from the antiwar, anti–Red bashing movement.

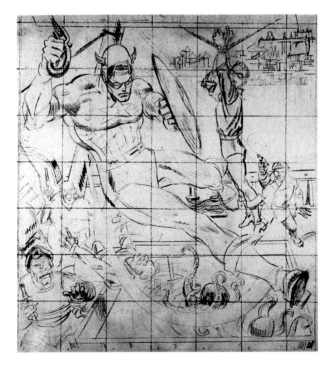

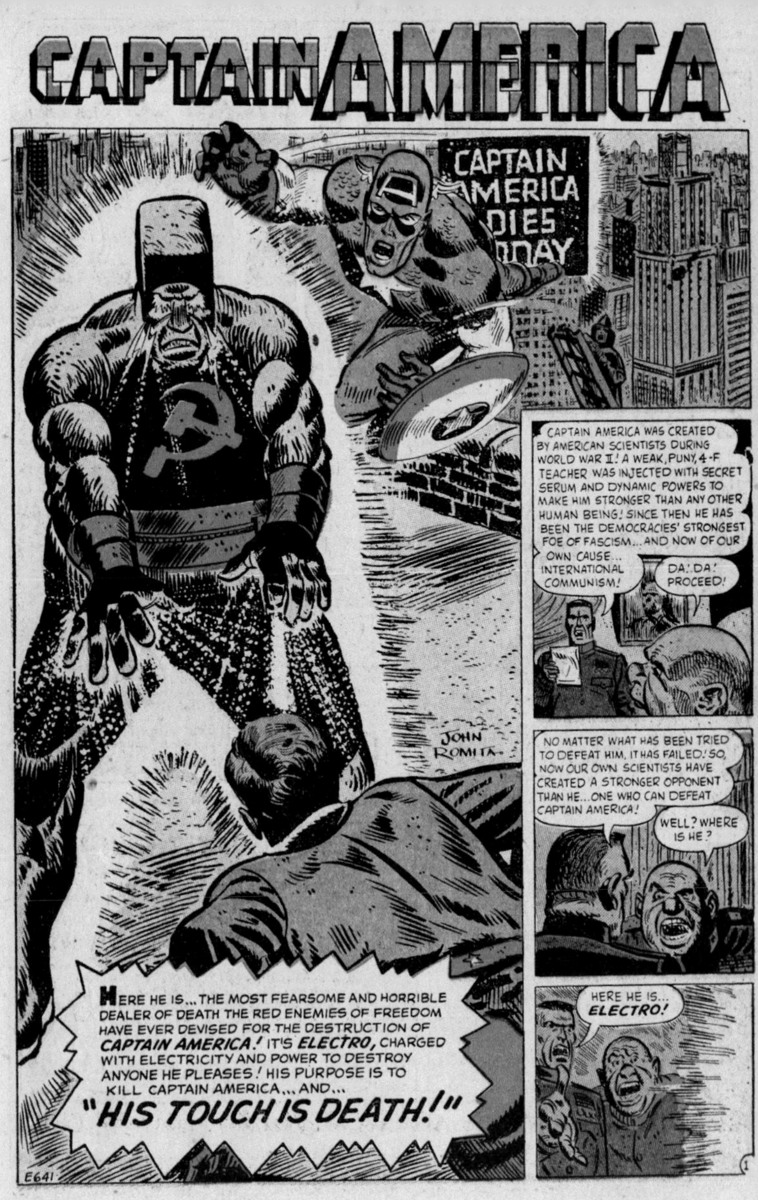
CAPTAIN AMERICA
CAPTAIN AMERICA DIES TODAY
JOHN ROMITA
CAPTAIN AMERICA WAS CREATED BY AMERICAN SCIENTISTS DURING WORLD WAR II! A WEAK, PUNY, 4-F TEACHER WAS INJECTED WITH SECRET SERUM AND DYNAMIC POWERS TO MAKE HIM STRONGER THAN ANY OTHER HUMAN BEING! SINCE THEN HE HAS BEEN THE DEMOCRACIES' STRONGEST FOE OF FASCISM... AND NOW OF OUR OWN CAUSE... INTERNATIONAL COMMUNISM!
DA! DA! PROCEED!
NO MATTER WHAT HAS BEEN TRIED TO DEFEAT HIM, IT HAS FAILED! SO, NOW OUR OWN SCIENTISTS HAVE CREATED A STRONGER OPPONENT THAN HE... ONE WHO CAN DEFEAT CAPTAIN AMERICA!
WELL? WHERE IS HE?
HERE HE IS... THE MOST FEARSOME AND HORRIBLE DEALER OF DEATH THE RED ENEMIES OF FREEDOM HAVE EVER DEVISED FOR THE DESTRUCTION OF CAPTAIN AMERICA! IT'S ELECTRO, CHARGED WITH ELECTRICITY AND POWER TO DESTROY ANYONE HE PLEASES! HIS PURPOSE IS TO KILL CAPTAIN AMERICA... AND...
"HIS TOUCH IS DEATH!"
HERE HE IS... ELECTRO!
E641
1

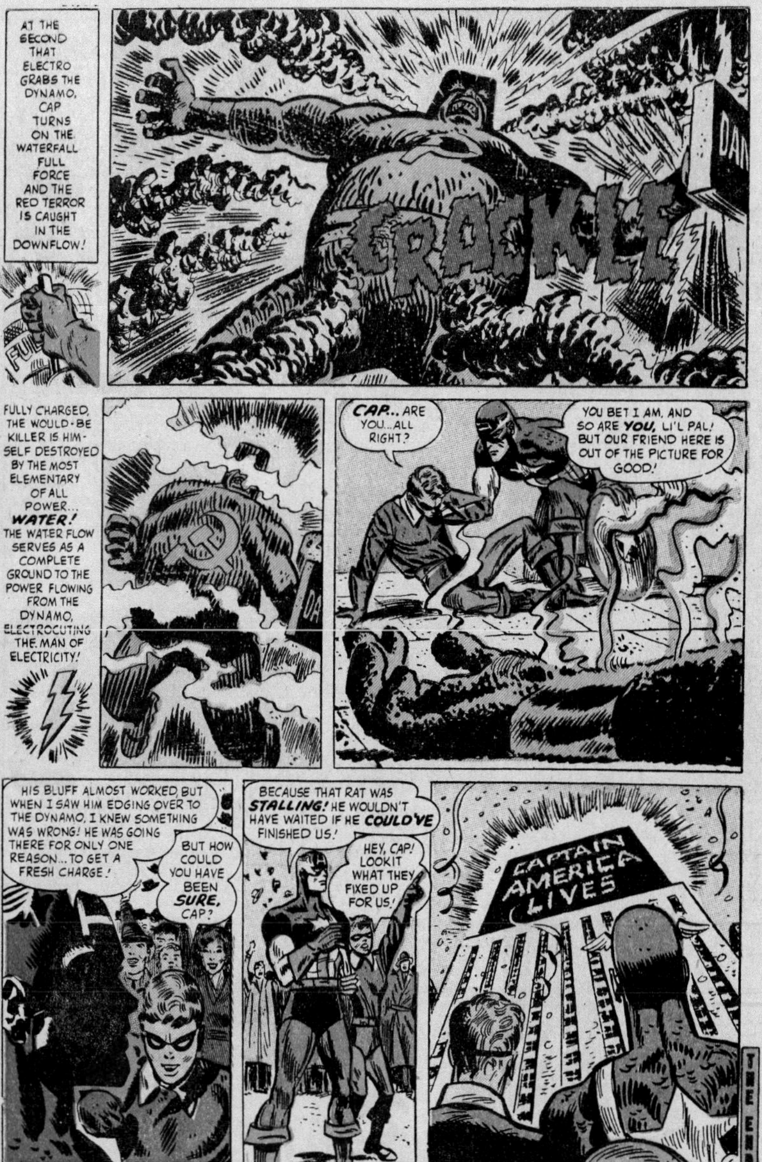
AT THE SECOND THAT ELECTRO GRABS THE DYNAMO, CAP TURNS ON THE WATERFALL FULL FORCE AND THE RED TERROR IS CAUGHT IN THE DOWNFLOW!
CRACKLE
FULLY CHARGED, THE WOULD-BE KILLER IS HIMSELF DESTROYED BY THE MOST ELEMENTARY OF ALL POWER... WATER! THE WATER FLOW SERVES AS A COMPLETE GROUND TO THE POWER FLOWING FROM THE DYNAMO, ELECTROCUTING THE MAN OF ELECTRICITY!
CAP... ARE YOU...ALL RIGHT?
YOU BET I AM. AND SO ARE YOU, LI'L PAL! BUT OUR FRIEND HERE IS OUT OF THE PICTURE FOR GOOD!
HIS BLUFF ALMOST WORKED, BUT WHEN I SAW HIM EDGING OVER TO THE DYNAMO, I KNEW SOMETHING WAS WRONG! HE WAS GOING THERE FOR ONLY ONE REASON... TO GET A FRESH CHARGE!
BUT HOW COULD YOU HAVE BEEN SURE, CAP?
BECAUSE THAT RAT WAS STALLING! HE WOULDN'T HAVE WAITED IF HE COULD'VE FINISHED US!
HEY, CAP! LOOKIT WHAT THEY FIXED UP FOR US!
CAPTAIN AMERICA LIVES
THE END
6
YOU CAN'T AFFORD TO MISS THE NEXT THRILLED-PACKED ISSUE OF "CAPTAIN AMERICA"! IT'S FULL OF SURPRISES AND DANGER!

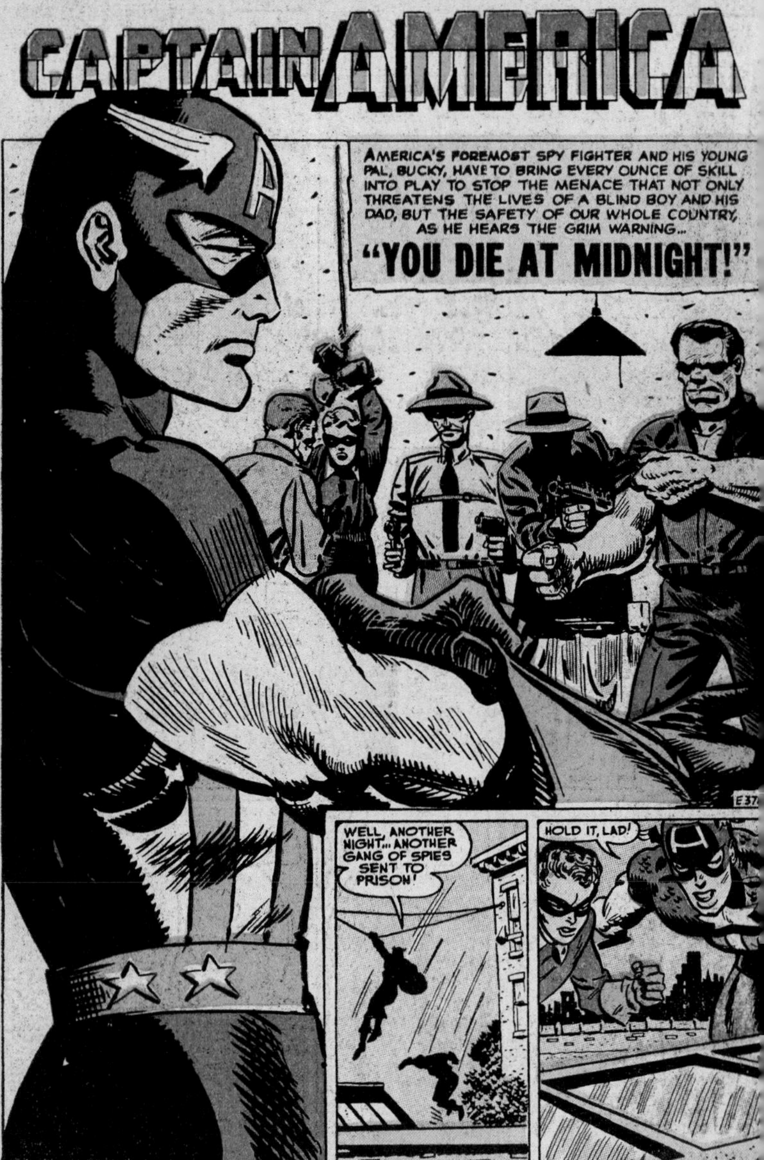
CAPTAIN AMERICA
AMERICA'S FOREMOST SPY FIGHTER AND HIS YOUNG PAL, BUCKY, HAVE TO BRING EVERY OUNCE OF SKILL INTO PLAY TO STOP THE MENACE THAT NOT ONLY THREATENS THE LIVES OF A BLIND BOY AND HIS DAD, BUT THE SAFETY OF OUR WHOLE COUNTRY, AS HE HEARS THE GRIM WARNING...
"YOU DIE AT MIDNIGHT!"
WELL, ANOTHER NIGHT... ANOTHER GANG OF SPIES SENT TO PRISON!
HOLD IT, LAD!

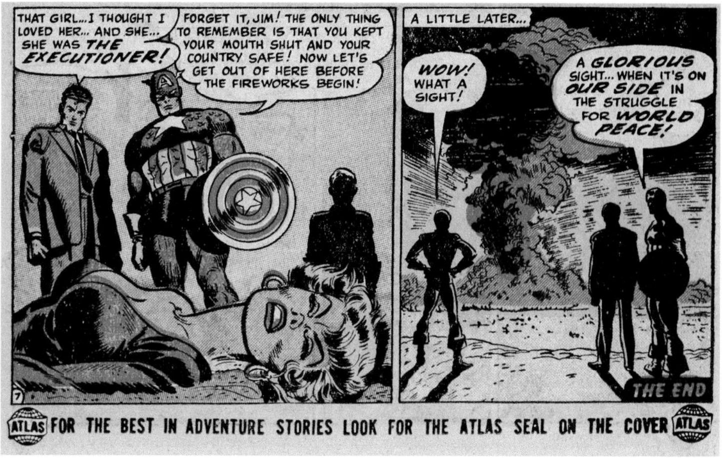
THAT GIRL...I THOUGHT I LOVED HER... AND SHE... SHE WAS THE EXECUTIONER!
FORGET IT, JIM! THE ONLY THING TO REMEMBER IS THAT YOU KEPT YOUR MOUTH SHUT AND YOUR COUNTRY SAFE! NOW LET'S GET OUT OF HERE BEFORE THE FIREWORKS BEGIN!
7
A LITTLE LATER...
WOW! WHAT A SIGHT!
A GLORIOUS SIGHT... WHEN IT'S ON OUR SIDE IN THE STRUGGLE FOR WORLD PEACE!
THE END
ATLAS
FOR THE BEST IN ADVENTURE STORIES LOOK FOR THE ATLAS SEAL ON THE COVER
ATLAS

CAPTAIN AMERICA No. 78

Pages 66–67: *Interiors, "His Touch Is Death"; script, unknown; pencils, John Romita and attributed Carl Burgos (Cap image); inks, John Romita; September 1954.* Cap battles the Communist prototype of Electro, who will later be Spider-Man's foe. As the climactic battle ends, "Captain America Lives" is plastered across the top of the building in the last panel—possibly a way to say goodbye to the character. He was canceled after this issue, and this time Cap would remain on ice for nearly a decade.

CAPTAIN AMERICA No. 77

Opposite: *Interior, "You Die at Midnight"; script, unknown; pencils and inks, John Romita; July 1954.* Cap and Bucky spend all their time routing out Commie spies. This time they take on the case of a blind boy being ransomed so his father will turn over atomic secrets. Cap is pretty tough on the father, telling himself that even if the father turned over the secrets because his son's life was in danger, he'd be as guilty as the actual spies! No compassion at all, these Cold Warriors!

YOUNG MEN No. 25

Above: *Interior, "Top Secret"; script, unknown; pencils and inks, John Romita; February 1954.* John Romita does his best impression of Milton Caniff as he gets the best of the deadly femme fatale Red spy, the Executioner.

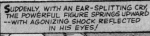

SUDDENLY, WITH AN EAR-SPLITTING CRY, THE POWERFUL FIGURE SPRINGS UPWARD --WITH AGONIZING SHOCK REFLECTED IN HIS EYES!

BUCKY-- BUCKY! LOOK OUT!

YOU CAN'T KILL HIM! YOU CAN'T KILL BUCKY! I WON'T LET YOU! I'LL SMASH YOU ALL!

THOR! IRON MAN! STOP HIM! HE'S GONE MAD!

BUT, AS SUDDENLY AS IT STARTED, THE LEGENDARY HERO'S WRATH SUBSIDES, AND THEN...

IT'S USELESS! I REMEMBER NOW! HE IS DEAD--HE IS! AND NOTHING ON EARTH CAN CHANGE THAT!

AND THEN, AS REALIZATION DAWNS, THE HANDSOME HEAD SLOWLY TURNS... THE CLEAR BLUE EYES TAKE IN THE AWESOME FIGURES SUR-ROUNDING HIM...

WHERE AM I? HOW DID I GET HERE? WHO ARE YOU??

THAT'S WHAT WE WERE ABOUT TO ASK YOU!

WHO AM I??

FOR A MOMENT, I HAD ALMOST FORGOTTEN MYSELF!

BUT I AM NOT LUCKY ENOUGH TO FORGET FOREVER!

--TO FORGET THAT I WAS ONCE THE MAN THE WORLD CALLED--CAPTAIN AMERICA!

5

THE AVENGERS No. 4

Opposite and below: *Cover; pencils, Jack Kirby; inks, George Roussos. Interior, "Captain America Joins the Avengers!"; script, Stan Lee; pencils, Jack Kirby; inks, George Roussos; March 1964.* Marvel trumpets Cap's return: "Jack Kirby drew the original Captain America during the Golden Age of Comics...and now he draws it again. Stan Lee's first script during those fabled days was in *Captain America*—and now he authors it again, in this, The Marvel Age." Forgetting Captain America's postwar appearances (he was published by Timely until 1949 and revived in the Atlas era for a few adventures in 1953–54) we learn that *this* Captain America was frozen in ice since 1944.

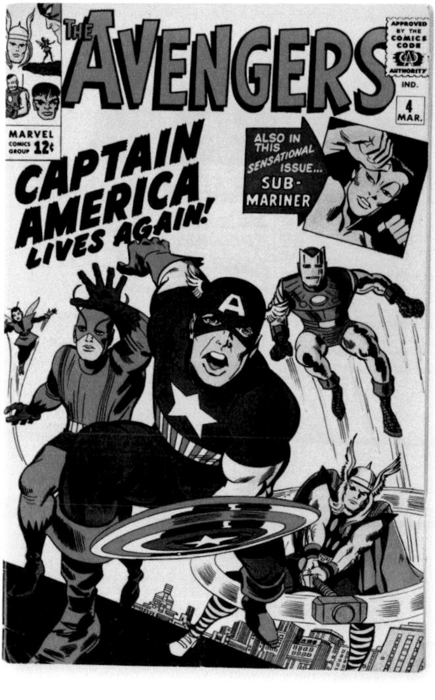
THE AVENGERS
APPROVED BY THE COMICS CODE AUTHORITY
IND.
4 MAR.
MARVEL COMICS GROUP 12¢
CAPTAIN AMERICA LIVES AGAIN!
ALSO IN THIS SENSATIONAL ISSUE... SUB-MARINER

THE AVENGERS No. 18

Below: *Interior, "When the Commissar Commands!"; script, Stan Lee; pencils, Don Heck; inks, Dick Ayers; July 1965.* "[Captain America] felt he was an anachronism. He realized that he was thinking like somebody in the late '30s and early '40s, but here he was living in the '60s, and he felt he'd never quite be on the same wavelength as the people. You know, he had been…frozen in a glacier for about 20 years.…[T]here was one line I wrote where he said maybe he should have battled less and questioned more, and that was the philosophy we tried to give him, but he couldn't really change his nature." —Stan Lee

TALES OF SUSPENSE No. 63

Opposite: *Interior, "The Origin of Captain America!"; script, Stan Lee; pencils, Jack Kirby; inks, Frank Giacoia; March 1963.* "I'll have a sort of choreographed action…like a ballet. In other words, if Captain America hits a man and he falls on the floor and some guy is coming up behind Captain, he'll already know what he's going to do with this guy.…It becomes a ballet and it's acted out on the paper." —Jack Kirby

HOW MUCH LONGER CAN I GO ON THIS WAY--BEING A LIVING SYMBOL TO MILLIONS--AND YET, A FRUSTRATED ANACHRONISM TO MYSELF!

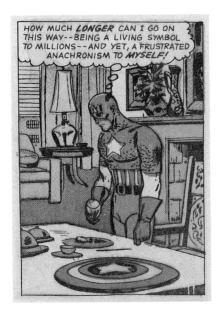

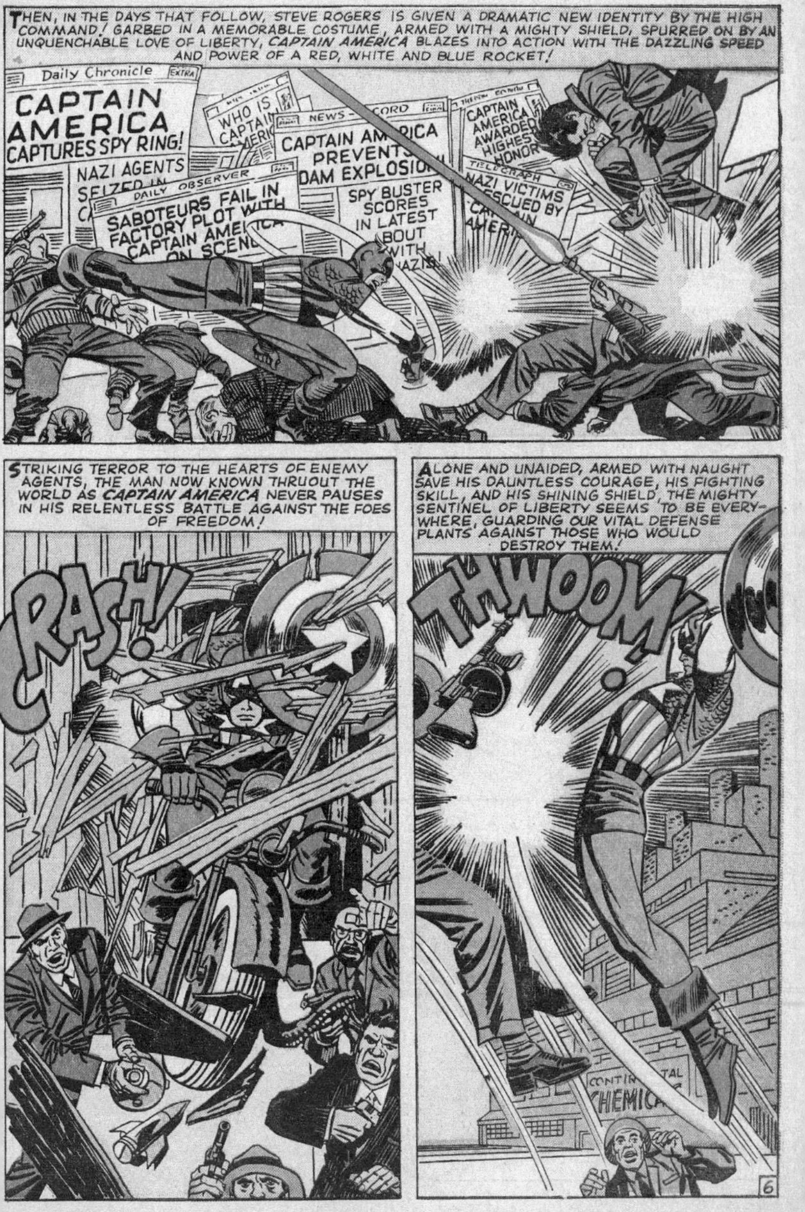
THEN, IN THE DAYS THAT FOLLOW, STEVE ROGERS IS GIVEN A DRAMATIC NEW IDENTITY BY THE HIGH COMMAND! GARBED IN A MEMORABLE COSTUME, ARMED WITH A MIGHTY SHIELD, SPURRED ON BY AN UNQUENCHABLE LOVE OF LIBERTY, CAPTAIN AMERICA BLAZES INTO ACTION WITH THE DAZZLING SPEED AND POWER OF A RED, WHITE AND BLUE ROCKET!
Daily Chronicle EXTRA
CAPTAIN AMERICA CAPTURES SPY RING!
NAZI AGENTS
WHO IS
CAPTAIN AMERICA PREVENTS DAM EXPLOSION
CAPTAIN AMERICA AWARDED HIGHEST HONOR
TELEGRAPH
NAZI VICTIMS
DAILY OBSERVER
SABOTEURS FAIL IN FACTORY PLOT WITH CAPTAIN AMERICA ON SCENE
SPY BUSTER SCORES IN LATEST BOUT WITH NAZIS!
STRIKING TERROR TO THE HEARTS OF ENEMY AGENTS, THE MAN NOW KNOWN THRUOUT THE WORLD AS CAPTAIN AMERICA NEVER PAUSES IN HIS RELENTLESS BATTLE AGAINST THE FOES OF FREEDOM!
CRASH!
ALONE AND UNAIDED, ARMED WITH NAUGHT SAVE HIS DAUNTLESS COURAGE, HIS FIGHTING SKILL, AND HIS SHINING SHIELD, THE MIGHTY SENTINEL OF LIBERTY SEEMS TO BE EVERYWHERE, GUARDING OUR VITAL DEFENSE PLANTS AGAINST THOSE WHO WOULD DESTROY THEM!
THWOOM!
6

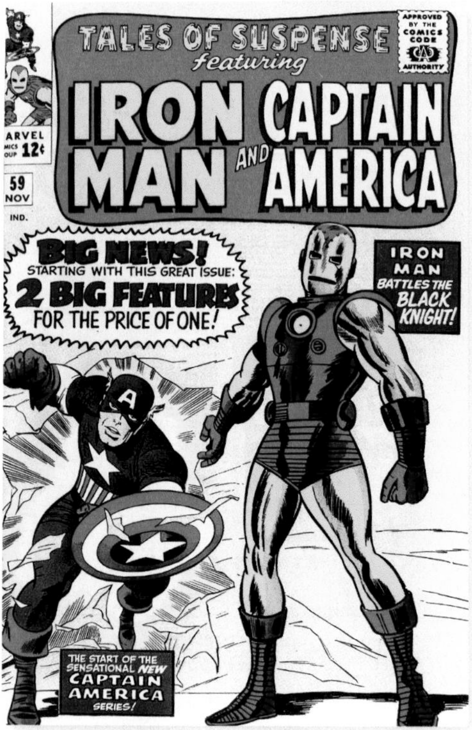
TALES OF SUSPENSE
featuring
IRON MAN AND CAPTAIN AMERICA
APPROVED BY THE COMICS CODE AUTHORITY
12¢
59 NOV
IND.
BIG NEWS! STARTING WITH THIS GREAT ISSUE: 2 BIG FEATURES FOR THE PRICE OF ONE!
IRON MAN BATTLES THE BLACK KNIGHT!
THE START OF THE SENSATIONAL NEW CAPTAIN AMERICA SERIES!

TALES OF SUSPENSE No. 59

Above: *Cover; pencils, Jack Kirby; inks, Dick Ayers; November 1964.*

THE ORIGIN OF CAPTAIN AMERICA!

Opposite: *Original interior art, "The Origin of Captain America!,"* Tales of Suspense *No. 63; script, Stan Lee; pencils, Jack Kirby; inks, Frank Giacoia; March 1963.* "When you look at the earliest great directors — D.W. Griffith or Eisenstein, their work — you can't touch and even see anymore how radical it was, how extraordinary and trippy it was to encounter for the first time, because everything rests on those innovations, everyone's followed them. Early John Ford films, everything looks like that now. It became the language of cinema. And Kirby's accomplishments, I think, reside in that same kind of relationship to the culture at large." — Jonathan Lethem

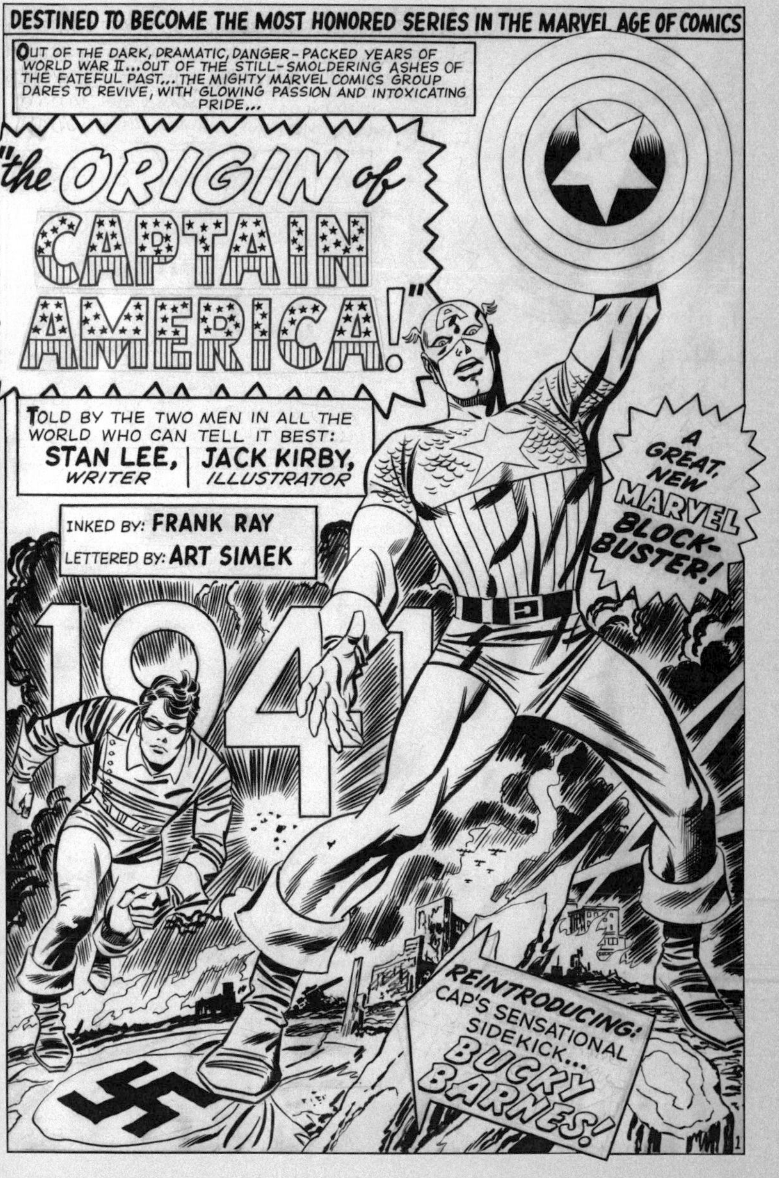

DESTINED TO BECOME THE MOST HONORED SERIES IN THE MARVEL AGE OF COMICS
OUT OF THE DARK, DRAMATIC, DANGER-PACKED YEARS OF WORLD WAR II...OUT OF THE STILL-SMOLDERING ASHES OF THE FATEFUL PAST... THE MIGHTY MARVEL COMICS GROUP DARES TO REVIVE, WITH GLOWING PASSION AND INTOXICATING PRIDE...
"the ORIGIN of CAPTAIN AMERICA!"
TOLD BY THE TWO MEN IN ALL THE WORLD WHO CAN TELL IT BEST: STAN LEE, WRITER | JACK KIRBY, ILLUSTRATOR
INKED BY: FRANK RAY
LETTERED BY: ART SIMEK
A GREAT, NEW MARVEL BLOCK-BUSTER!
1941
REINTRODUCING: CAP'S SENSATIONAL SIDEKICK... BUCKY BARNES!
1

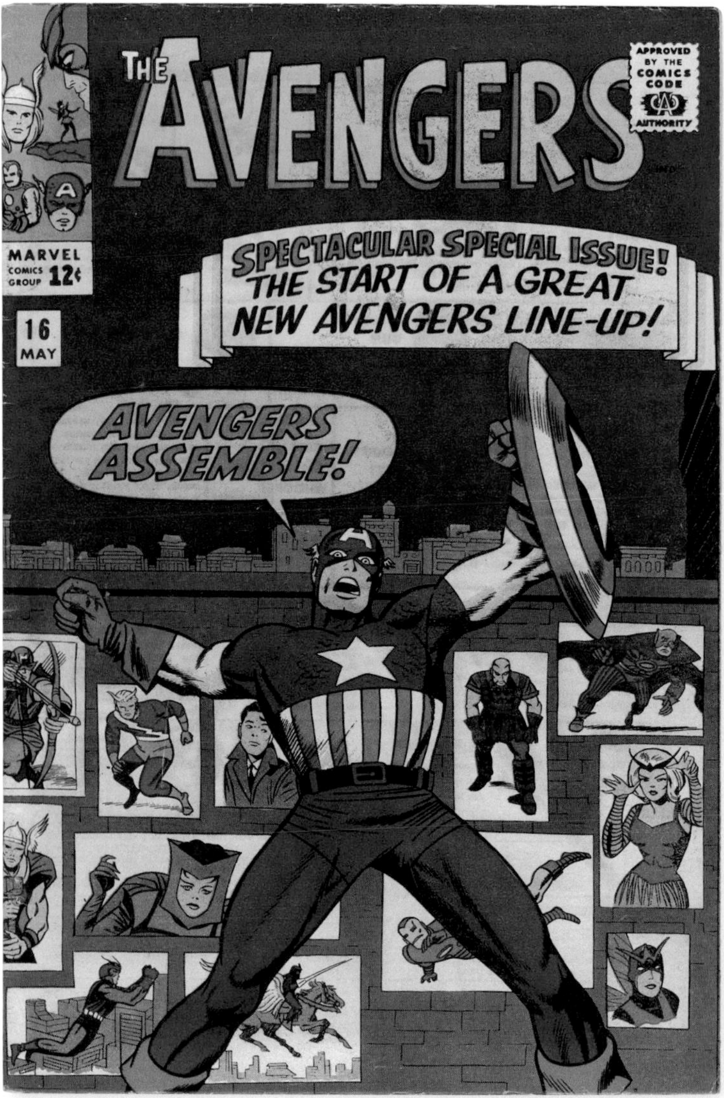
THE AVENGERS
APPROVED BY THE COMICS CODE AUTHORITY
MARVEL COMICS GROUP 12¢
16 MAY
SPECTACULAR SPECIAL ISSUE!
THE START OF A GREAT NEW AVENGERS LINE-UP!
AVENGERS ASSEMBLE!

THE AVENGERS No. 16

Opposite: *Cover; pencils, Jack Kirby; inks, Sol Brodsky; May 1965.* "Did you know the real reason we changed the Avengers lineup? Iron Man, Thor and Giant-Man were all starring in their own mags. After a while it didn't seem right to have one of them captured in Transylvania in his own mag while he might be taking in the *Late Show* on TV in *The Avengers*. The truth is it seemed to kill all the realism." — Stan Lee

THE MAN AND THE KING

Above: *Photograph, Stan Lee and Jack Kirby, 1966.*

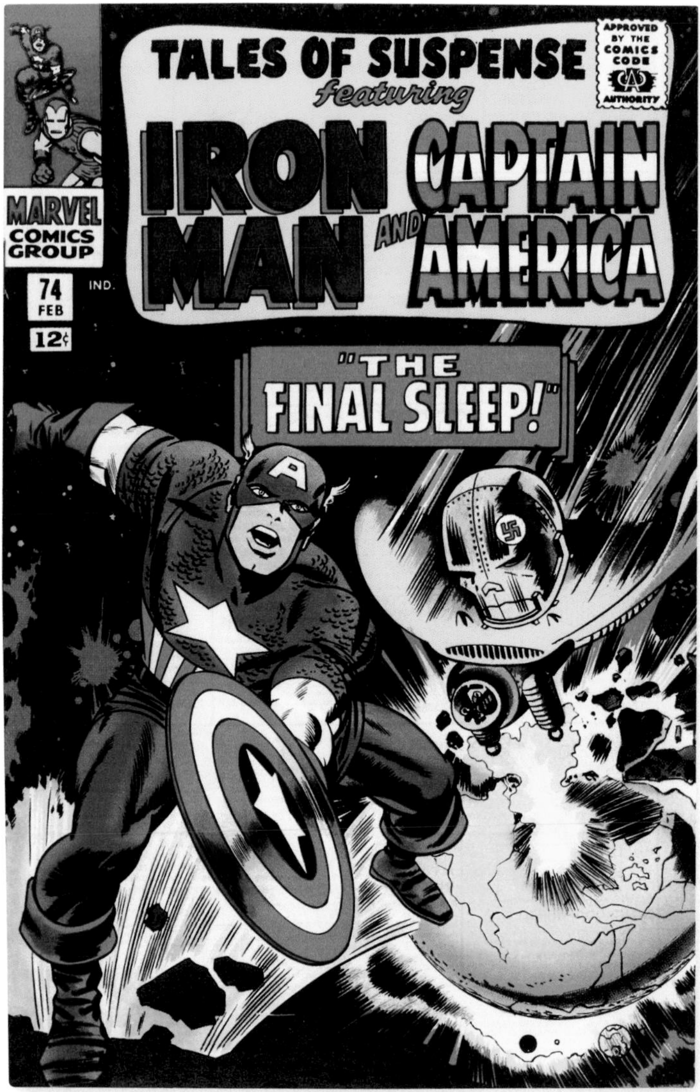
TALES OF SUSPENSE
featuring
IRON MAN AND CAPTAIN AMERICA
APPROVED BY THE COMICS CODE AUTHORITY
MARVEL COMICS GROUP
74 FEB
IND.
12¢
"THE FINAL SLEEP!"

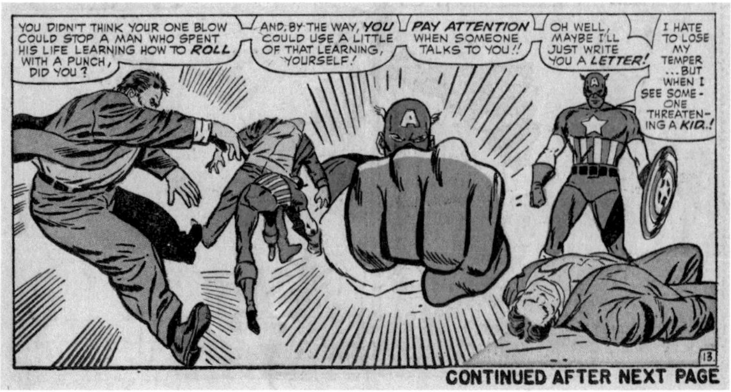
YOU DIDN'T THINK YOUR ONE BLOW COULD STOP A MAN WHO SPENT HIS LIFE LEARNING HOW TO ROLL WITH A PUNCH, DID YOU?
AND, BY THE WAY, YOU COULD USE A LITTLE OF THAT LEARNING, YOURSELF!
PAY ATTENTION WHEN SOMEONE TALKS TO YOU!!
OH WELL, MAYBE I'LL JUST WRITE YOU A LETTER!
I HATE TO LOSE MY TEMPER ...BUT WHEN I SEE SOME-ONE THREATEN-ING A KID!
13
CONTINUED AFTER NEXT PAGE

TALES OF SUSPENSE No. 74

Opposite: *Cover; pencils, Jack Kirby; inks, Sol Brodsky; February 1966.* In a cover heavy on symbolism, a swastikaed sleeper robot explodes planet Earth by crashing into it.

THE AVENGERS No. 12

Above: *Interior, "This Hostage Earth!"; script, Stan Lee; pencils, Don Heck; inks, Dick Ayers; January 1965.* Don Heck takes an incredibly violent moment—Captain America losing his temper and taking it out on a man to the point of unconsciousness—and deconstructs it.

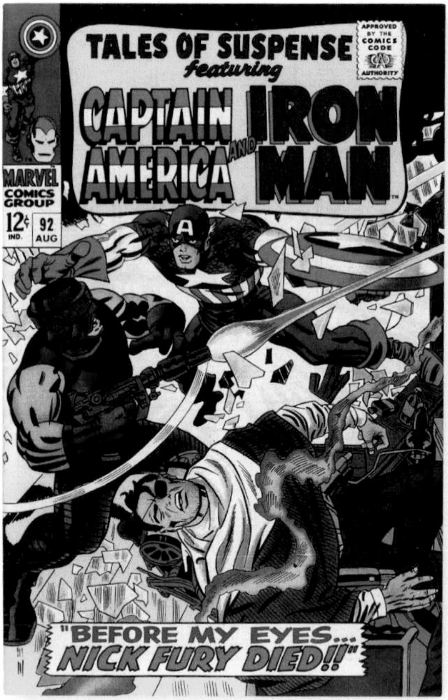
TALES OF SUSPENSE
featuring
CAPTAIN AMERICA AND IRON MAN
MARVEL COMICS GROUP
12¢ 92 IND. AUG
APPROVED BY THE COMICS CODE AUTHORITY
"BEFORE MY EYES...
NICK FURY DIED!!"

TALES OF SUSPENSE No. 92

Above: *Cover; pencils, Jack Kirby; inks, Frank Giacoia; August 1967.* Despite the cover copy, Cap manages to prevent scientific supervillain network AIM (Advanced Idea Mechanics) from assassinating Nick Fury.

STRANGE TALES No. 114

Opposite: *Interior, "The Human Torch Meets... Captain America"; script, Stan Lee; pencils, Jack Kirby; inks, Dick Ayers; November 1963.* Kirby's use of perspective and camera angles was clearly influenced by the movies. Within the frame of a comic book panel, Kirby used all the tools at his disposal to create visual excitement without getting in the way of telling a story. This is not the "real" Captain America. One of the Torch's villains, the Acrobat, disguises himself as the good Captain. At the end of the story Stan and Jack ask the fans if they'd like to see the real Captain America return. Not waiting for their response, just four months later, Cap is defrosted in *The Avengers* No. 4.

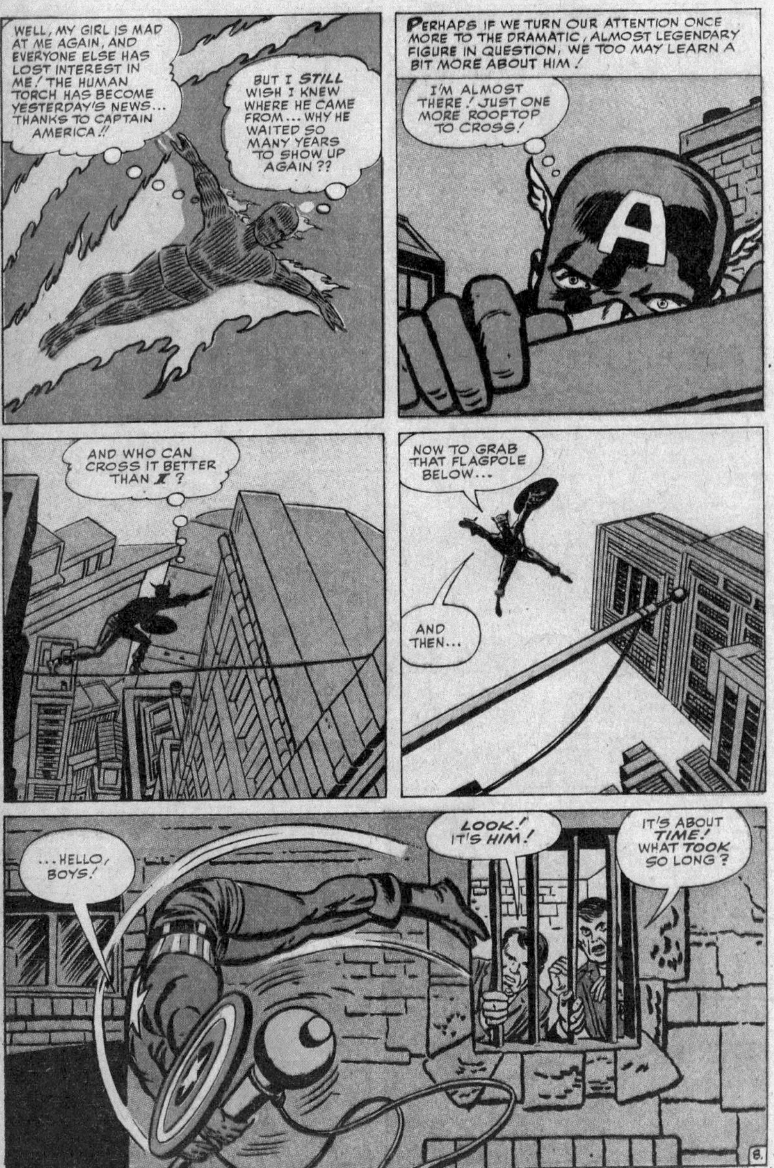
WELL, MY GIRL IS MAD AT ME AGAIN, AND EVERYONE ELSE HAS LOST INTEREST IN ME! THE HUMAN TORCH HAS BECOME YESTERDAY'S NEWS... THANKS TO CAPTAIN AMERICA!!
BUT I STILL WISH I KNEW WHERE HE CAME FROM... WHY HE WAITED SO MANY YEARS TO SHOW UP AGAIN??
PERHAPS IF WE TURN OUR ATTENTION ONCE MORE TO THE DRAMATIC, ALMOST LEGENDARY FIGURE IN QUESTION, WE TOO MAY LEARN A BIT MORE ABOUT HIM!
I'M ALMOST THERE! JUST ONE MORE ROOFTOP TO CROSS!
AND WHO CAN CROSS IT BETTER THAN I?
NOW TO GRAB THAT FLAGPOLE BELOW...
AND THEN...
...HELLO, BOYS!
LOOK! IT'S HIM!
IT'S ABOUT TIME! WHAT TOOK SO LONG?
8.

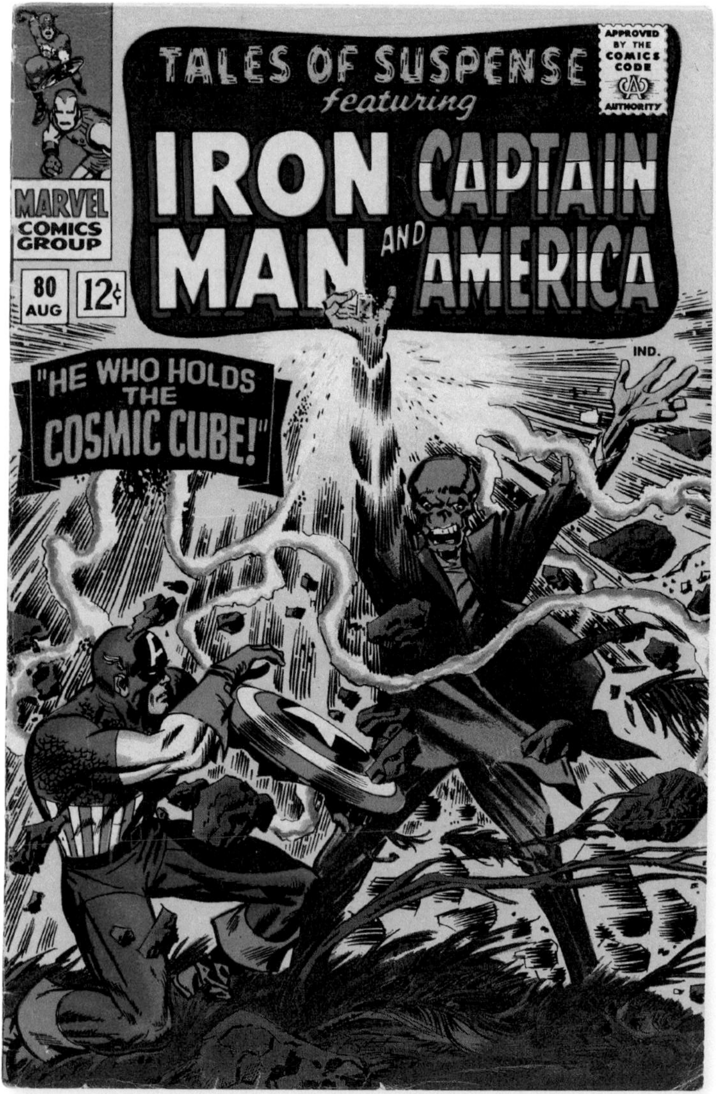
TALES OF SUSPENSE
featuring
IRON MAN AND CAPTAIN AMERICA
APPROVED BY THE COMICS CODE AUTHORITY
MARVEL COMICS GROUP
80 AUG
12¢
IND.
"HE WHO HOLDS THE COSMIC CUBE!"

CAPTAIN AMERICA
MARVEL COMICS GROUP
12¢ IND.
103 JULY
THE WEAKEST LINK!

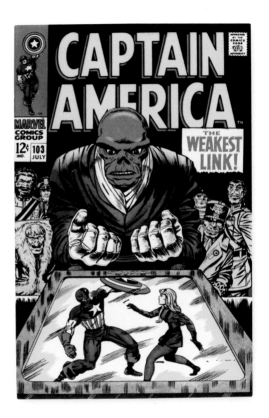

TALES OF SUSPENSE No. 80

Opposite: *Cover; pencils, Jack Kirby; inks, Don Heck; August 1966.* The Comics Code would have vetoed the Red Skull's original 1940s visage — in fact, it had to be redrawn for reprints because it looked too much like a real skull — but, despite the restriction, Kirby manages to retain the sense of menace in the evil Skull's face.

CAPTAIN AMERICA No. 103

Above: *Cover; pencils, Jack Kirby; inks, Syd Shores; July 1968.* Cap's archenemy was the Red Skull, a Nazi with whom he has had many epic battles for more than 75 years.

TALES OF SUSPENSE No. 76

Below: *Cover; pencils, Jack Kirby; inks, John Romita; April 1966.* Batroc the Leaper, the French master of *savate* (French kickboxing) and acrobatics, was an ongoing foe of Cap's. Lacking super powers, his formidable martial arts abilities—writer Mark Waid would joke in 1997, "Jean-Claude Van Damme, but he was in the '60s"—provided a perfect foil for Cap's physicality, and allowed Kirby to choreograph some of his most fantastic fight scenes.

TALES OF SUSPENSE No. 85

Opposite: *Interior, "The Blitzkrieg of Batroc!"; script, Stan Lee; pencils, Jack Kirby; inks, Frank Giacoia; January 1967.* This nine-panel sequence illustrates how much movement Kirby could bring to a single page. Having gotten his start "in-betweening" animation cels in the 1930s at the legendary Fleischer Studios, Kirby understood how to bring a story to life, and Lee wisely stood back and let Kirby's images speak for themselves.

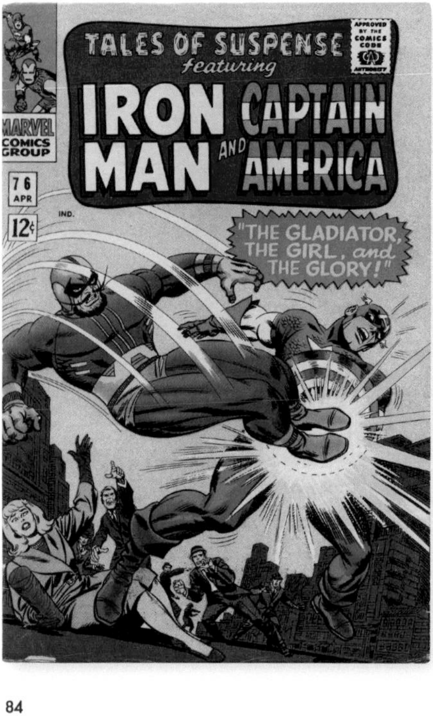
TALES OF SUSPENSE
featuring
IRON MAN AND CAPTAIN AMERICA
APPROVED BY THE COMICS CODE AUTHORITY
MARVEL COMICS GROUP
76 APR
12¢
IND.
"THE GLADIATOR, THE GIRL, and THE GLORY!"

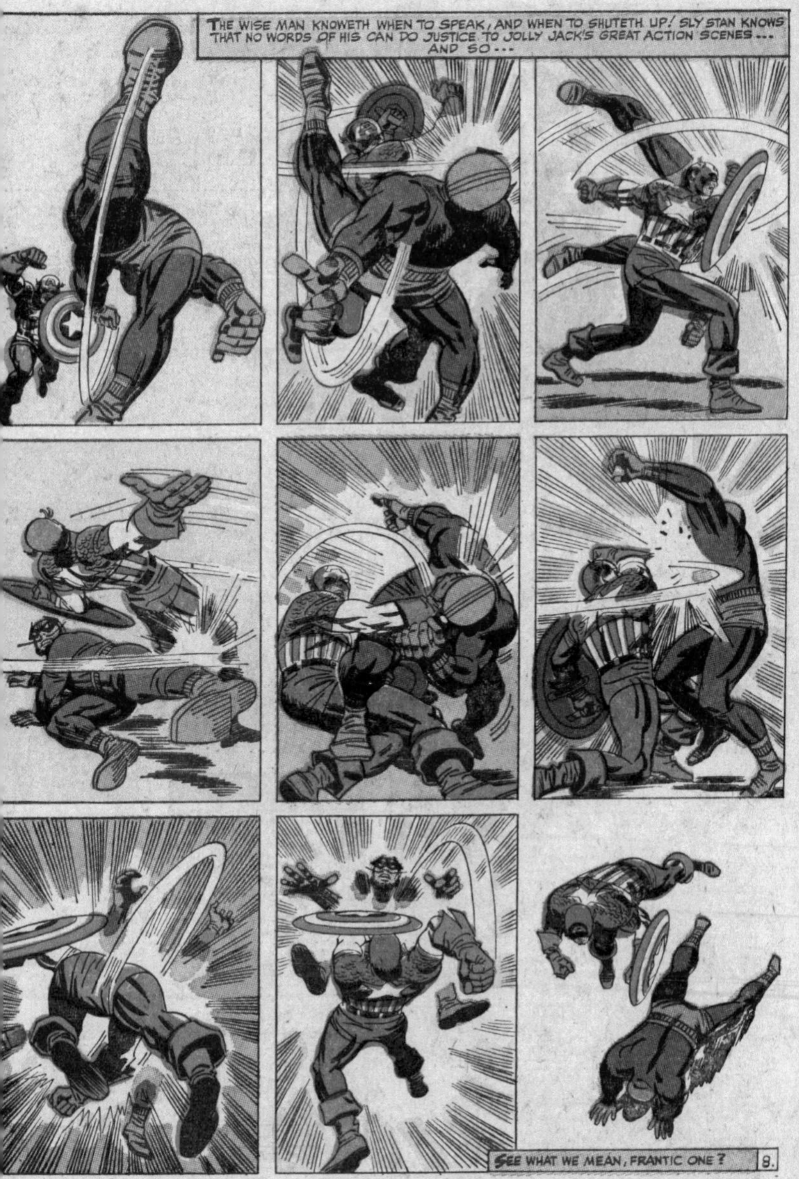
THE WISE MAN KNOWETH WHEN TO SPEAK, AND WHEN TO SHUTETH UP! SLY STAN KNOWS THAT NO WORDS OF HIS CAN DO JUSTICE TO JOLLY JACK'S GREAT ACTION SCENES... AND SO...
SEE WHAT WE MEAN, FRANTIC ONE?

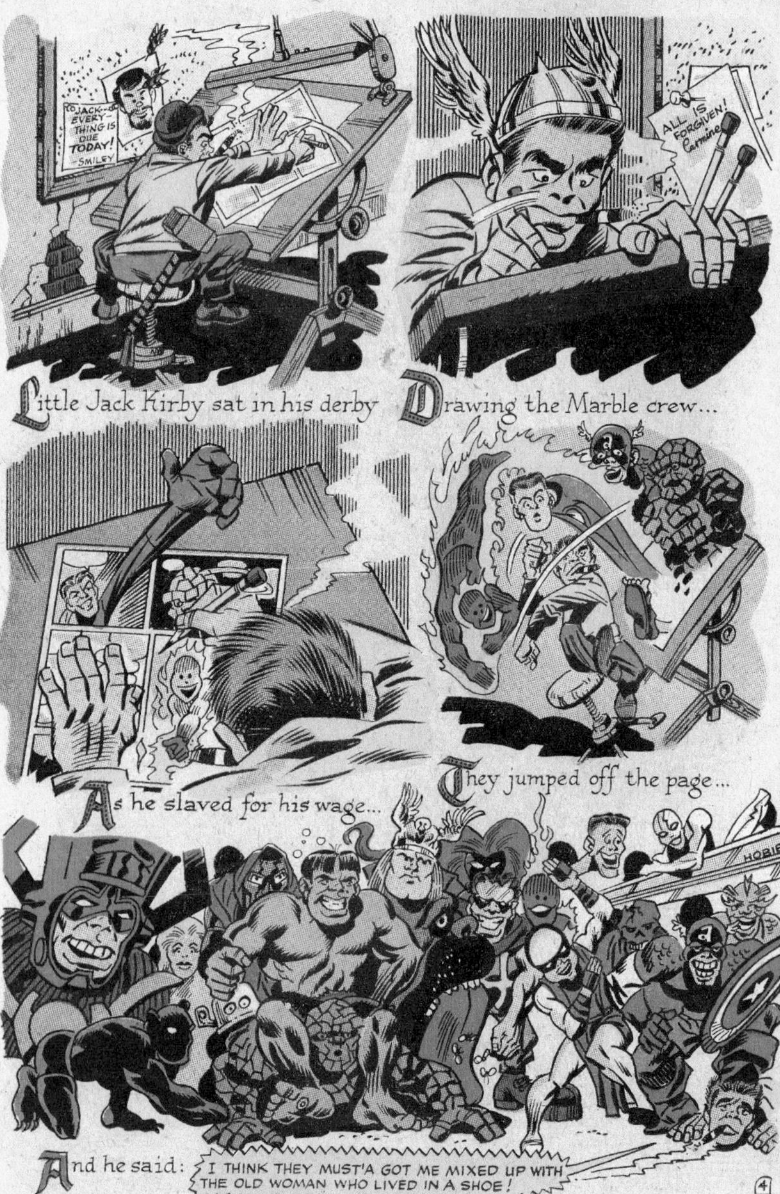

TO JACK-- EVERYTHING IS DUE TODAY! -SMILEY
ALL IS FORGIVEN! Carmine
Little Jack Kirby sat in his derby
Drawing the Marble crew...
As he slaved for his wage...
They jumped off the page...
HOBIE'
And he said:
I THINK THEY MUST'A GOT ME MIXED UP WITH THE OLD WOMAN WHO LIVED IN A SHOE!

Text in image: CAPTIVE AMERICAN — WHY WON'T THEY LET ME JOIN THE JESTER'S LEAGUE OF AMERICA? — ©T.C.G. PRTD. IN U.S.A.

NOT BRAND ECHH No. 11

Opposite: *Interior, "Auntie Goose Rhymes Dept.";* script, *Roy Thomas; pencils and inks, John Verpoorten; December 1968.* Roy Thomas and Verpoorten transform the nursery rhyme "Little Miss Muffett" into a satirical tribute to Jack Kirby that shows a parade of Marvel characters who come to life at his drawing board.

KRAZY LITTLE COMICS

Above: *Cover, Topps Krazy Little Comics; dialogue, Len Brown; pencils and inks, Wally Wood; 1967.* Len Brown and Roy Thomas teamed up with Wally Wood and Gil Kane for a line of mini-comics for Topps, which included parodies of Marvel characters and back cover ads by Art Spiegelman. They were test marketed but did not receive national distribution.

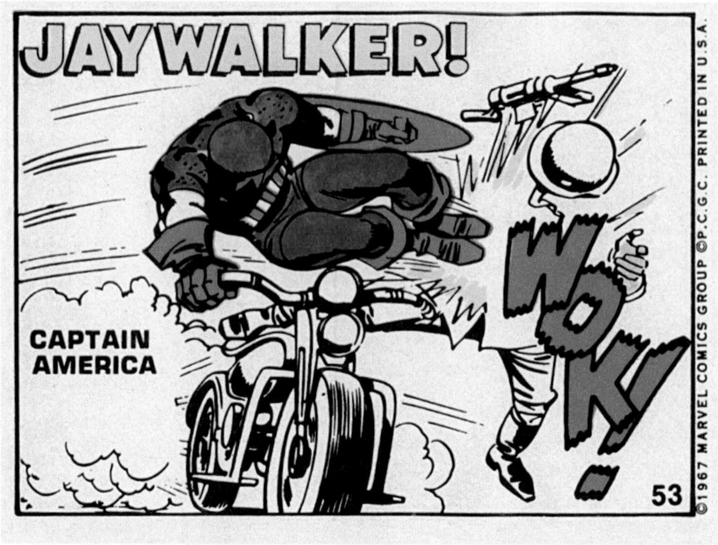
JAYWALKER!
CAPTAIN AMERICA
WOK!
53
©1967 MARVEL COMICS GROUP ©P.C.G.C. PRINTED IN U.S.A.

ALL THIS AND A STICK OF GUM!

Above and opposite: *Super Hero stickers, 1967.* Donruss may have released the first Marvel trading card set a year earlier, but the Philadelphia Chewing Gum Company was the first to produce a set of Marvel Comics trading cards that were all stickers (55 of them in total). They featured Marvel's most popular super heroes, using art from the comic books and adding funny captions. For just a nickel kids could go to the corner drugstore and buy a pack, which consisted of five stickers and a stick of gum.

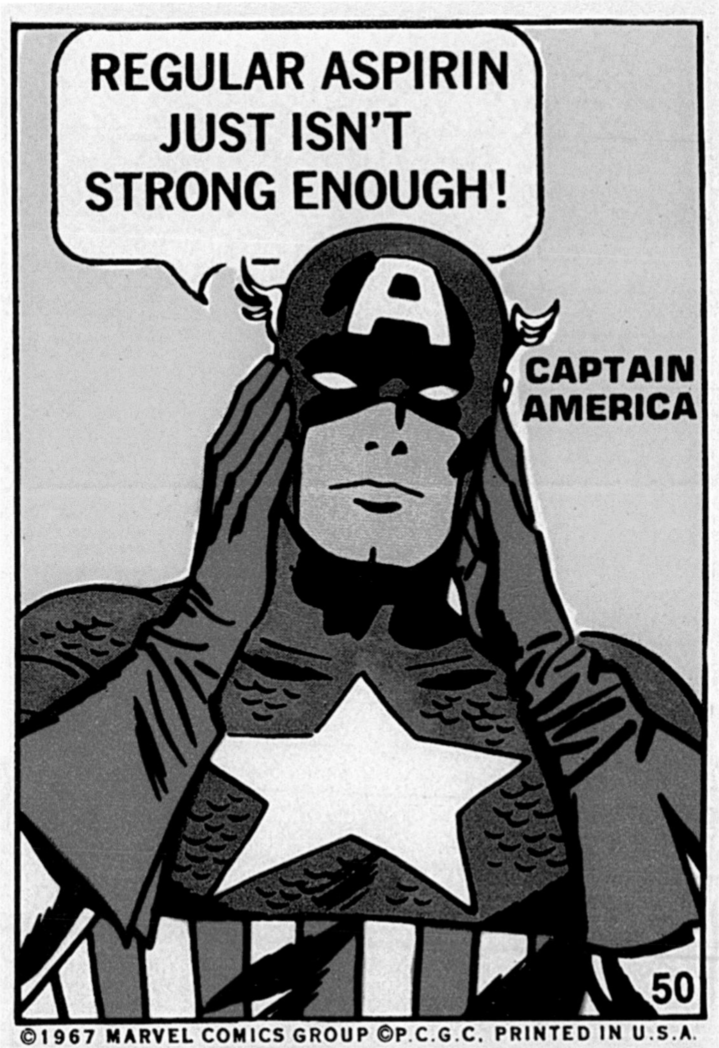

REGULAR ASPIRIN JUST ISN'T STRONG ENOUGH!
CAPTAIN AMERICA
50
©1967 MARVEL COMICS GROUP ©P.C.G.C. PRINTED IN U.S.A.

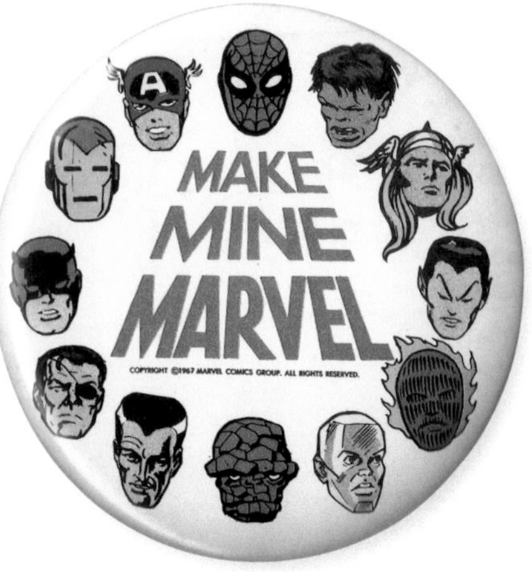
MAKE
MINE
MARVEL
COPYRIGHT ©1967 MARVEL COMICS GROUP. ALL RIGHTS RESERVED.

MAKE MINE MARVEL

Above: *Promotional button, 1967.* Stan Lee first used this phrase in Marvel's "Bullpen Bulletins" page in June/July 1965. It became so popular that it was used on a button for Marvel's first fan club, the Merry Marvel Marching Society (M.M.M.S.).

MOVING MARVEL MERCHANDISE

Opposite: *House ad; pencils, Jack Kirby and Don Heck; inks, Frank Giacoia, Don Heck, and attributed Marie Severin; lettering, Artie Simek; September 1965.* By mid-decade, Marvel was selling products to a growing and enthusiastic public, including T-shirts advertised throughout the line. Along with the Avengers, there were designs for the FF, Spider-Man, Daredevil, Iron Man, Thor, the Hulk, the X-Men, Dr. Strange, Sgt. Fury, and even Marvel's top Western Kids: Rawhide, Two-Gun Kid, and Kid Colt (poor Patsy Walker and Millie the Model were left out).

COMING TO A TV NEAR YOU

Pages 92–93: *Advertisement; pencils and inks, Jack Kirby and Gene Colan; ca. 1966. Marvel Super-Heroes* was a syndicated cartoon that landed on television screens across America in fall 1966. Five nights a week, Iron Man, Captain America, the Sub-Mariner, the Hulk, and Thor starred in stories adapted (and utilizing artwork) from the comics. The Grantray-Lawrence series had very limited, rudimentary animation, but it brought greater recognition to Marvel's line, and the shows did have catchy theme songs!

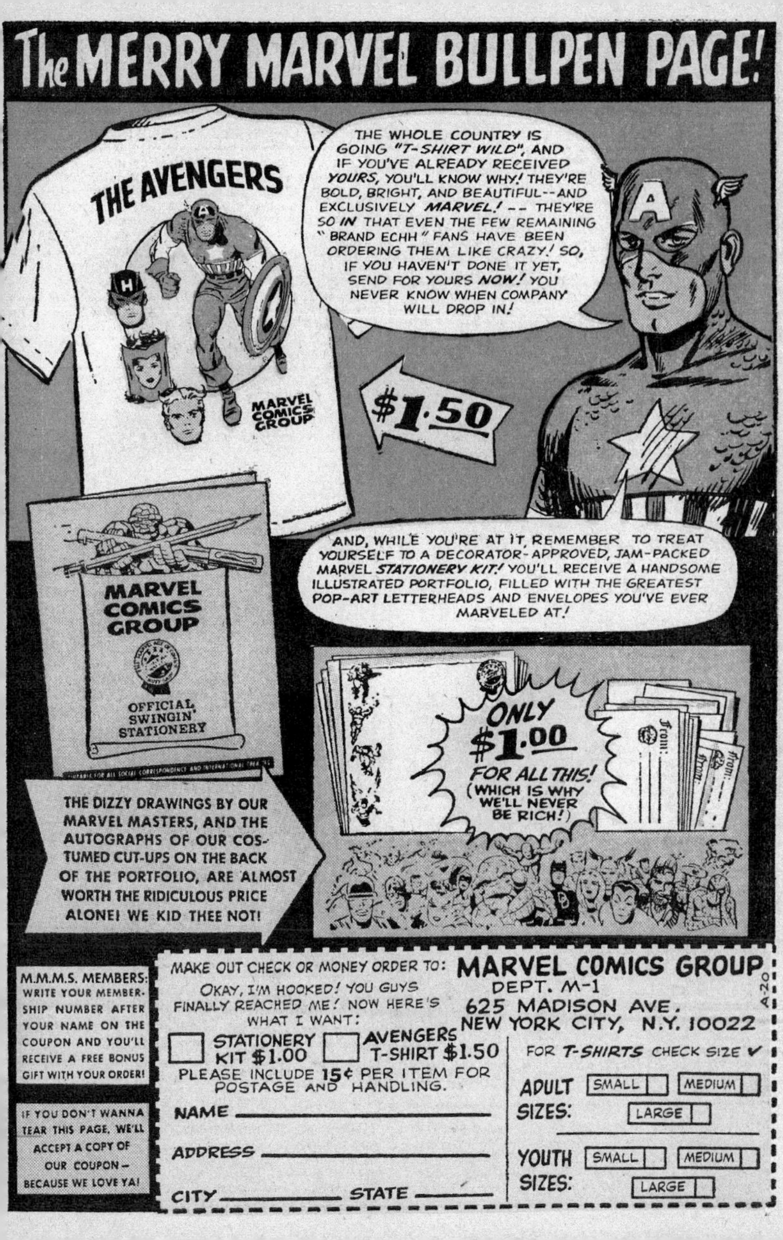

The MERRY MARVEL BULLPEN PAGE!
THE AVENGERS
MARVEL COMICS GROUP
THE WHOLE COUNTRY IS GOING "T-SHIRT WILD", AND IF YOU'VE ALREADY RECEIVED YOURS, YOU'LL KNOW WHY! THEY'RE BOLD, BRIGHT, AND BEAUTIFUL--AND EXCLUSIVELY MARVEL! -- THEY'RE SO IN THAT EVEN THE FEW REMAINING "BRAND ECHH" FANS HAVE BEEN ORDERING THEM LIKE CRAZY! SO, IF YOU HAVEN'T DONE IT YET, SEND FOR YOURS NOW! YOU NEVER KNOW WHEN COMPANY WILL DROP IN!
$1.50
AND, WHILE YOU'RE AT IT, REMEMBER TO TREAT YOURSELF TO A DECORATOR-APPROVED, JAM-PACKED MARVEL STATIONERY KIT! YOU'LL RECEIVE A HANDSOME ILLUSTRATED PORTFOLIO, FILLED WITH THE GREATEST POP-ART LETTERHEADS AND ENVELOPES YOU'VE EVER MARVELED AT!
MARVEL COMICS GROUP
OFFICIAL SWINGIN' STATIONERY
ONLY $1.00 FOR ALL THIS! (WHICH IS WHY WE'LL NEVER BE RICH!)
From:
THE DIZZY DRAWINGS BY OUR MARVEL MASTERS, AND THE AUTOGRAPHS OF OUR COSTUMED CUT-UPS ON THE BACK OF THE PORTFOLIO, ARE ALMOST WORTH THE RIDICULOUS PRICE ALONE! WE KID THEE NOT!
M.M.M.S. MEMBERS: WRITE YOUR MEMBERSHIP NUMBER AFTER YOUR NAME ON THE COUPON AND YOU'LL RECEIVE A FREE BONUS GIFT WITH YOUR ORDER!
IF YOU DON'T WANNA TEAR THIS PAGE, WE'LL ACCEPT A COPY OF OUR COUPON—BECAUSE WE LOVE YA!
MAKE OUT CHECK OR MONEY ORDER TO: MARVEL COMICS GROUP
DEPT. M-1
625 MADISON AVE.
NEW YORK CITY, N.Y. 10022
A-20
OKAY, I'M HOOKED! YOU GUYS FINALLY REACHED ME! NOW HERE'S WHAT I WANT:
STATIONERY KIT $1.00
AVENGERS T-SHIRT $1.50
PLEASE INCLUDE 15¢ PER ITEM FOR POSTAGE AND HANDLING.
NAME
ADDRESS
CITY
STATE
FOR T-SHIRTS CHECK SIZE ✔
ADULT SIZES: SMALL MEDIUM LARGE
YOUTH SIZES: SMALL MEDIUM LARGE

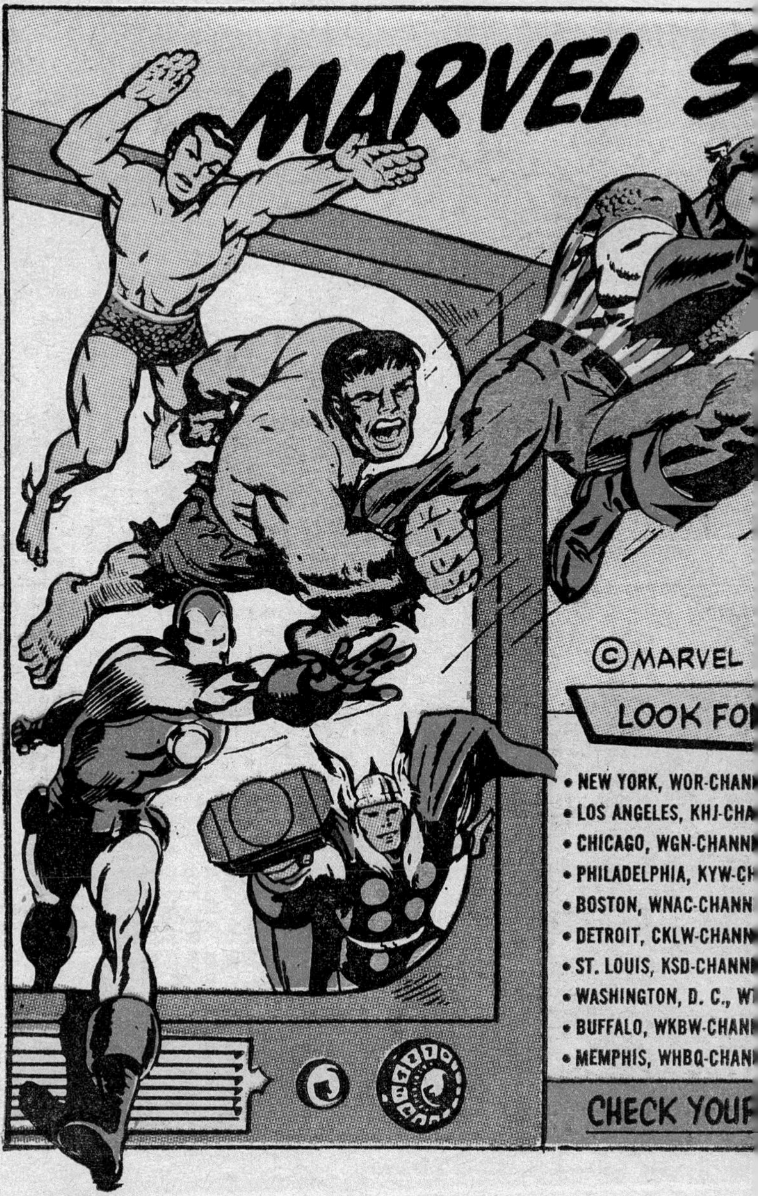

MARVEL S
©MARVEL
LOOK FO
• NEW YORK, WOR-CHAN
• LOS ANGELES, KHJ-CHA
• CHICAGO, WGN-CHANN
• PHILADELPHIA, KYW-CH
• BOSTON, WNAC-CHANN
• DETROIT, CKLW-CHANN
• ST. LOUIS, KSD-CHANN
• WASHINGTON, D. C., W
• BUFFALO, WKBW-CHAN
• MEMPHIS, WHBQ-CHAN
CHECK YOUR

PER-HEROES ARE ON TV

- **CAPTAIN AMERICA!**
- **THE SUB-MARINER!**
- **THE INCREDIBLE HULK!**
- **THE MIGHTY THOR!**
- **IRON MAN!**

ON THE FOLLOWING TELEVISION STATIONS:

- SYRACUSE, WHEN-CHANNEL 5
- PROVIDENCE, WPRO-CHANNEL 12
- BALTIMORE, WBAL-CHANNEL 11
- MILWAUKEE, WUHF-CHANNEL 18
- MINNEAPOLIS/ST. PAUL, WCCO-CHANNEL 4
- NEW ORLEANS, WVUE-CHANNEL 12
- ALBANY, WTEN-CHANNEL 10
- CHARLESTON, W. VA., WSAZ-CHANNEL 3

- SALT LAKE CITY, KCPX-CHANNEL 4
- ROCHESTER, WHEC-CHANNEL 10
- SAN JUAN, P. R., WAPA-CHANNEL 4
- SAGINAW/BAY CITY, WNEM-CHANNEL 5
- PORTLAND, ME., WGAN-CHANNEL 13
- TAMPA, WTVT-CHANNEL 13
- LITTLE ROCK, KATV, CHANNEL 7
- SPRINGFIELD, MASS., WHYN-CHANNEL 40
- EVANSVILLE, IND., WEHT-CHANNEL 50
- HARRISONBURG, VA., WSVA-CHANNEL 3

LISTING FOR TIME | THIS LIST IS INCOMPLETE AT TIME OF PUBLICATION.

AS.

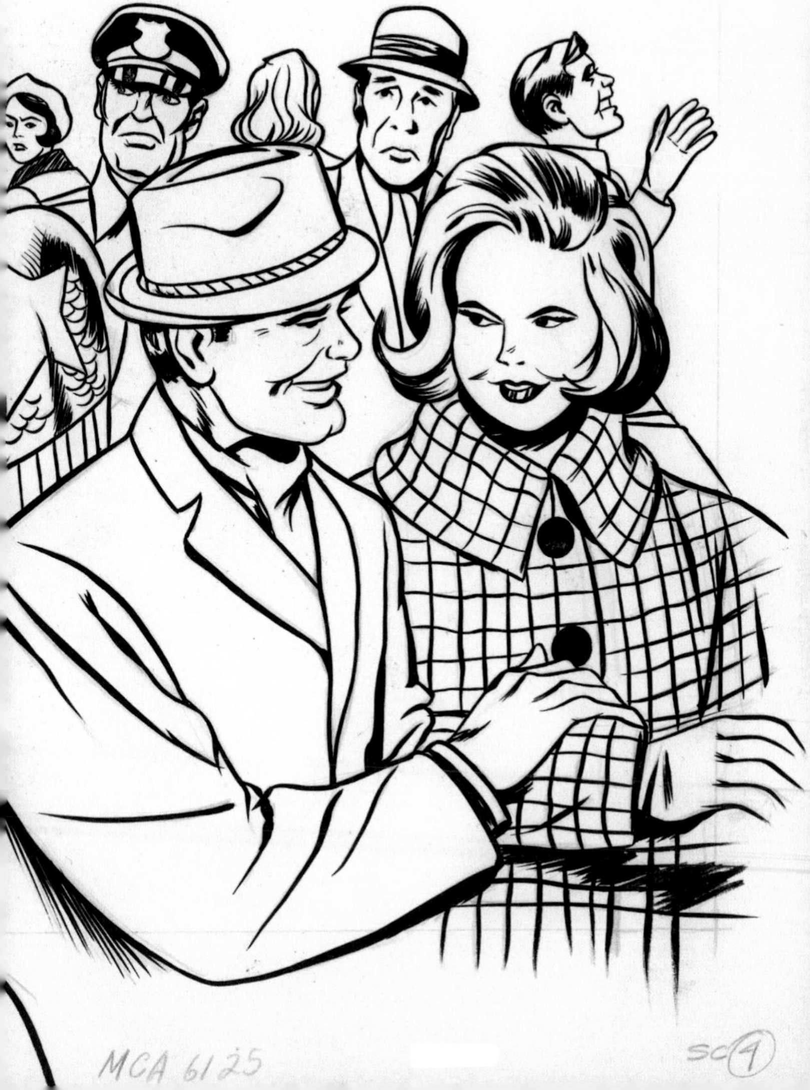
MCA 6125
SC (7)

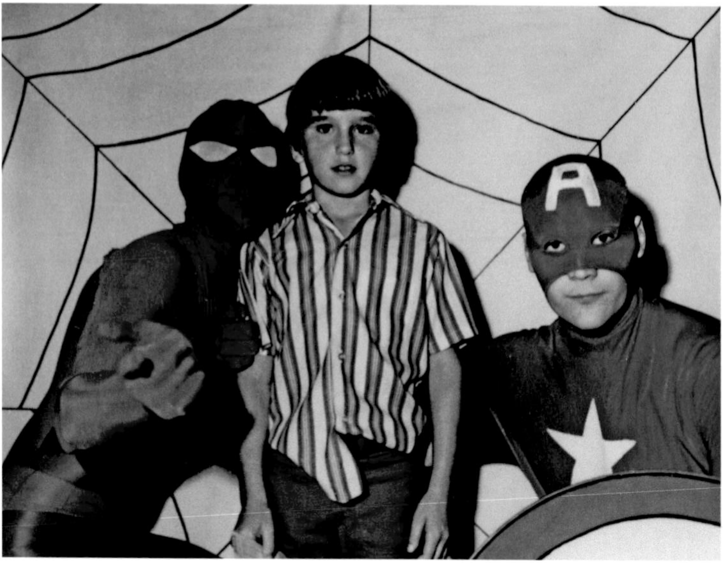

A

ASTONISHING ANIMATION

Pages 94–95: *Animation still,* Marvel Super-Heroes*; Grantray-Lawrence Animation; 1966.* Grantray-Lawrence produced cartoons for television on a budget, and their Marvel shows employed art from the comics, altered and expanded to work on the screen, rather than animation cels. This is an expanded version of a Jack Kirby *Tales of Suspense* panel, with additional art possibly by animator Mike Royer, who would later go on to ink Jack Kirby's work in the 1970s.

HEROES UNITED!

Above: *Photograph, ca. 1968.* A young boy is thrilled to be in the presence of Spidey and Cap at the Michigan State Fair.

CAPTAIN AMERICA CALLING

Opposite: *Captain America promotional postcard, ca. 1966.* Many local networks employed actors to dress up as Marvel characters and appear as hosts in between the *Marvel Super-Heroes* cartoons.

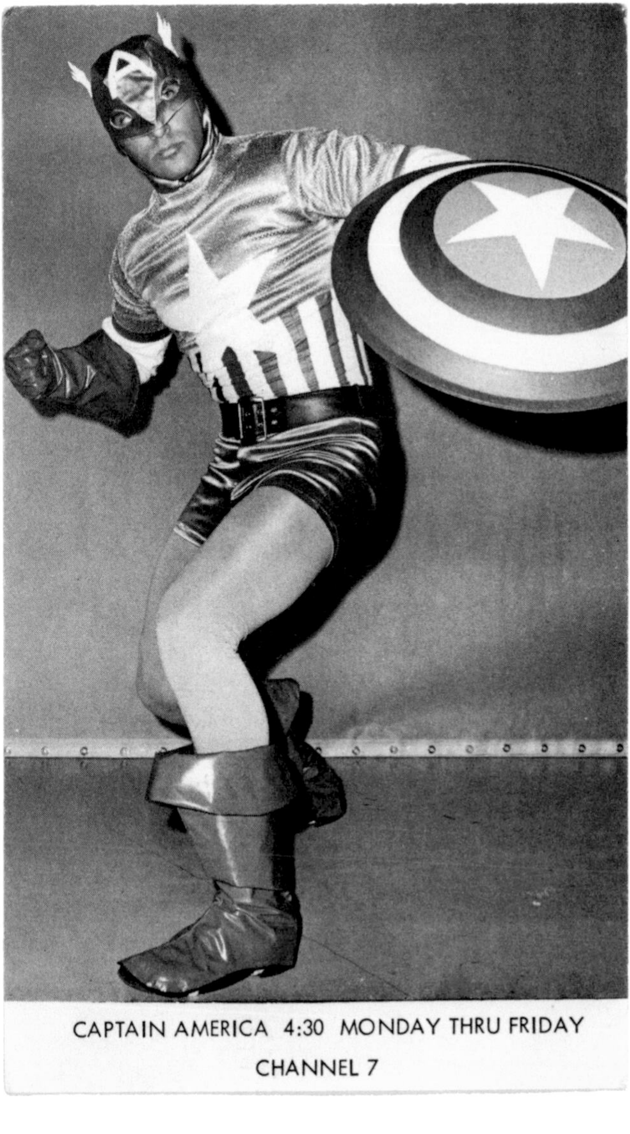
CAPTAIN AMERICA 4:30 MONDAY THRU FRIDAY
CHANNEL 7

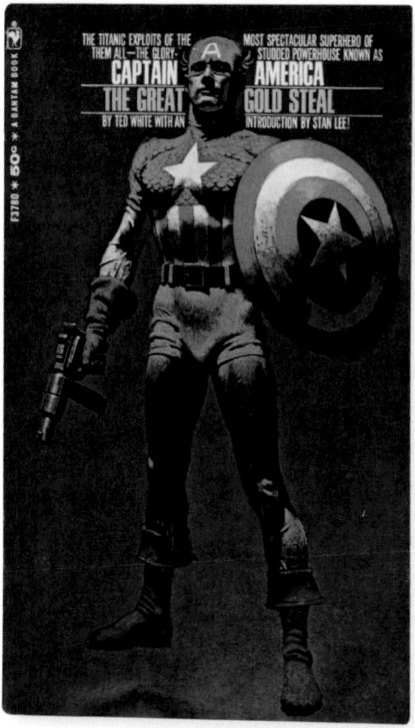
F3780 ★ 50¢ ★ A BANTAM BOOK
THE TITANIC EXPLOITS OF THE MOST SPECTACULAR SUPERHERO OF THEM ALL—THE GLORY-STUDDED POWERHOUSE KNOWN AS
CAPTAIN AMERICA
THE GREAT GOLD STEAL
BY TED WHITE WITH AN INTRODUCTION BY STAN LEE!

THE GLORY-STUDDED POWERHOUSE

Above: *Book cover, Ted White,* Captain America: The Great Gold Steal*; art, Peter Carras; Bantam, 1968.* Hugo Award–winning sci-fi writer Ted Knight penned this Captain America novel. Among the hard-boiled prose, one tidbit unexplored by the comics is explained: those target-like concentric circles on Cap's shield compel his enemies to shoot at *it*, and not *him*.

STRANGE TALES No. 162

Opposite: *Interior, "So Evil, the Night!"; script and pencils, Jim Steranko; inks, Frank Giacoia; November 1967.* In true Bond fashion, Steranko gives Fury a new toy after he crashes his Kirby-designed flying Porsche: a customized Ferrari 330/P4 Berlinetta with "vortex beam devices in the wheel rims" and "hydrolic-mounted cannons." Oh, and did we mention it's invisible? (Even Bond didn't get an invisible car for another 40 years....)

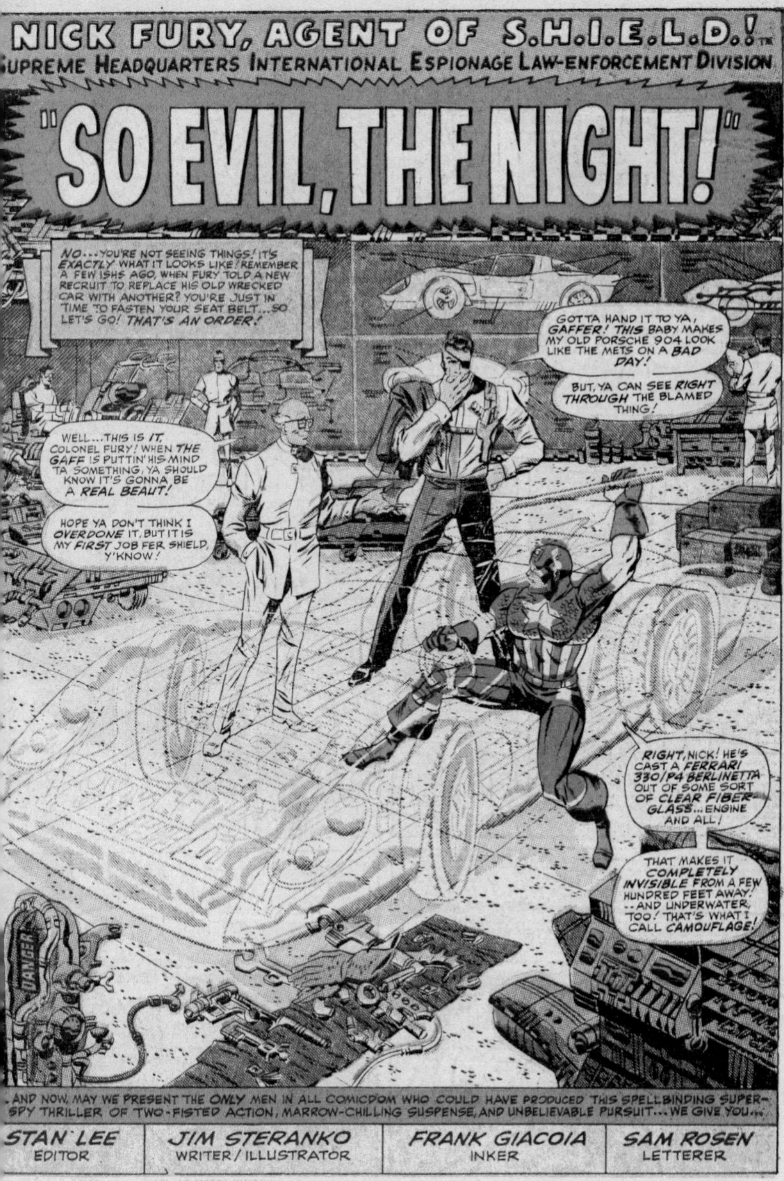
NICK FURY, AGENT OF S.H.I.E.L.D.!™
SUPREME HEADQUARTERS INTERNATIONAL ESPIONAGE LAW-ENFORCEMENT DIVISION
"SO EVIL, THE NIGHT!"
NO... YOU'RE NOT SEEING THINGS! IT'S EXACTLY WHAT IT LOOKS LIKE! REMEMBER A FEW ISHS AGO, WHEN FURY TOLD A NEW RECRUIT TO REPLACE HIS OLD WRECKED CAR WITH ANOTHER? YOU'RE JUST IN TIME TO FASTEN YOUR SEAT BELT... SO LET'S GO! THAT'S AN ORDER!
WELL... THIS IS IT, COLONEL FURY! WHEN THE GAFF IS PUTTIN' HIS MIND TA SOMETHING, YA SHOULD KNOW IT'S GONNA BE A REAL BEAUT!
HOPE YA DON'T THINK I OVERDONE IT, BUT IT IS MY FIRST JOB FER SHIELD, Y'KNOW!
GOTTA HAND IT TO YA, GAFFER! THIS BABY MAKES MY OLD PORSCHE 904 LOOK LIKE THE METS ON A BAD DAY!
BUT, YA CAN SEE RIGHT THROUGH THE BLAMED THING!
RIGHT, NICK! HE'S CAST A FERRARI 330/P4 BERLINETTA OUT OF SOME SORT OF CLEAR FIBER-GLASS... ENGINE AND ALL!
THAT MAKES IT COMPLETELY INVISIBLE FROM A FEW HUNDRED FEET AWAY! ...AND UNDERWATER, TOO! THAT'S WHAT I CALL CAMOUFLAGE!
DANGER
...AND NOW, MAY WE PRESENT THE ONLY MEN IN ALL COMICDOM WHO COULD HAVE PRODUCED THIS SPELLBINDING SUPER-SPY THRILLER OF TWO-FISTED ACTION, MARROW-CHILLING SUSPENSE, AND UNBELIEVABLE PURSUIT... WE GIVE YOU...
STAN LEE EDITOR
JIM STERANKO WRITER/ILLUSTRATOR
FRANK GIACOIA INKER
SAM ROSEN LETTERER

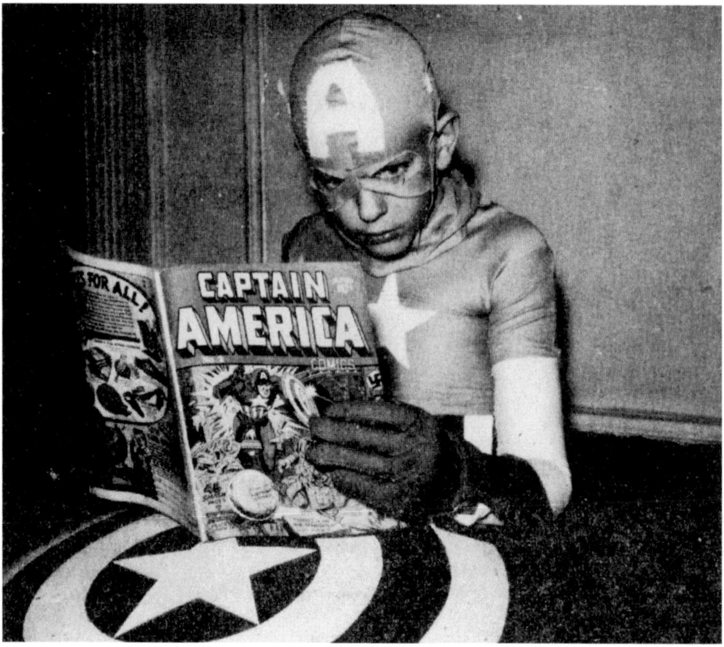
CAPTAIN
AMERICA
COMICS

YOUNG AVENGER

Above: *Photograph, Park Sheraton Hotel, July 23, 1966.* Clad in a homemade Captain America costume, 14-year-old David Armstrong devours a Golden Age issue of Captain America Comics at an early New York Comic-Con. Armstrong would grow up to be a passionate collector; he was the last president of the American Association of Comic Collectors.

STRANGE TALES No. 161

Opposite: *Cover; pencils and inks, Jim Steranko; October 1967.* Here Steranko takes a romp through time in a mash-up featuring characters from Marvel's three decades in publishing: Captain America from the Timely era, the Yellow Claw from the Atlas '50s, and Nick Fury representing the current Marvel Age.

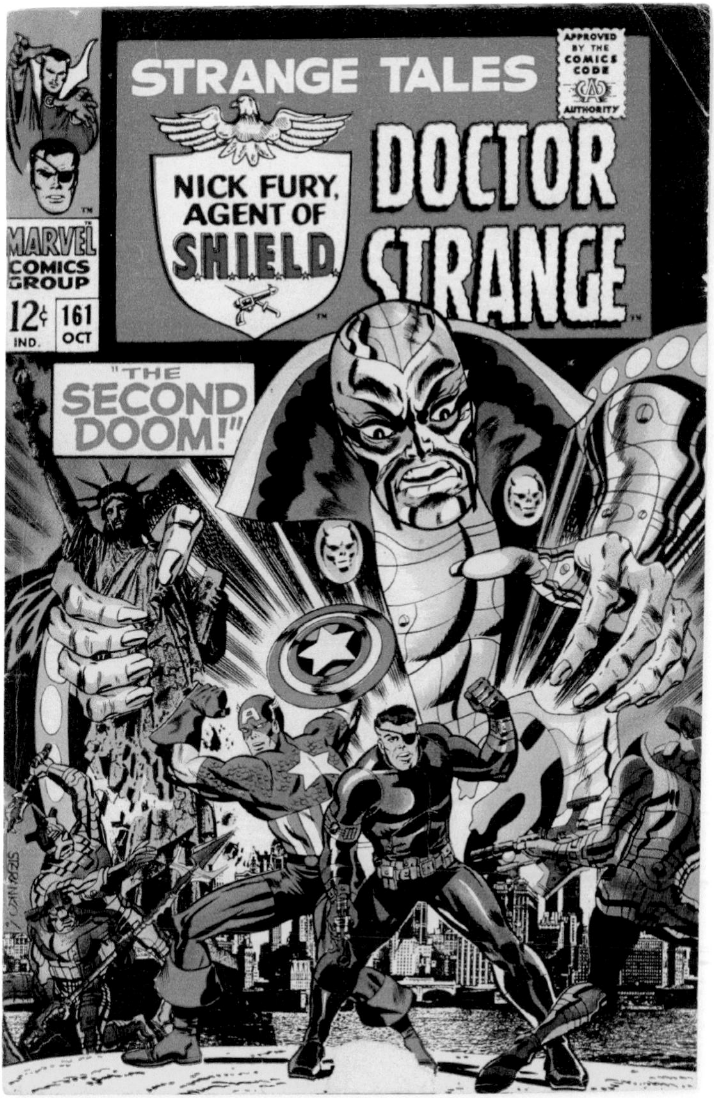
STRANGE TALES
APPROVED BY THE COMICS CODE AUTHORITY
NICK FURY, AGENT OF S.H.I.E.L.D.
DOCTOR STRANGE
MARVEL COMICS GROUP
12¢ IND.
161 OCT
"THE SECOND DOOM!"
STERANKO

STERANKO THE GREAT

Above: *Photograph, 1965.* "Jim was, in essence, the Will Eisner of his generation…Steranko laid it down, providing us then-budding artists with a road map for the future of comic illustration that a few of us are just now catching up to."
—Dave Stevens

CAPTAIN AMERICA No.111

Opposite: *Cover; pencils and inks, Jim Steranko; March 1969.*

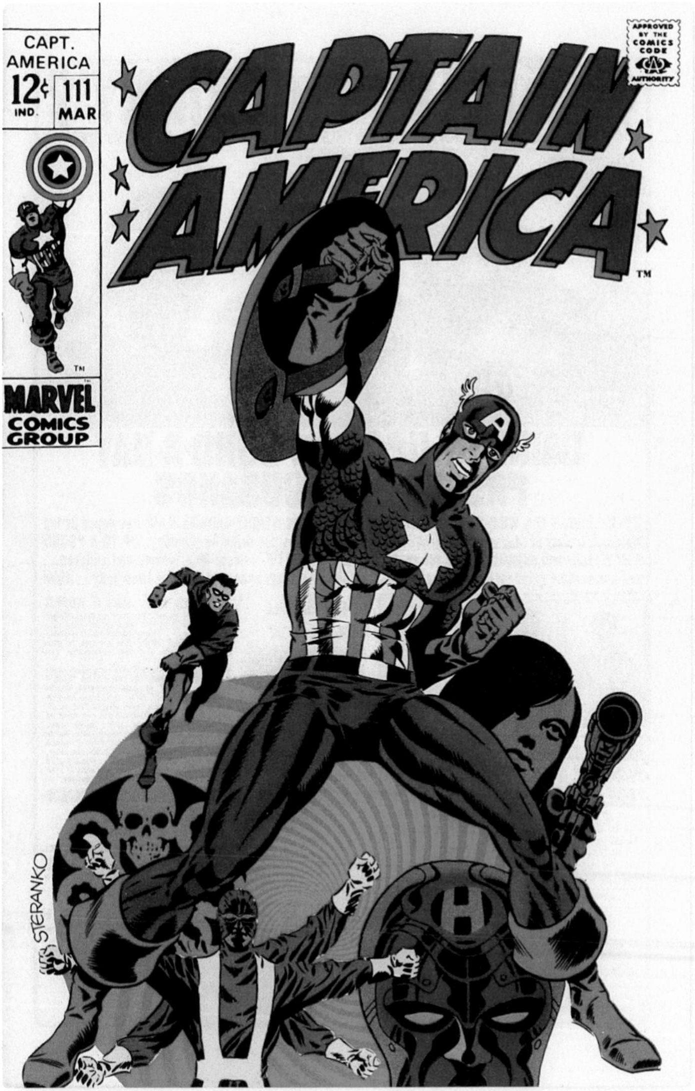
CAPT. AMERICA
12¢ IND.
111 MAR
APPROVED BY THE COMICS CODE AUTHORITY
CAPTAIN AMERICA
MARVEL COMICS GROUP
STERANKO

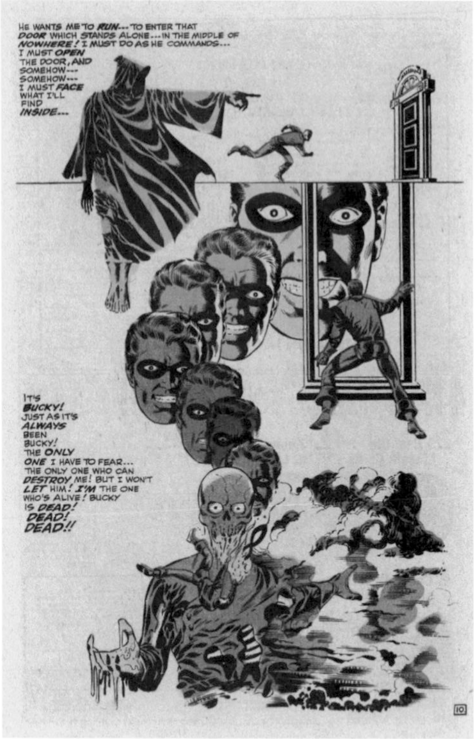
HE WANTS ME TO RUN--- TO ENTER THAT DOOR WHICH STANDS ALONE---IN THE MIDDLE OF NOWHERE! I MUST DO AS HE COMMANDS... I MUST OPEN THE DOOR, AND SOMEHOW--- SOMEHOW--- I MUST FACE WHAT I'LL FIND INSIDE...
IT'S BUCKY! JUST AS IT'S ALWAYS BEEN BUCKY! THE ONLY ONE I HAVE TO FEAR... THE ONLY ONE WHO CAN DESTROY ME! BUT I WON'T LET HIM! I'M THE ONE WHO'S ALIVE! BUCKY IS DEAD! DEAD! DEAD!!
10

CAPTAIN AMERICA No. 111

Above: *Interior, "Tomorrow You Live, Tonight I Die!"; script, Stan Lee; pencils, Jim Steranko; inks, Joe Sinnott; March 1969.* Panel borders disappear and words become subsumed within Steranko's hallucinogenic illustrations, disrupting the usual pacing of the comics while conveying loss and sinister meaning as only Steranko can.

CAPTAIN AMERICA No. 113

Opposite: *Cover; pencils and inks, Jim Steranko. May 1969.*

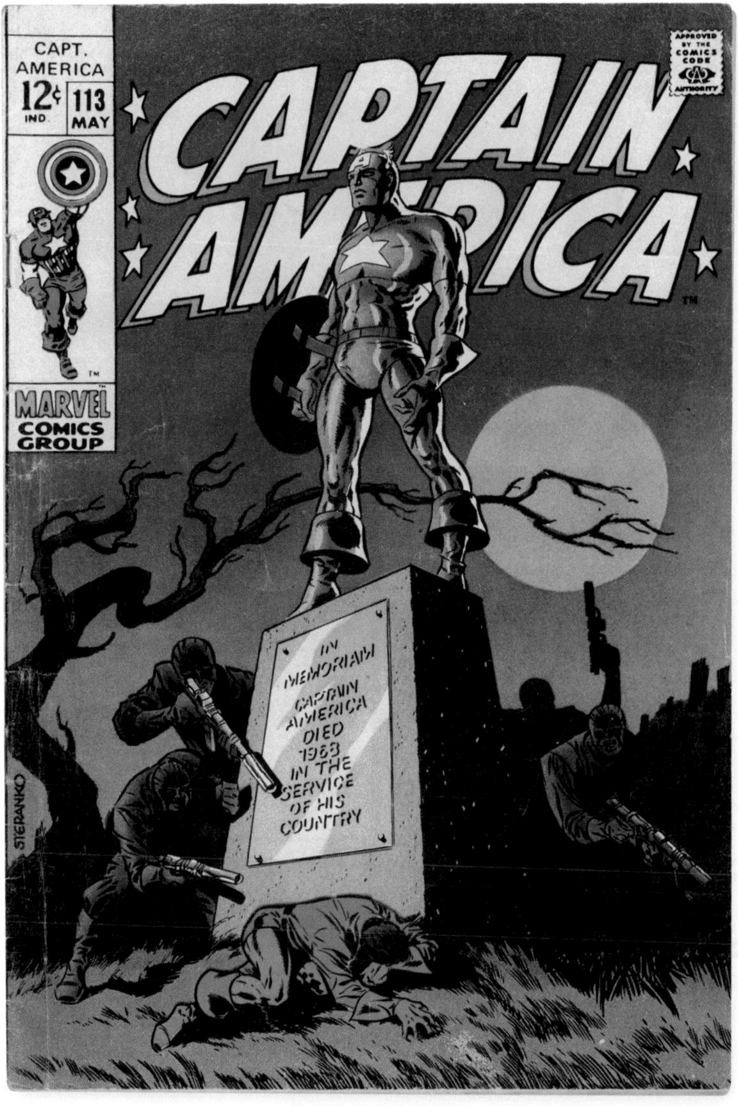
CAPT.
AMERICA
12¢ IND.
113 MAY
CAPTAIN AMERICA
MARVEL COMICS GROUP
APPROVED BY THE COMICS CODE AUTHORITY
IN MEMORIAM
CAPTAIN AMERICA
DIED
1968
IN THE
SERVICE
OF HIS
COUNTRY
STERANKO

CAPT. AMERICA

WORLD COLOR

YELLOW T S

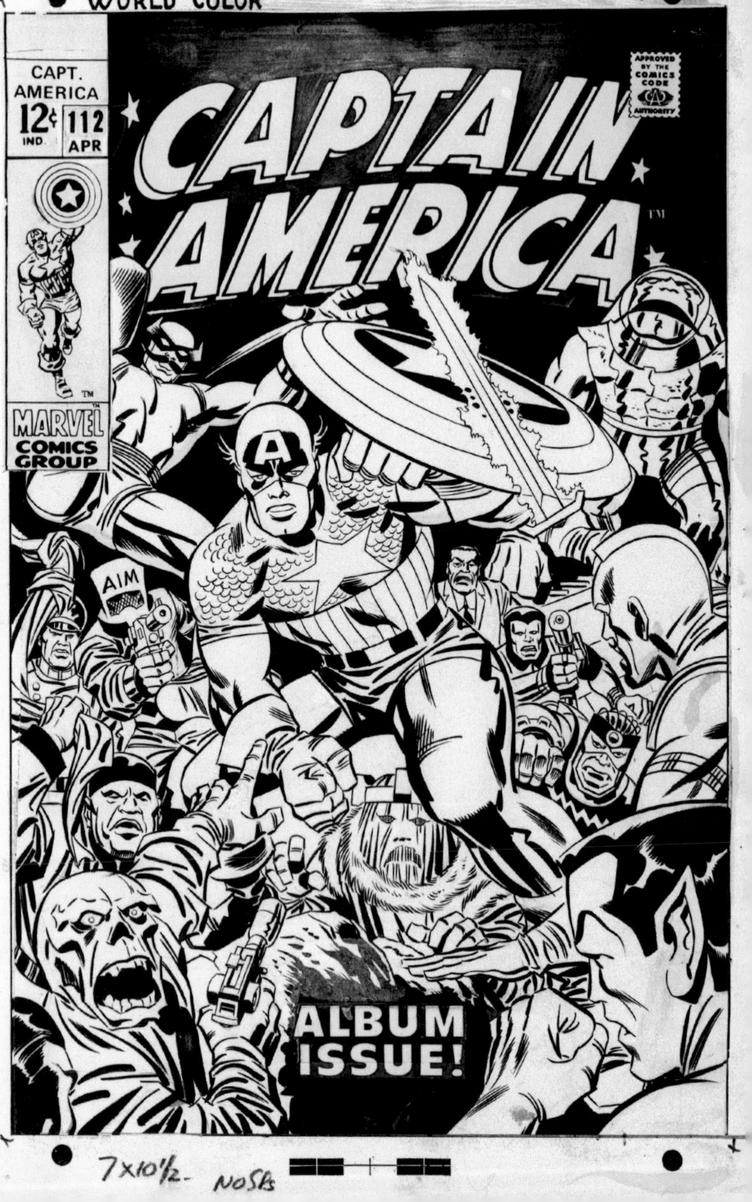

CAPT.
AMERICA
12¢
IND.
112
APR
TM
MARVEL
COMICS
GROUP
APPROVED BY THE COMICS CODE AUTHORITY
CAPTAIN AMERICA
TM
AIM
ALBUM ISSUE!

RED T S

7x10½

NO SPs

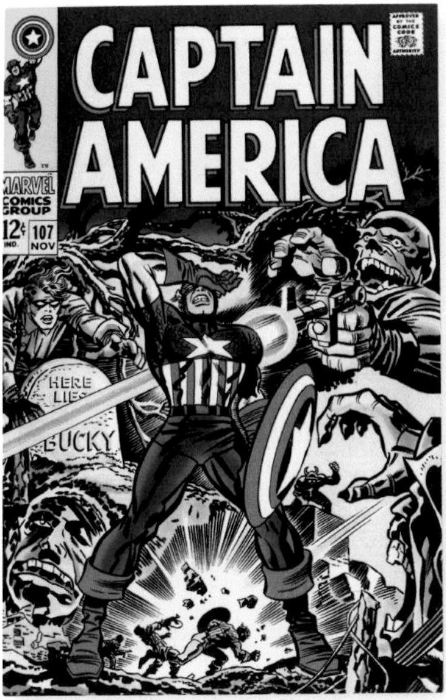
CAPTAIN AMERICA
MARVEL COMICS GROUP
12¢
107
NOV
HERE LIES
BUCKY

A STORY BEHIND EVERY COVER

Opposite: *Original cover art,* Captain America *No. 112; pencils, Jack Kirby; inks, Frank Giacoia; April 1969.* Steranko ended *Cap* No. 111 on a cliff-hanger, but Stan Lee worried he was going to miss the deadline for the next issue. The Marvel office called Kirby in a panic, asking if he could pencil an issue of Captain America in a hurry. It was explained, "Captain America's dead." Kirby responded, "Do I have to bring him back?" No, he was told, he had to keep him dead. In two days Kirby reportedly penciled the entire story, along with this cover.

CAPTAIN AMERICA No. 107

Above: *Cover; pencils, Jack Kirby; inks, Frank Giacoia; November 1968.*

THE AVENGERS No. 100

Pages 108–09: *Interior, "Whatever Gods There Be!"; script, Roy Thomas; pencils and inks, Barry Smith; June 1972.* Loyal Avengers readers might not have been aware of the Conan phenomenon, but in the series' 100th issue they got to behold a precious six pages of art penciled and inked by Smith, including this double-page spread.

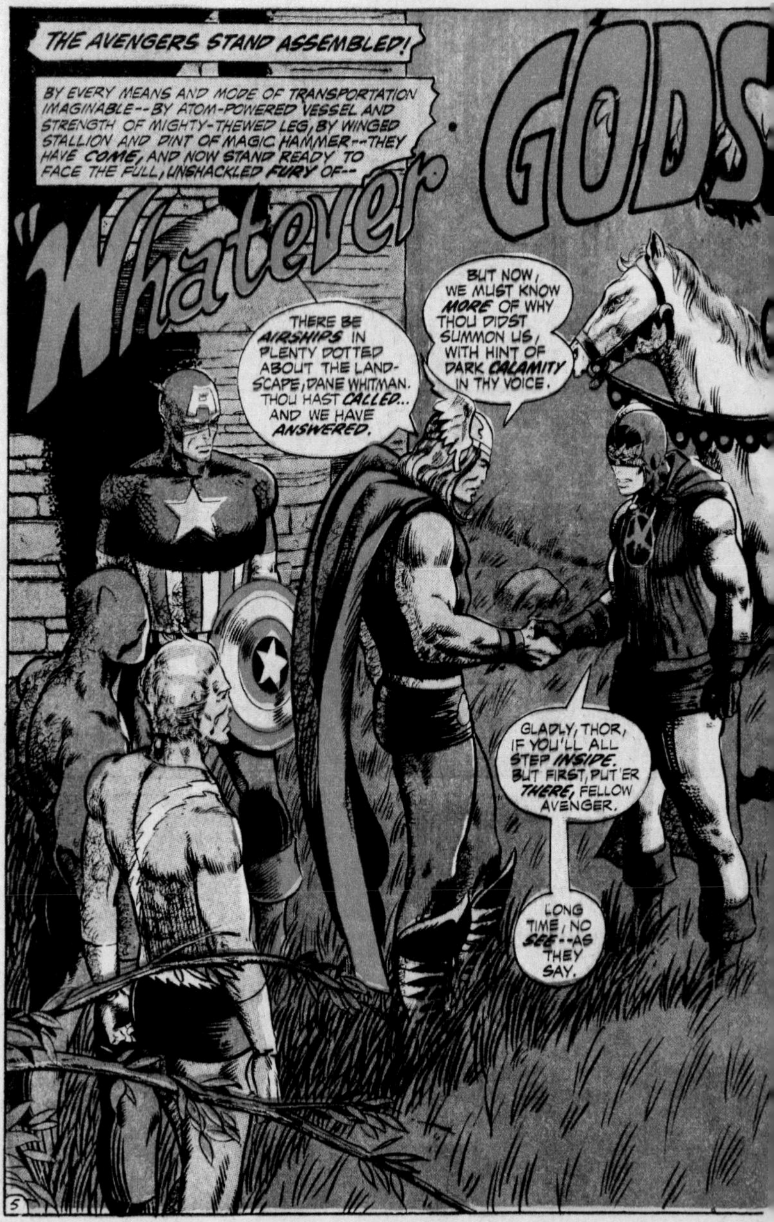
THE AVENGERS STAND ASSEMBLED!
BY EVERY MEANS AND MODE OF TRANSPORTATION IMAGINABLE--BY ATOM-POWERED VESSEL AND STRENGTH OF MIGHTY-THEWED LEG, BY WINGED STALLION AND DINT OF MAGIC HAMMER--THEY HAVE COME, AND NOW STAND READY TO FACE THE FULL, UNSHACKLED FURY OF--
"Whatever GODS
THERE BE AIRSHIPS IN PLENTY DOTTED ABOUT THE LANDSCAPE, DANE WHITMAN. THOU HAST CALLED... AND WE HAVE ANSWERED.
BUT NOW, WE MUST KNOW MORE OF WHY THOU DIDST SUMMON US, WITH HINT OF DARK CALAMITY IN THY VOICE.
GLADLY, THOR, IF YOU'LL ALL STEP INSIDE. BUT FIRST, PUT'ER THERE, FELLOW AVENGER.
LONG TIME, NO SEE--AS THEY SAY.
5

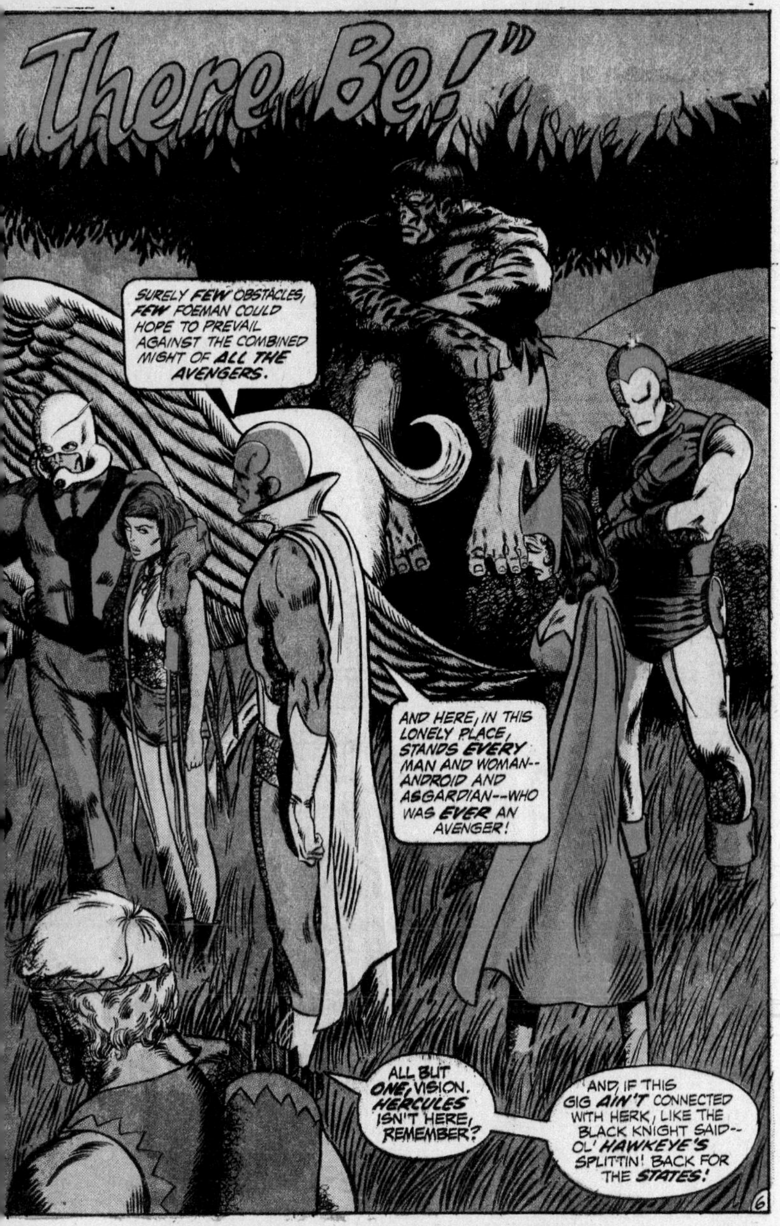

There Be!"
SURELY FEW OBSTACLES, FEW FOEMAN COULD HOPE TO PREVAIL AGAINST THE COMBINED MIGHT OF ALL THE AVENGERS.
AND HERE, IN THIS LONELY PLACE, STANDS EVERY MAN AND WOMAN--ANDROID AND ASGARDIAN--WHO WAS EVER AN AVENGER!
ALL BUT ONE, VISION. HERCULES ISN'T HERE, REMEMBER?
AND, IF THIS GIG AIN'T CONNECTED WITH HERK, LIKE THE BLACK KNIGHT SAID--OL' HAWKEYE'S SPLITTIN' BACK FOR THE STATES!
6

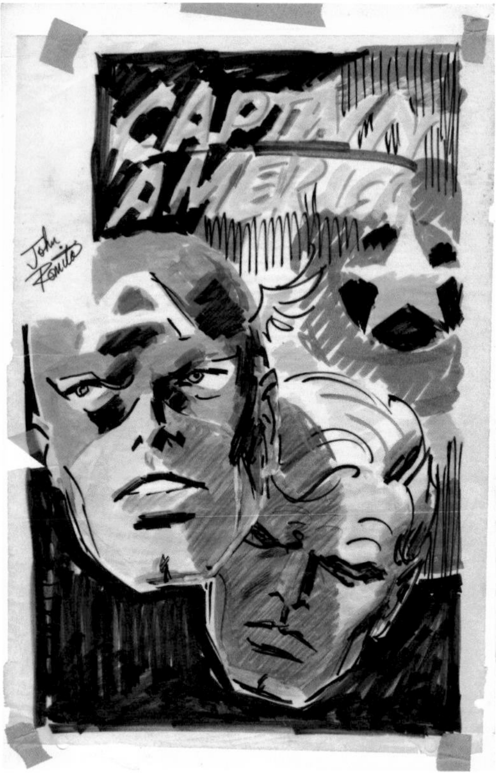
John Romita

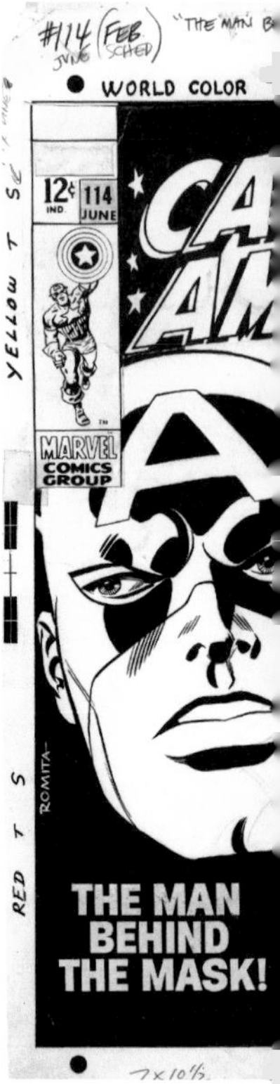
#114 (FEB SCHED)
WORLD COLOR
12¢ IND.
114 JUNE
MARVEL COMICS GROUP
YELLOW T S
RED T S
ROMITA
THE MAN BEHIND THE MASK!

CAPTAIN AMERICA No. 114

Above, sequence: *Cover rough, original art, and published cover; pencils, inks, and coloring, John Romita; June 1969.* These three images show the evolution of a comic book cover, from initial rough to printed book. Romita first sketches out an idea, complete with color guide, leaving room for the logo and corner image. After it is approved, Romita pencils and then inks the art, modifying it as necessary for reproduction. It is then lettered, a colorist completes the job, and off to the printer it goes.

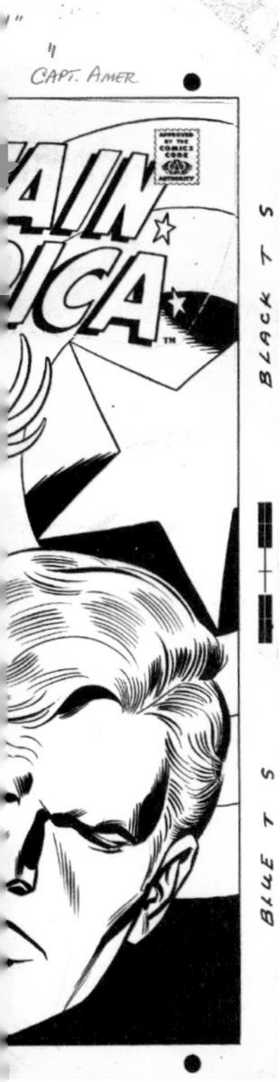
CAPT. AMER
BLACK T S
BLUE T S

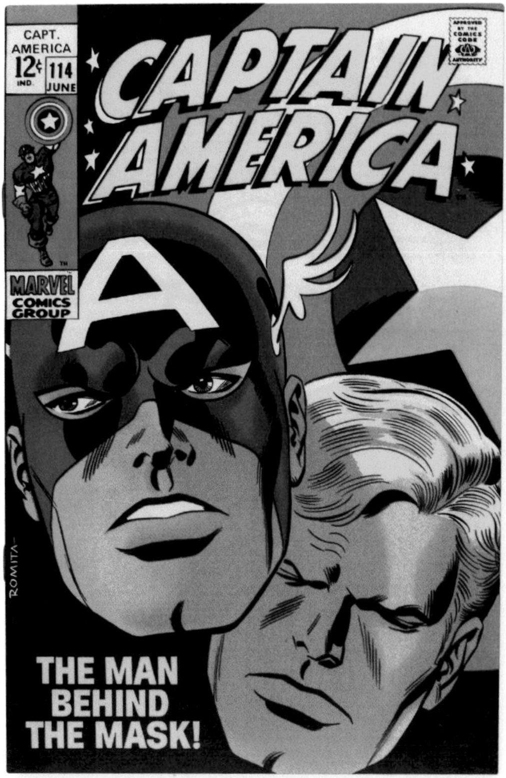
CAPT. AMERICA
12¢ IND.
114 JUNE
CAPTAIN AMERICA
MARVEL COMICS GROUP
ROMITA
THE MAN BEHIND THE MASK!

TALES OF SUSPENSE No. 98

Below: *Cover; pencils, Jack Kirby; inks, Frank Giacoia; February 1968.* The Black Panther was the first black super hero in mainstream comics, an African king with a tremendous range of skills, powers, and abilities.

CAPTAIN AMERICA No. 117

Opposite: *Cover; pencils, Gene Colan and John Romita; inks, Joe Sinnott and John Romita; September 1969.* This issue marks the first appearance of the Falcon, who would become Cap's partner for many years, even for a time becoming Captain America himself. He is the first African-American super hero in mainstream comics—although Black Panther made his debut three years earlier, he wasn't American.

TALES OF SUSPENSE
CAPTAIN AMERICA
AND
IRON MAN
APPROVED BY THE COMICS CODE AUTHORITY
MARVEL COMICS GROUP
12¢ IND.
98 FEB
MCG
CAP VS.... THE PANTHER

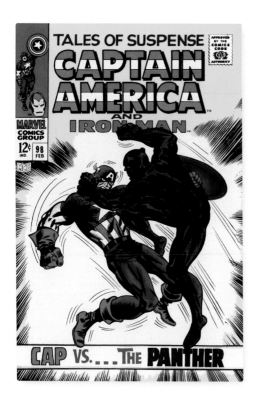

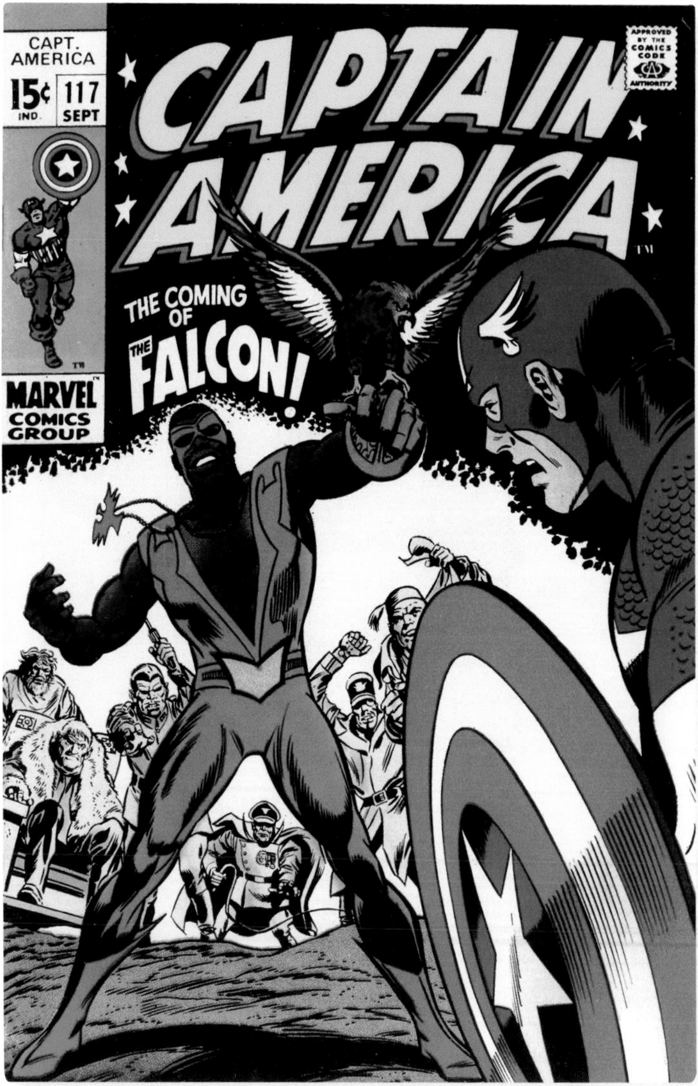
CAPT. AMERICA
15¢ IND.
117 SEPT
MARVEL COMICS GROUP
APPROVED BY THE COMICS CODE AUTHORITY
CAPTAIN AMERICA
THE COMING OF THE FALCON!

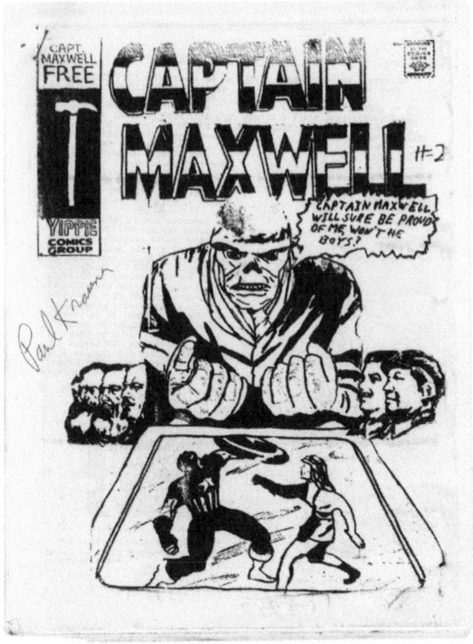
CAPT. MAXWELL
FREE
YIPPIE COMICS GROUP
CAPTAIN MAXWELL
#2
CAPTAIN MAXWELL WILL SURE BE PROUD OF ME WON'T HE BOYS?
Paul Krassner

NEWS FROM THE UNDERGROUND

Above: *'Zine cover,* Captain Maxwell*, Yippie Comics; art, Paul Krassner; 1968.* Marvel may have been big business, but its outsider approach lent the publisher an air of street cred, even with the burgeoning counterculture movement. Krassner, a founding member of the Youth International Party (Yippies), one of Ken Kesey's Merry Pranksters, and a leading figure of the counterculture movement, co-opted Kirby's cover of *Captain America* No. 103 as the cover of one of the Yippies' many satirical underground publications.

CAPTAIN AMERICA No. 120

Opposite: *Interior, "Crack-Up on Campus!"; script, Stan Lee; pencils, Gene Colan; inks, Joe Sinnott; December 1969.* While the Falcon would depart after his first encounter with Captain America, he soon returned as his full-time partner. The idea of adding an African-American hero to the strip helped make Cap a more contemporary hero, and their stories would often address relevant social issues like bigotry. Colan's splash page, with its varied background characters' emotions, touches on both the optimism and the distrust that plagued race relations in the 1960s.

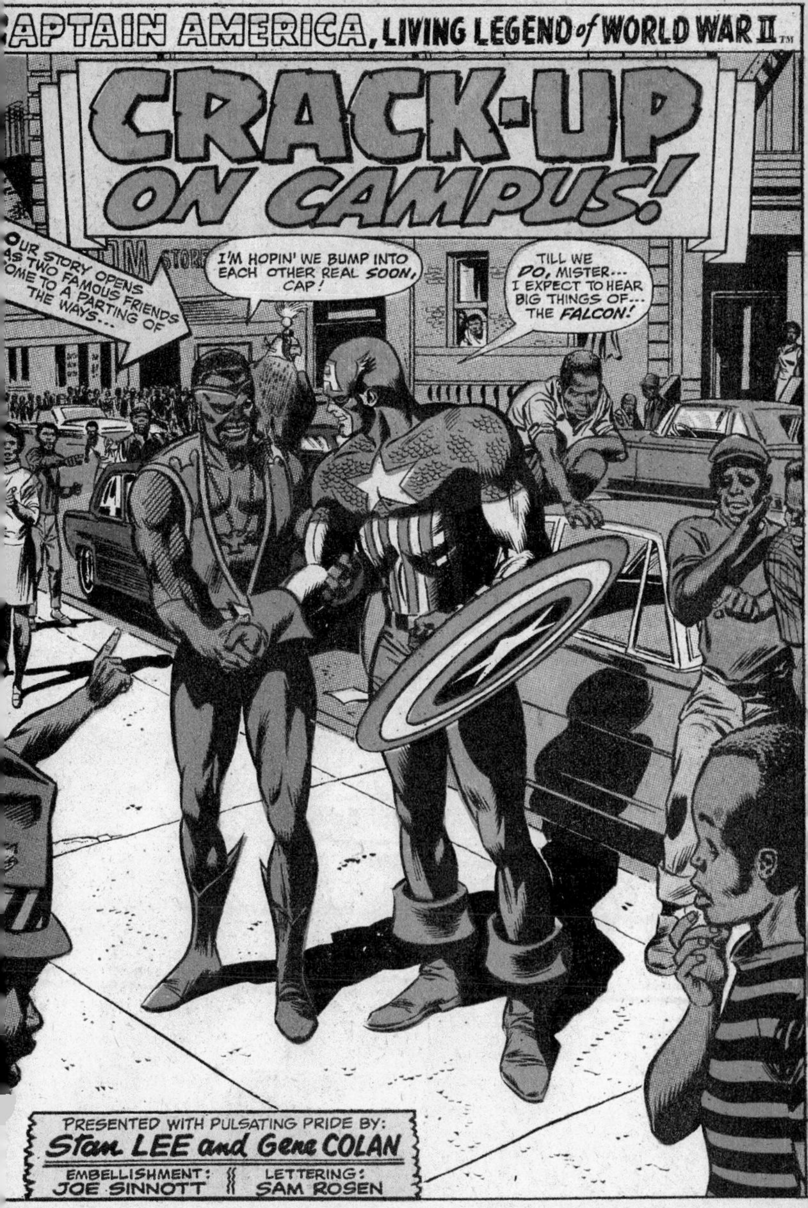
CAPTAIN AMERICA, LIVING LEGEND of WORLD WAR II TM
CRACK-UP ON CAMPUS!
OUR STORY OPENS AS TWO FAMOUS FRIENDS COME TO A PARTING OF THE WAYS...
I'M HOPIN' WE BUMP INTO EACH OTHER REAL SOON, CAP!
TILL WE DO, MISTER... I EXPECT TO HEAR BIG THINGS OF... THE FALCON!
PRESENTED WITH PULSATING PRIDE BY:
Stan LEE and Gene COLAN
EMBELLISHMENT: JOE SINNOTT
LETTERING: SAM ROSEN

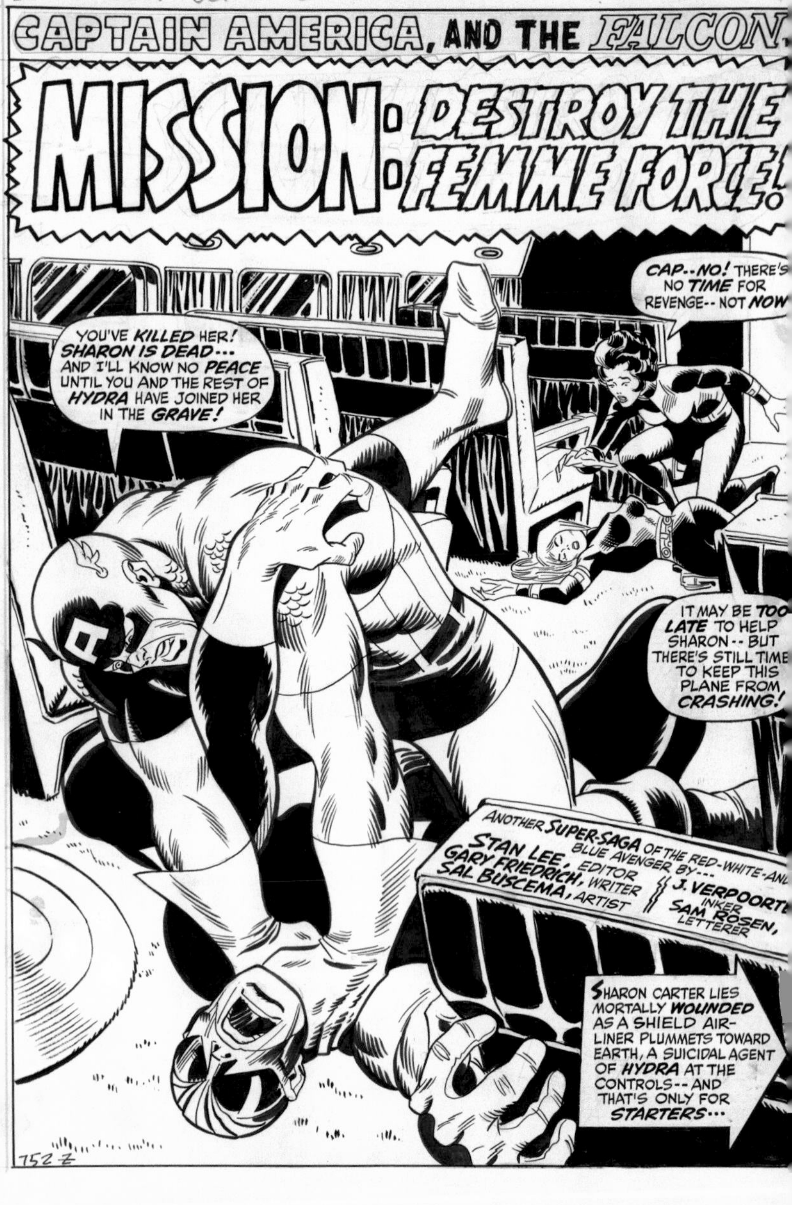
CAPTAIN AMERICA, AND THE FALCON
MISSION: DESTROY THE FEMME FORCE!
YOU'VE KILLED HER! SHARON IS DEAD... AND I'LL KNOW NO PEACE UNTIL YOU AND THE REST OF HYDRA HAVE JOINED HER IN THE GRAVE!
CAP--NO! THERE'S NO TIME FOR REVENGE-- NOT NOW
IT MAY BE TOO LATE TO HELP SHARON -- BUT THERE'S STILL TIME TO KEEP THIS PLANE FROM CRASHING!
ANOTHER SUPER-SAGA OF THE RED-WHITE-AND BLUE AVENGER BY---
STAN LEE, EDITOR
GARY FRIEDRICH, WRITER
SAL BUSCEMA, ARTIST
J. VERPOORTE INKER
SAM ROSEN, LETTERER
SHARON CARTER LIES MORTALLY WOUNDED AS A SHIELD AIR-LINER PLUMMETS TOWARD EARTH, A SUICIDAL AGENT OF HYDRA AT THE CONTROLS-- AND THAT'S ONLY FOR STARTERS...
752 Z

CAPTAIN AMERICA No. 146

Opposite: *Original interior art, "Mission: Destroy the Femme Force!"; script, Gary Friedrich; pencils, Sal Buscema; inks, John Verpoorten; February 1972.* Years before the American military integrated its battle forces with women, Marvel showed a great deal of faith in its similar female characters. The moniker Femme Force was given to the S.H.I.E.L.D. team composed of Agent 13 and the Contessa — each an elite, battle-hardened field agent more than capable of taking on Hydra.

CAPTAIN AMERICA No. 156

Below: *Interior, "Two into One Won't Go!"; script, Steve Englehart; pencils, Sal Buscema; inks, Frank McLaughlin; December 1972.* By the middle of 1972, Cap's floundering title was reportedly on the verge of cancellation. Englehart's masterstroke was to take Steve Rogers's quest for meaning and infuse it irrevocably into his character. America was a country that sought change — and so Captain America would be emblematic of that change. Within months, the team of Englehart and Buscema had turned *Captain America* into a top seller.

CAPTAIN AMERICA No. 144

Opposite: *Cover; pencils and inks, John Romita; December 1971.* The Falcon debuts his red and white costume in this story, in which he parts ways with Captain America. The split on the cover is both figurative and literal, with each character having their own 10-page story in the issue.

HE DOESN'T KNOW I'M THE MAN HE IDOLIZED -- BUT I KNOW IT!
IN A VERY REAL WAY, I'M RE-SPONSIBLE FOR ALL THE EVIL HE'S DONE!
NOW I HAVE TO FACE HIM, AND FINISH THIS.
BUT CAN I FINISH A MAN WHO'S MY BIGGEST FAN?

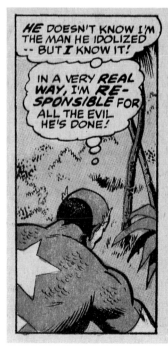

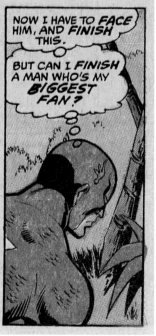

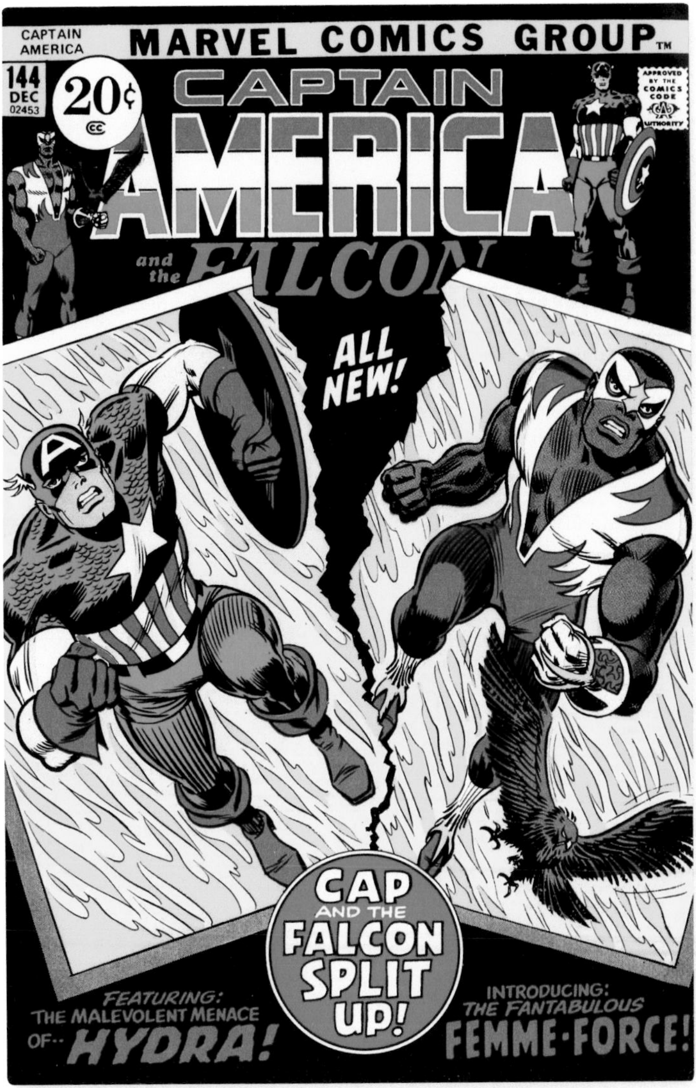
CAPTAIN AMERICA
MARVEL COMICS GROUP™
144 DEC 02453
20¢
CC
APPROVED BY THE COMICS CODE AUTHORITY
CAPTAIN AMERICA
and the FALCON
ALL NEW!
CAP AND THE FALCON SPLIT UP!
FEATURING: THE MALEVOLENT MENACE OF-- HYDRA!
INTRODUCING: THE FANTABULOUS FEMME-FORCE!

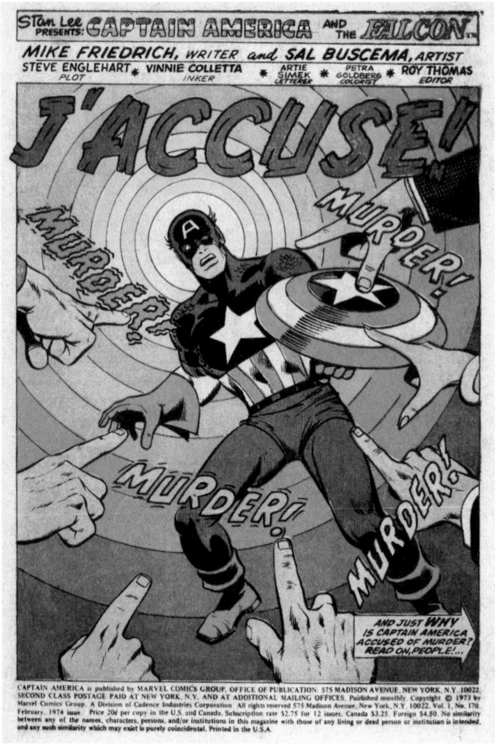
STAN LEE PRESENTS: CAPTAIN AMERICA AND THE FALCON
MIKE FRIEDRICH, WRITER and SAL BUSCEMA, ARTIST
STEVE ENGLEHART PLOT * VINNIE COLLETTA INKER * ARTIE SIMEK LETTERER * PETRA GOLDBERG COLORIST * ROY THOMAS EDITOR
J'ACCUSE!
MURDER!
MURDER!
MURDER!
MURDER!
MURDER!
AND JUST WHY IS CAPTAIN AMERICA ACCUSED OF MURDER? READ ON, PEOPLE!...
CAPTAIN AMERICA is published by MARVEL COMICS GROUP, OFFICE OF PUBLICATION: 575 MADISON AVENUE, NEW YORK, N.Y. 10022. SECOND CLASS POSTAGE PAID AT NEW YORK, N.Y. AND AT ADDITIONAL MAILING OFFICES. Published monthly. Copyright © 1973 by Marvel Comics Group, A Division of Cadence Industries Corporation. All rights reserved 575 Madison Avenue, New York, N.Y. 10022. Vol. 1, No. 170, February, 1974 issue. Price 20¢ per copy in the U.S. and Canada. Subscription rate $2.75 for 12 issues, Canada $3.25, Foreign $4.50. No similarity between any of the names, characters, persons, and/or institutions in this magazine with those of any living or dead person or institution is intended, and any such similarity which may exist is purely coincidental. Printed in the U.S.A.

CAPTAIN AMERICA No. 170

Above: *Interior, "J'Accuse!"; plot, Steve Englehart; script, Mike Friedrich; pencils, Sal Buscema; inks, Vince Colletta; February 1974.* As Marvel's most traditional and heroic super hero, writers always had a field day putting Captain America in the middle of real world politics, from Vietnam War-era protests and "dropouts" to post-Watergate disillusionment.

CAPTAIN AMERICA No. 169

Opposite: *Interior, "When a Legend Dies"; plot and script, Steve Englehart; script, Mike Friedrich; pencils, Sal Buscema; inks, Frank McLaughlin; January 1974.*

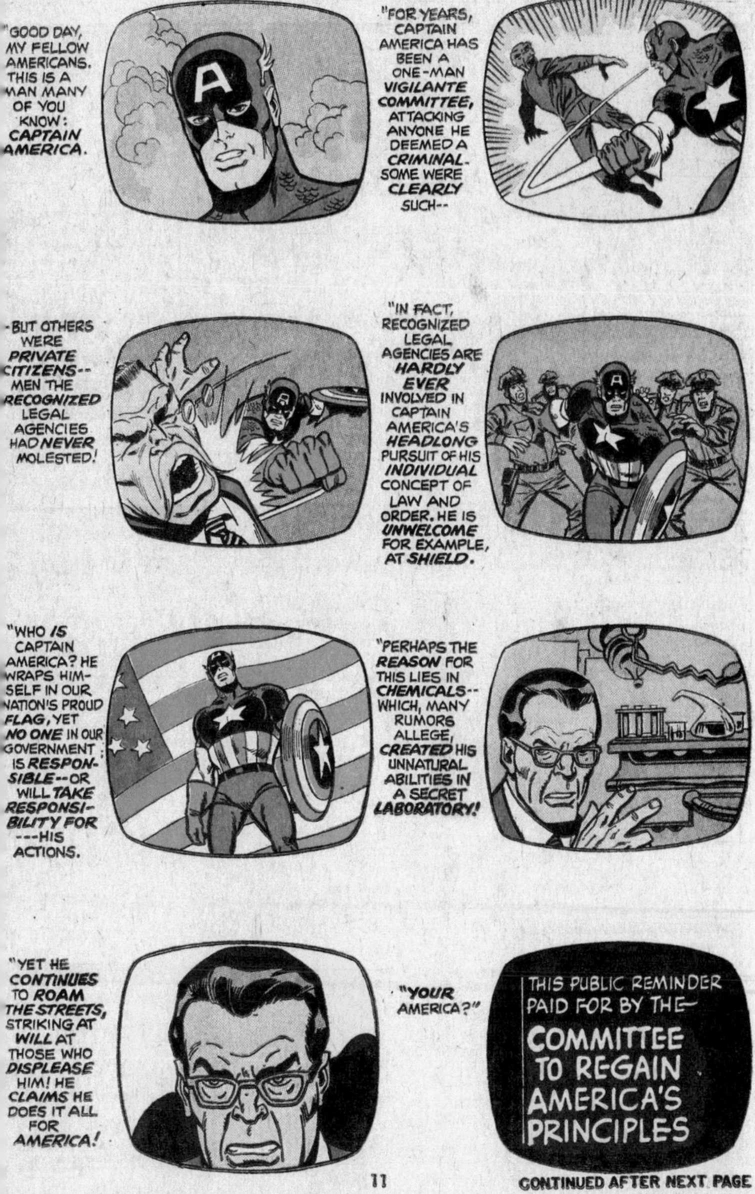
"GOOD DAY, MY FELLOW AMERICANS. THIS IS A MAN MANY OF YOU KNOW: CAPTAIN AMERICA.
"FOR YEARS, CAPTAIN AMERICA HAS BEEN A ONE-MAN VIGILANTE COMMITTEE, ATTACKING ANYONE HE DEEMED A CRIMINAL- SOME WERE CLEARLY SUCH--
-BUT OTHERS WERE PRIVATE CITIZENS-- MEN THE RECOGNIZED LEGAL AGENCIES HAD NEVER MOLESTED!
"IN FACT, RECOGNIZED LEGAL AGENCIES ARE HARDLY EVER INVOLVED IN CAPTAIN AMERICA'S HEADLONG PURSUIT OF HIS INDIVIDUAL CONCEPT OF LAW AND ORDER. HE IS UNWELCOME FOR EXAMPLE, AT SHIELD.
"WHO IS CAPTAIN AMERICA? HE WRAPS HIMSELF IN OUR NATION'S PROUD FLAG, YET NO ONE IN OUR GOVERNMENT IS RESPONSIBLE--OR WILL TAKE RESPONSIBILITY FOR ---HIS ACTIONS.
"PERHAPS THE REASON FOR THIS LIES IN CHEMICALS-- WHICH, MANY RUMORS ALLEGE, CREATED HIS UNNATURAL ABILITIES IN A SECRET LABORATORY!
"YET HE CONTINUES TO ROAM THE STREETS, STRIKING AT WILL AT THOSE WHO DISPLEASE HIM! HE CLAIMS HE DOES IT ALL FOR AMERICA!
"YOUR AMERICA?"
THIS PUBLIC REMINDER PAID FOR BY THE—
COMMITTEE TO RE-GAIN AMERICA'S PRINCIPLES

CONTINUED AFTER NEXT PAGE

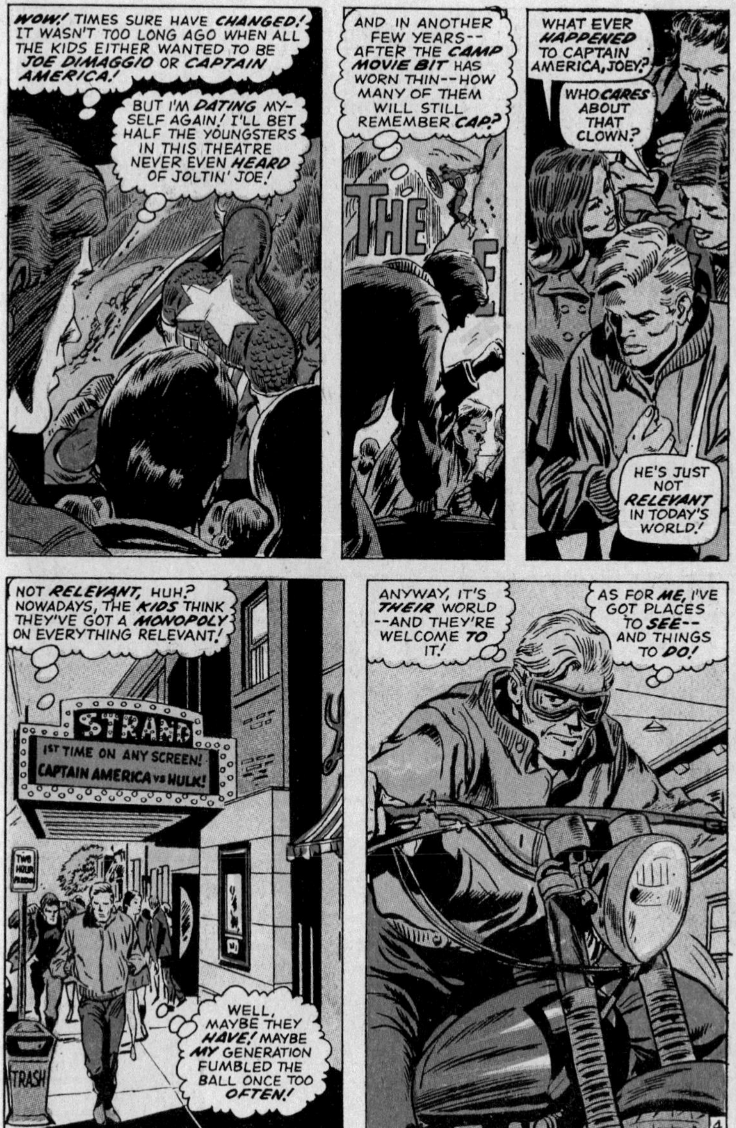

WOW! TIMES SURE HAVE CHANGED! IT WASN'T TOO LONG AGO WHEN ALL THE KIDS EITHER WANTED TO BE JOE DIMAGGIO OR CAPTAIN AMERICA!
BUT I'M DATING MYSELF AGAIN! I'LL BET HALF THE YOUNGSTERS IN THIS THEATRE NEVER EVEN HEARD OF JOLTIN' JOE!
AND IN ANOTHER FEW YEARS-- AFTER THE CAMP MOVIE BIT HAS WORN THIN--HOW MANY OF THEM WILL STILL REMEMBER CAP?
THE
WHAT EVER HAPPENED TO CAPTAIN AMERICA, JOEY?
WHO CARES ABOUT THAT CLOWN?
HE'S JUST NOT RELEVANT IN TODAY'S WORLD!
NOT RELEVANT, HUH? NOWADAYS, THE KIDS THINK THEY'VE GOT A MONOPOLY ON EVERYTHING RELEVANT!
STRAND
1ST TIME ON ANY SCREEN!
CAPTAIN AMERICA vs HULK!
TRASH
WELL, MAYBE THEY HAVE! MAYBE MY GENERATION FUMBLED THE BALL ONCE TOO OFTEN!
ANYWAY, IT'S THEIR WORLD --AND THEY'RE WELCOME TO IT!
AS FOR ME, I'VE GOT PLACES TO SEE-- AND THINGS TO DO!
4

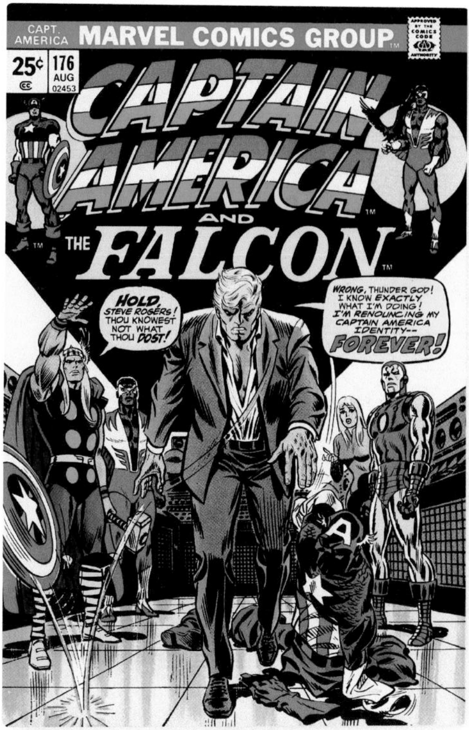
CAPT. AMERICA
MARVEL COMICS GROUP
25¢
176
AUG
02453
CAPTAIN AMERICA
AND
THE FALCON
HOLD, STEVE ROGERS! THOU KNOWEST NOT WHAT THOU DOST!
WRONG, THUNDER GOD! I KNOW EXACTLY WHAT I'M DOING! I'M RENOUNCING MY CAPTAIN AMERICA IDENTITY-- FOREVER!

CAPTAIN AMERICA No. 130

Opposite: *Interior, "Up Against the Wall!"; script, Stan Lee; pencils, Gene Colan; inks, Dick Ayers; October 1970.* "This is the day of the antihero — the age of the rebel — and the dissenter! ...In a world rife with injustice, greed, and endless war — who's to say the rebels are wrong?" — Captain America

CAPTAIN AMERICA No. 176

Above and pages 124–25: *Cover; pencils and inks, John Romita. Interiors, "Captain America Must Die!"; script, Steve Englehart; pencils, Sal Buscema; inks, Vince Colletta; August 1974.* Cap retires in this issue, leaving Falcon and a load of wannabe Captain Americas to handle the workload.

"FOR NEARLY TWO HUNDRED YEARS, THE SPIRIT OF FREEDOM HAS NEVER BEEN FORGOTTEN HERE--
"--AND FOR THAT REASON, COUNTLESS MEN AND WOMEN, CRUSHED UNDER THE BRUTAL HEEL OF TOTALITARIANISM, HAVE BEEN ABLE TO KEEP ALIVE THEIR DREAMS OF LIBERATION.'
"THIS IS BIGGER THAN YOU OR ANY OTHER INDIVIDUAL, CAP! IT'S BIGGER THAN ALL OF US!
"BUT YOU SYMBOLIZE ALL OF IT IN YOUR OWN WAY--AND YOU'RE THE ONLY ONE WHO DOES!'

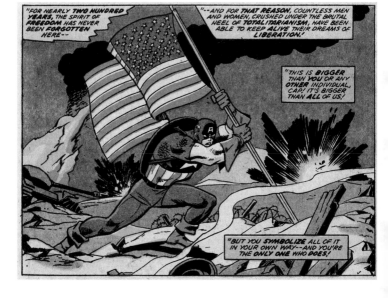

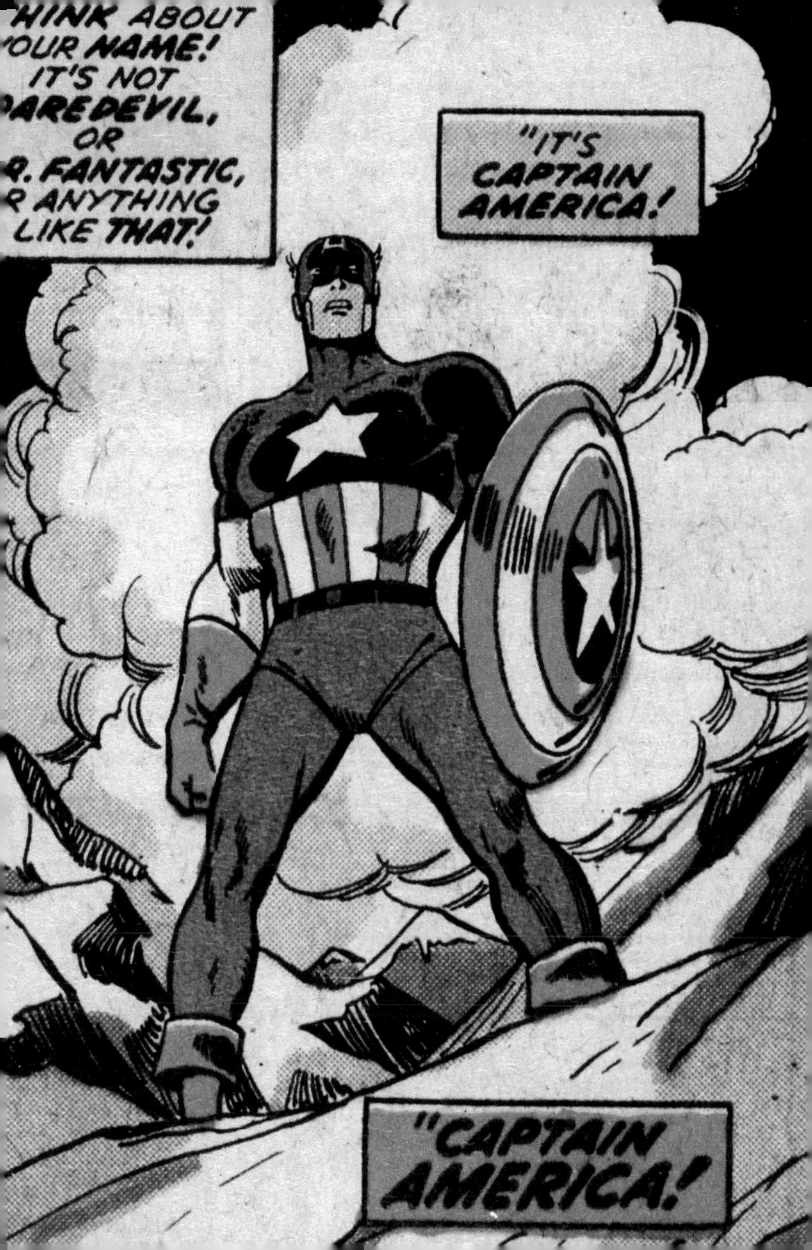

HINK ABOUT OUR NAME! IT'S NOT DAREDEVIL, OR R. FANTASTIC, R ANYTHING LIKE THAT!
"IT'S CAPTAIN AMERICA!
"CAPTAIN AMERICA!

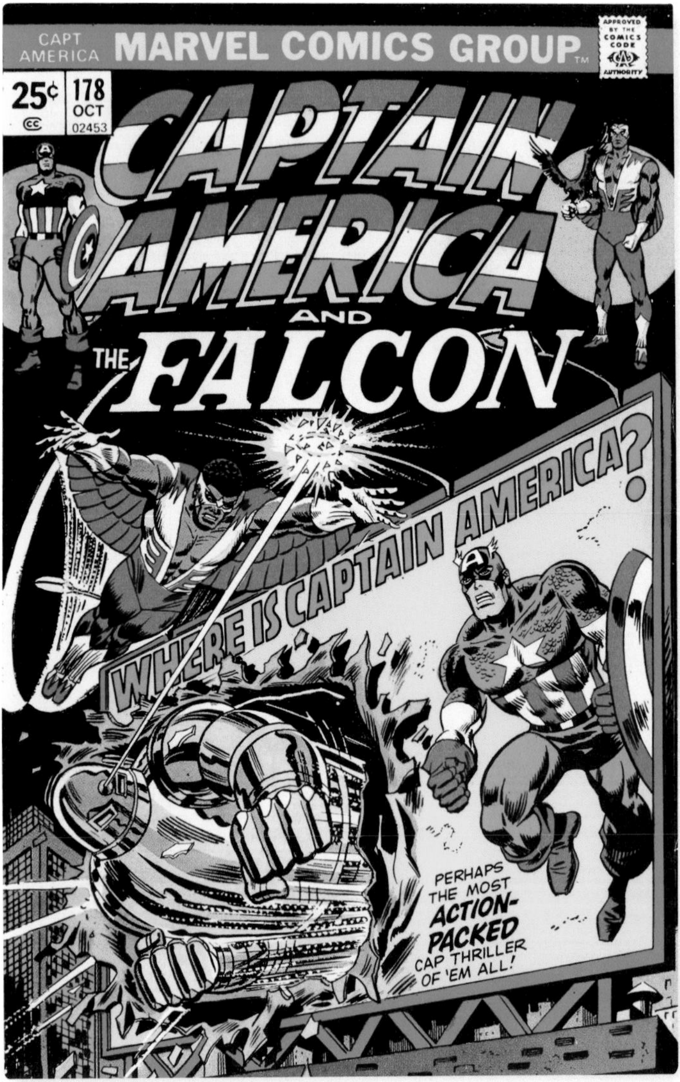

CAPT AMERICA
MARVEL COMICS GROUP
APPROVED BY THE COMICS CODE AUTHORITY
25¢
178 OCT
02453
CAPTAIN AMERICA
AND
THE FALCON
WHERE IS CAPTAIN AMERICA?
PERHAPS THE MOST ACTION-PACKED CAP THRILLER OF 'EM ALL!

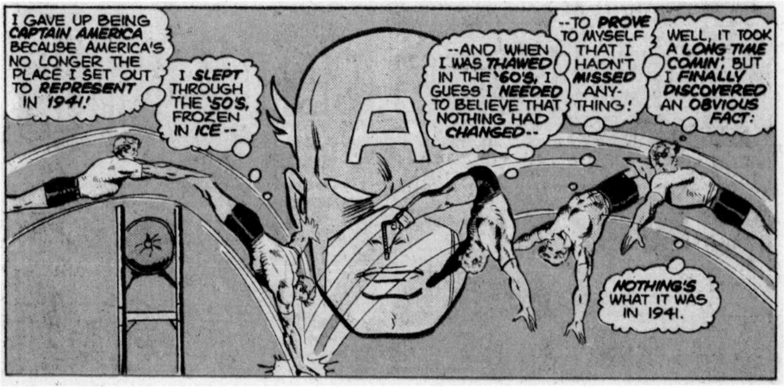
I GAVE UP BEING CAPTAIN AMERICA BECAUSE AMERICA'S NO LONGER THE PLACE I SET OUT TO REPRESENT IN 1941!
I SLEPT THROUGH THE '50'S, FROZEN IN ICE--
--AND WHEN I WAS THAWED IN THE '60'S, I GUESS I NEEDED TO BELIEVE THAT NOTHING HAD CHANGED--
--TO PROVE TO MYSELF THAT I HADN'T MISSED ANY-THING!
WELL, IT TOOK A LONG TIME COMIN', BUT I FINALLY DISCOVERED AN OBVIOUS FACT:
NOTHING'S WHAT IT WAS IN 1941.

CAPTAIN AMERICA No. 178

Opposite and above: *Interior, "If the Falcon Should Fall!"; script, Steve Englehart; pencils, Sal Buscema; inks, Vince Colletta; October 1974.* With a storyline centered around Cap's flagging spirits, Englehart's Nomad arc — which had the disillusioned Steve Rogers don *caped* crusading attire — was in tune with the political climate of early-'70s America.

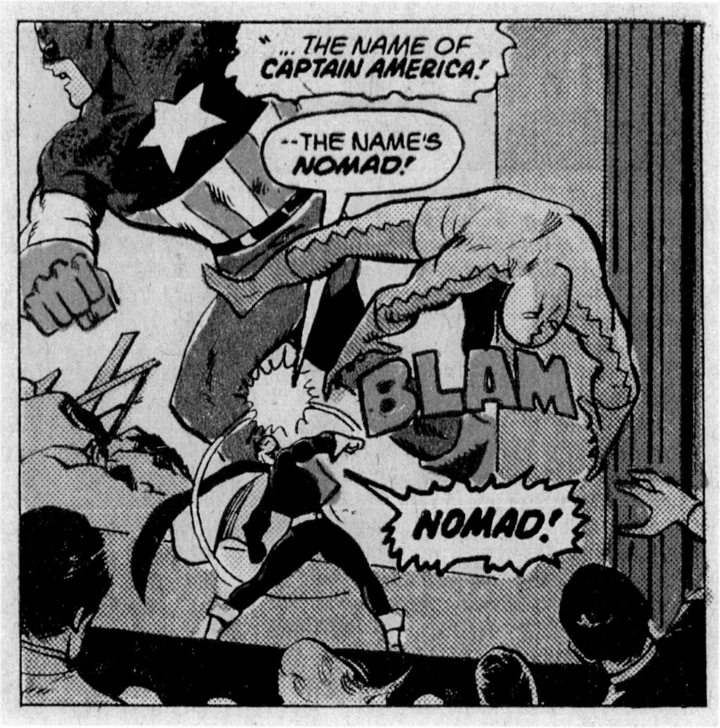

"... THE NAME OF CAPTAIN AMERICA!'
--THE NAME'S NOMAD!'
BLAM
NOMAD!

CAPTAIN AMERICA No. 180

Above and opposite: *Interiors, "The Coming of the Nomad!"; script, Steve Englehart; pencils, Sal Buscema; inks, Vince Colletta; December 1974.* As the tragedy of Vietnam made way for the travesty of Watergate, the most pointed change in comics may have been Steve Rogers's abandonment of his star-spangled identity and brief adoption of vigilante alter ego Nomad, who lasted only a few issues longer than the cape.

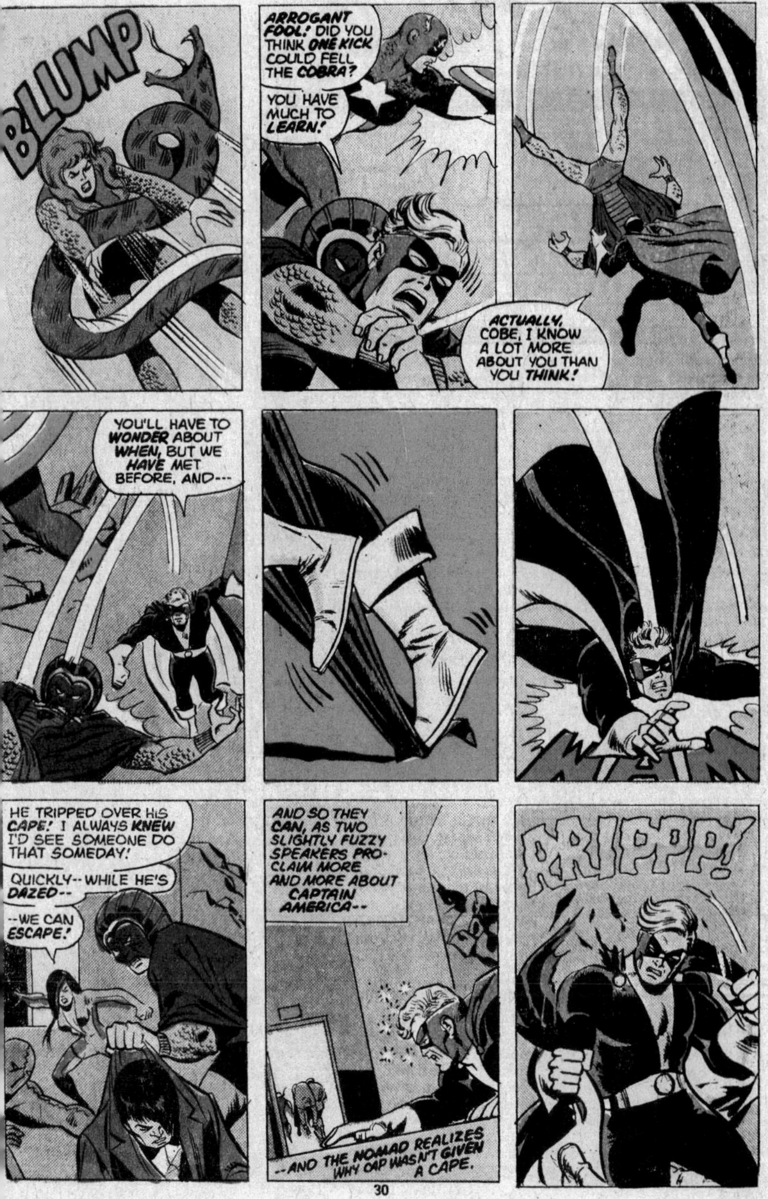

BLUMP
ARROGANT FOOL! DID YOU THINK ONE KICK COULD FELL THE COBRA?
YOU HAVE MUCH TO LEARN!
ACTUALLY, COBE, I KNOW A LOT MORE ABOUT YOU THAN YOU THINK!
YOU'LL HAVE TO WONDER ABOUT WHEN, BUT WE HAVE MET BEFORE, AND---
HE TRIPPED OVER HIS CAPE! I ALWAYS KNEW I'D SEE SOMEONE DO THAT SOMEDAY!
QUICKLY-- WHILE HE'S DAZED--
--WE CAN ESCAPE!
AND SO THEY CAN, AS TWO SLIGHTLY FUZZY SPEAKERS PROCLAIM MORE AND MORE ABOUT CAPTAIN AMERICA--
--AND THE NOMAD REALIZES WHY CAP WASN'T GIVEN A CAPE.
RRIPPP!

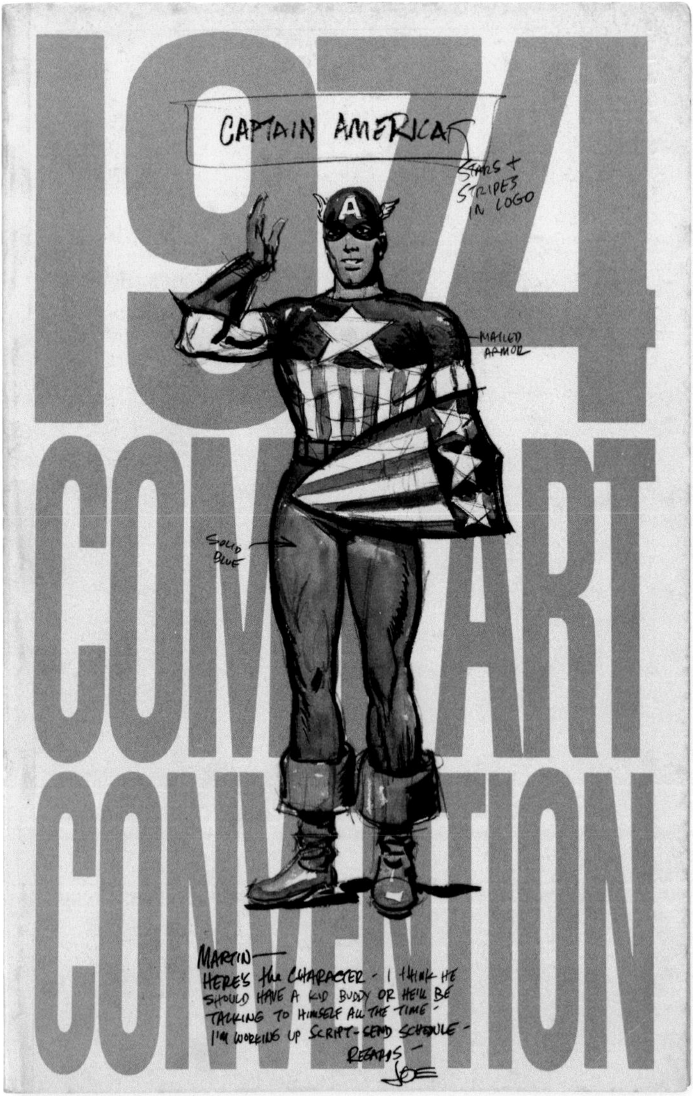
1974
CAPTAIN AMERICA
STARS + STRIPES IN LOGO
MAILED ARMOR
SOLID BLUE
MARTIN—
HERE'S the CHARACTER - I THINK HE SHOULD HAVE A KID BUDDY OR HE'LL BE TALKING TO HIMSELF ALL THE TIME - I'M WORKING UP SCRIPT - SEND SCHEDULE -
REGARDS -
JOE

REINTRODUCING CAPTAIN AMERICA

Opposite: *Cover, 1974 Comic Art Convention program; art, Joe Simon, originally ca. 1940.* So much had changed for Captain America since his Golden Age debut. Less popular wars in Korea and Vietnam—the latter winding down as this 1974 convention was under way—taxed the American psyche as the nation struggled to understand its involvement. Cap's revival in the Silver Age had been a huge success, but as the current war reached its height and the target market of comics aged, becoming more politically active, what role would the man wearing the red, white, and blue have in Marvel's Universe?

CA$H BONUS

Below: *Cover, Curtis incentive program brochure; pencils, Jack Kirby; inks, Syd Shores; November 1973.* "Wherever there is a trend that has been spotted, wherever there is a reading need to be satisfied amongst the 'now-generation' readership, Marvel will make every effort to capture such trends and to fill such needs." —Marvel marketing objectives plan, ca. 1970s

MARVEL TREASURY SPECIAL No. 1

Pages 132–33: *Cover; pencils, Jack Kirby and Marie Severin; inks, Frank Giacoia; September 1976.*

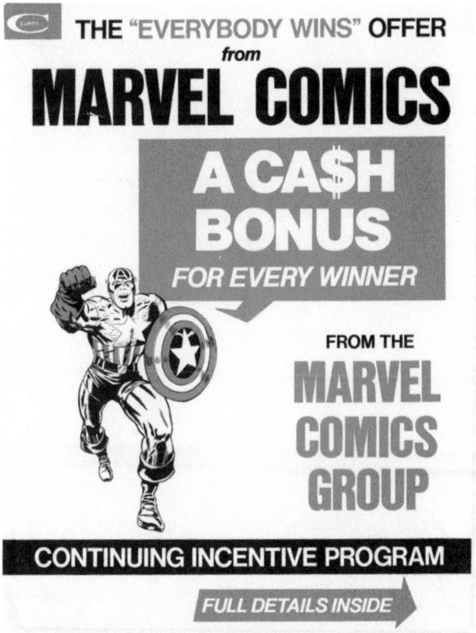
THE "EVERYBODY WINS" OFFER
from
MARVEL COMICS
A CA$H BONUS
FOR EVERY WINNER
FROM THE
MARVEL COMICS GROUP
CONTINUING INCENTIVE PROGRAM
FULL DETAILS INSIDE

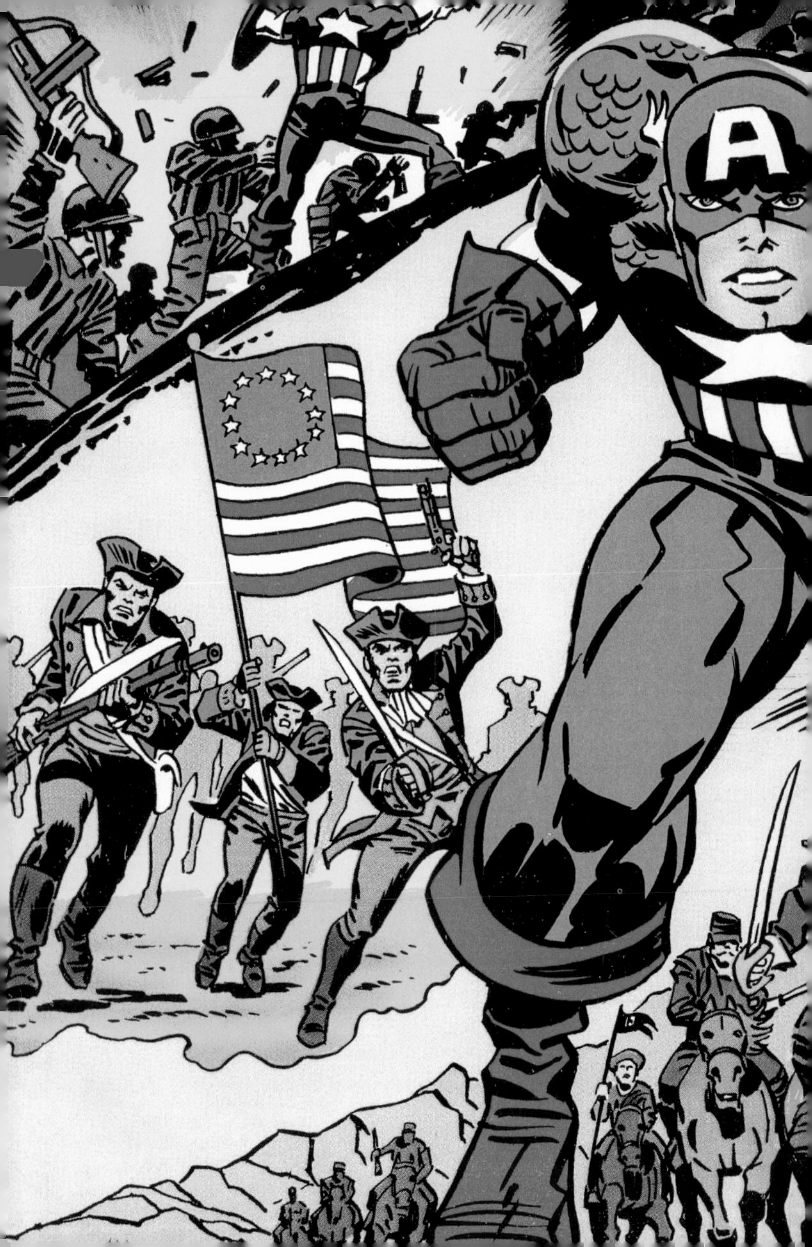

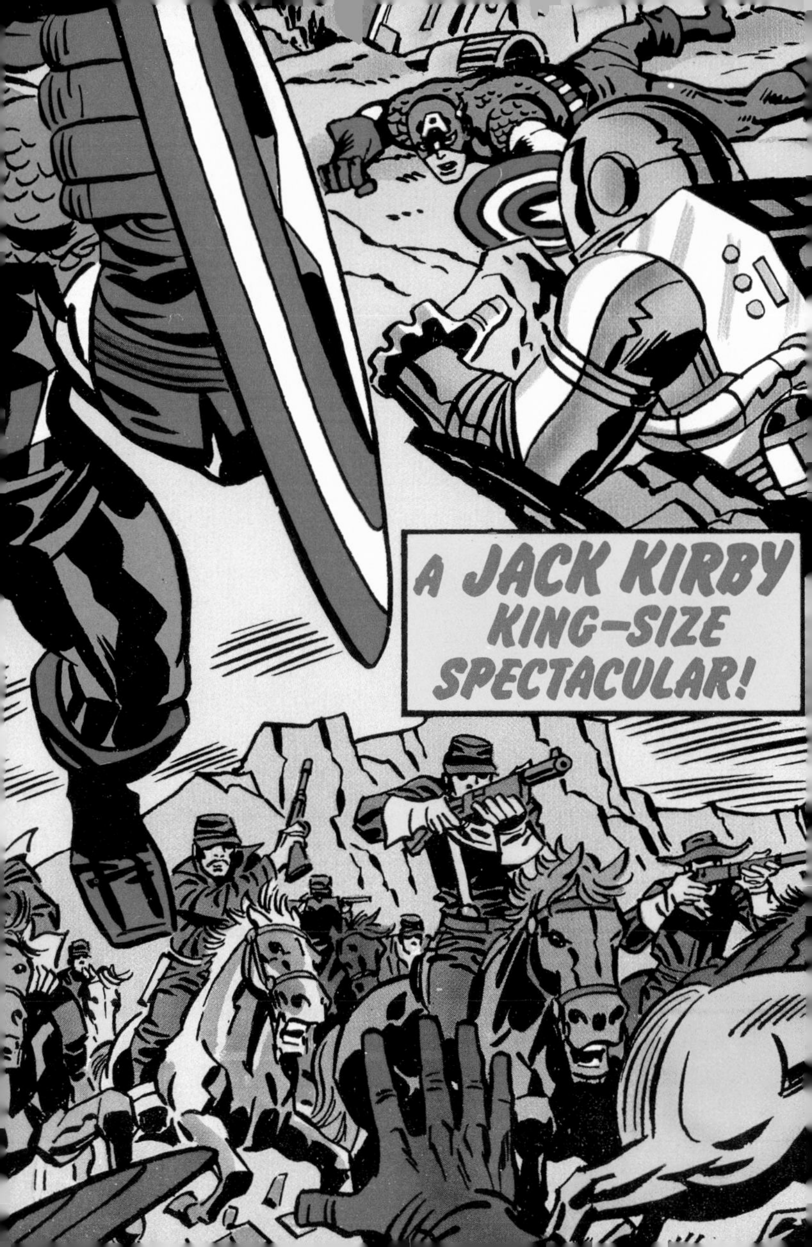
A JACK KIRBY
KING-SIZE
SPECTACULAR!

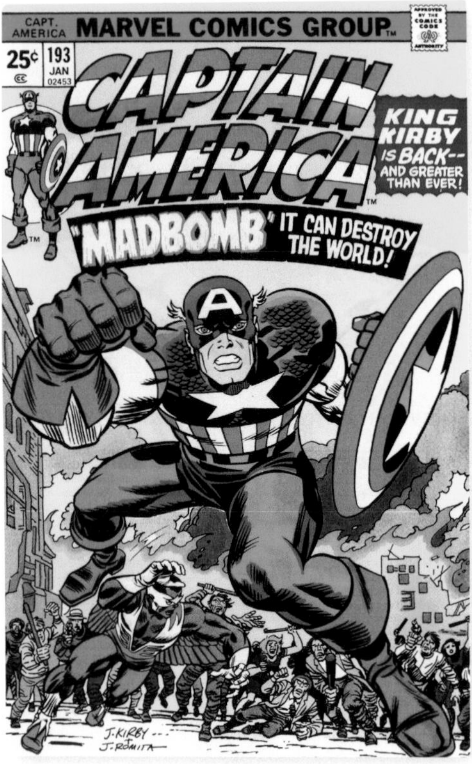
CAPT. AMERICA
MARVEL COMICS GROUP
25¢ 193 JAN 02453
CAPTAIN AMERICA
KING KIRBY IS BACK-- AND GREATER THAN EVER!
"MADBOMB" IT CAN DESTROY THE WORLD!
J. KIRBY
J. ROMITA

CAPTAIN AMERICA No. 193

Above: *Cover; pencils, Jack Kirby; inks, John Romita; January 1976.* Fresh off a five-year stint at DC, where he produced a tremendous amount of work—including the massive "Fourth World" saga—"King" Kirby returned to Marvel, and the character he co-created in 1941, for a 22-issue run as both writer and penciler.

CAPTAIN AMERICA No. 230

Opposite: *Cover; pencils, Ron Wilson; inks, Bob Layton; February 1979.* Luckily, Captain America's steel-and-vibranium shield keeps him from ending up red, white, and blue jelly on the wall.

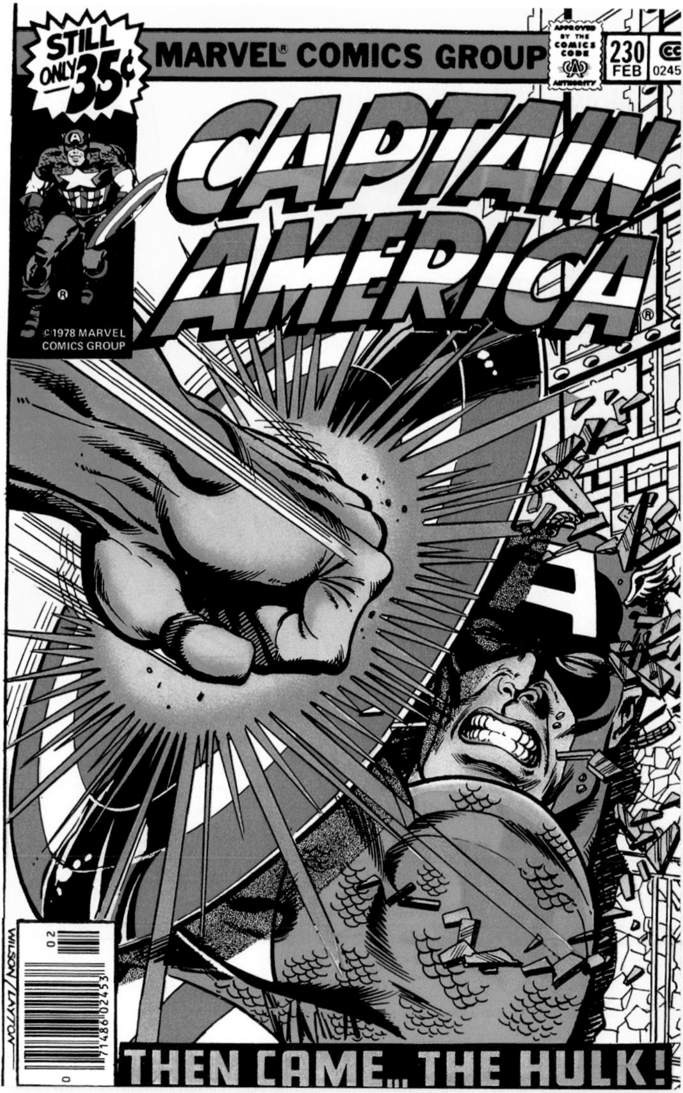
STILL ONLY 35¢
MARVEL COMICS GROUP
APPROVED BY THE COMICS CODE AUTHORITY
230
FEB
0245
CAPTAIN AMERICA
©1978 MARVEL COMICS GROUP
WILSON/LAYTON
THEN CAME... THE HULK!

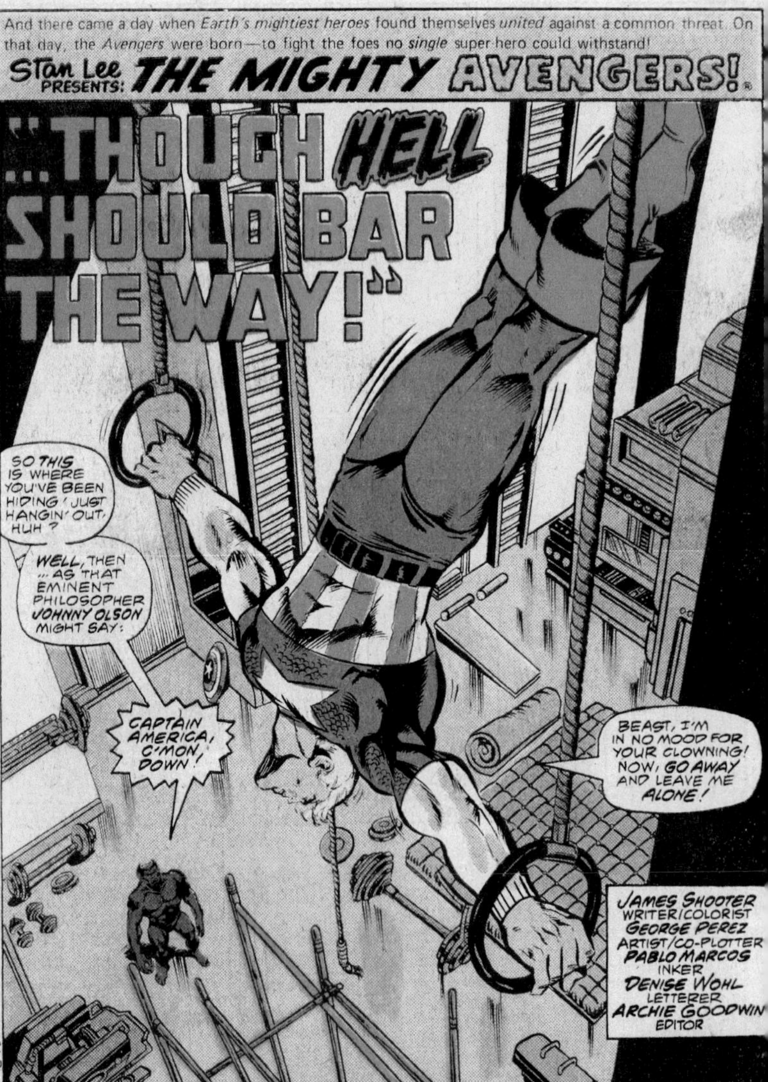

THE AVENGERS® is published by MARVEL COMICS GROUP, James E. Galton, President. Stan Lee, Publisher. OFFICE OF PUBLICATION 575 MADISON AVENUE, NEW YORK, N.Y. 10022. SECOND CLASS POSTAGE PAID AT NEW YORK, N.Y. AND AT ADDITIONAL MAILING OFFICES. Published monthly.

Vol. 1, No 170, April, 1978 issue. Price 35¢ per copy in the U.S. and Canada. Subscription rate $4.50 for 12 issues. Canada, $5.50. Foreign, $6.50.

THE AVENGERS No. 170

Opposite: *Interior, "... Though Hell Should Bar the Way!"; plot and script, Jim Shooter; plot and pencils, George Pérez; inks, Pablo Marcos; April 1978.*

CAPTAIN AMERICA AND HIS PAL

Below: *Picture frame; 1976.* Captain America was Marvel's earliest—and most successful—answer to the world's first super hero, Superman. A clean-cut, honorable, model citizen, Cap continues to be an inspiration to generations of kids and adults alike.

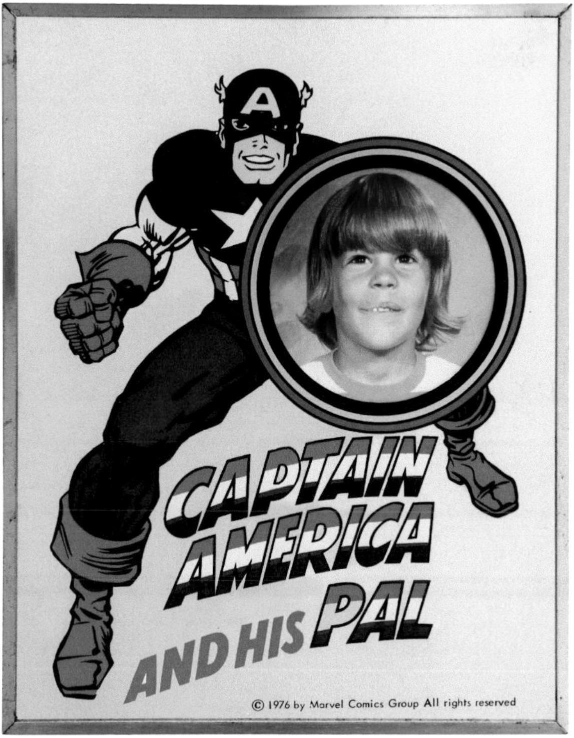
CAPTAIN AMERICA
AND HIS PAL
© 1976 by Marvel Comics Group All rights reserved

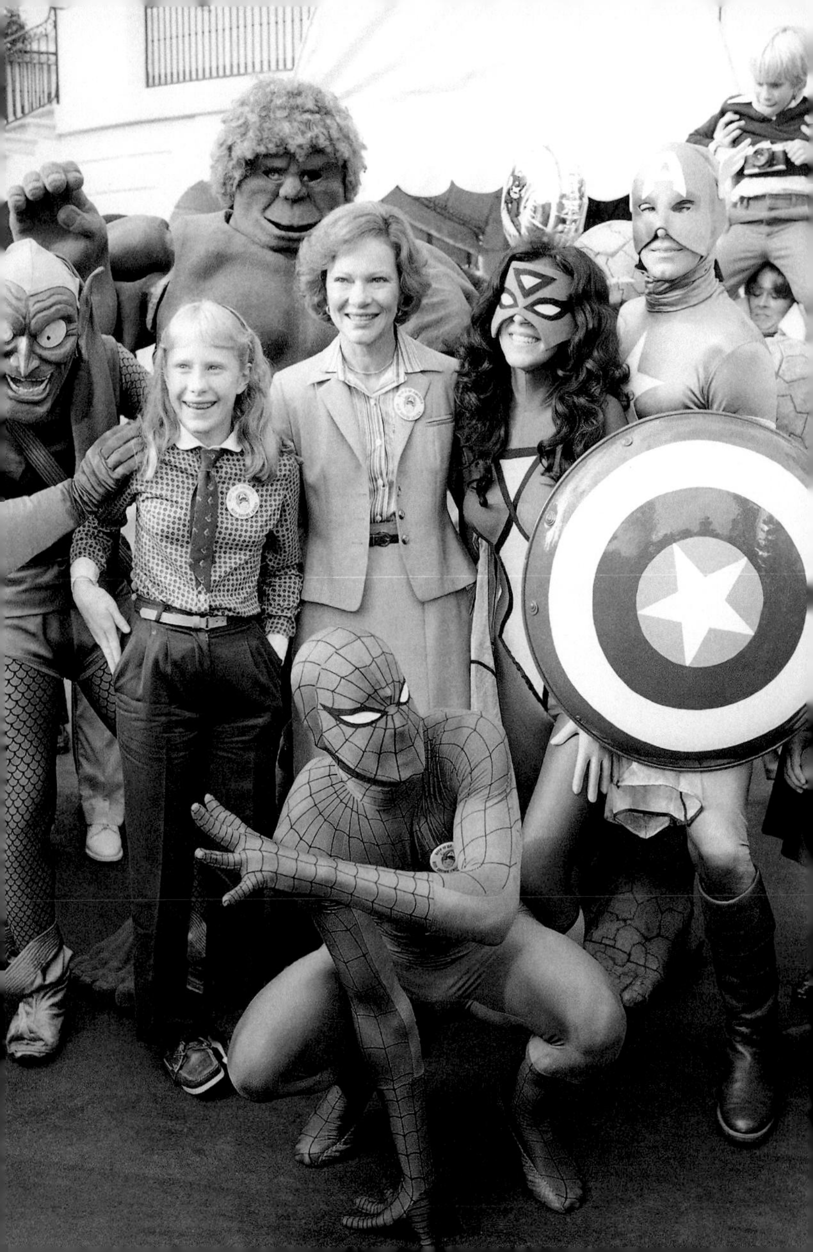

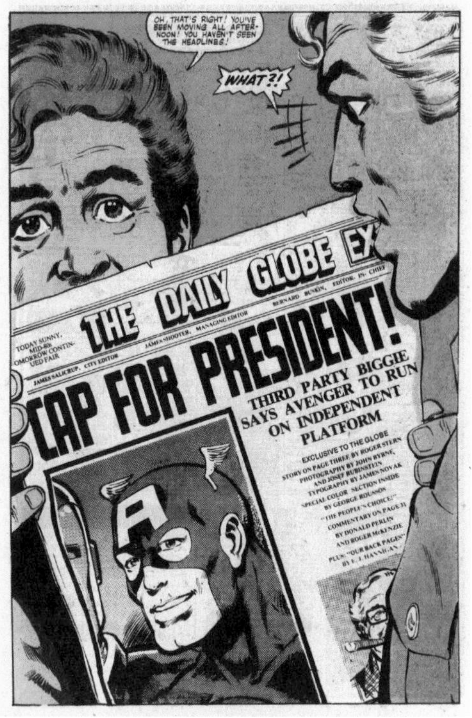

OH, THAT'S RIGHT! YOU'VE BEEN MOVING ALL AFTER-NOON! YOU HAVEN'T SEEN THE HEADLINES!
WHAT?!
THE DAILY GLOBE EX
BERNARD BUNKIN, EDITOR-IN-CHIEF
JAMES SHOOTER, MANAGING EDITOR
JAMES SALICRUP, CITY EDITOR
TODAY SUNNY, MID-80s
CAP FOR PRESIDENT!
THIRD PARTY BIGGIE SAYS AVENGER TO RUN ON INDEPENDENT PLATFORM
EXCLUSIVE TO THE GLOBE
STORY ON PAGE THREE BY ROGER STERN
PHOTOGRAPHY BY JOHN BYRNE, AND JOSEF RUBINSTEIN
TYPOGRAPHY BY JAMES NOVAK
SPECIAL COLOR SECTION INSIDE BY GEORGE ROUSSOS
"THE PEOPLE'S CHOICE!" COMMENTARY ON PAGE 31 BY DONALD PERLIN AND ROGER McKENZIE
PLUS: "OUR BACK PAGES"

MARVEL DOES THE WHITE HOUSE

Opposite: *Photograph; Amy Carter and her mother, First Lady Rosalynn Carter, with Marvel heroes; Associated Press; October 1980.* When the Department of Energy launched the Captain America Youth Energy Conservation Program, Cap and fellow Marvel heroes crashed the White House.

CAPTAIN AMERICA No. 250

Above: *Interior, "Cap for President!"; script, Roger Stern and John Byrne; pencils, Byrne; inks, Joe Rubinstein; October 1980.* "You need but to look within yourselves to find the people you need to keep this nation strong," Cap told the crowd at the New Populist Party convention. In a note at the end of the issue, Stern credited Roger McKenzie and Don Perlin with first pitching a Cap run for president, and Jim Shooter with suggesting that the issue be about why Steve Rogers won't run.

YOUR LUNCH IS SAFE WITH US

Below: *Lunch box, ca. 1976.* Marvel merchandising was already mighty by the 1970s. Not even Loki could get to a sandwich kept in one of these ubiquitous containers.

WAR AGAINST DRUGS

Opposite: *Cover,* Captain America Goes to War Against Drugs; *pencils, John Romita; inks, Jose Marzan Jr.; 1990.* This anti-drug promotional comic was reprinted several times as a giveaway for various markets.

STERANKO'S BACK!

Pages 142–43: *Cover;* Marvel Comics Index *No. 8; art, Jim Steranko; Pacific Comics, December 1979.* Steranko did his last work for Marvel's monthlies back in 1974, but he has since contributed a few covers, including this *Marvel Comics Index.*

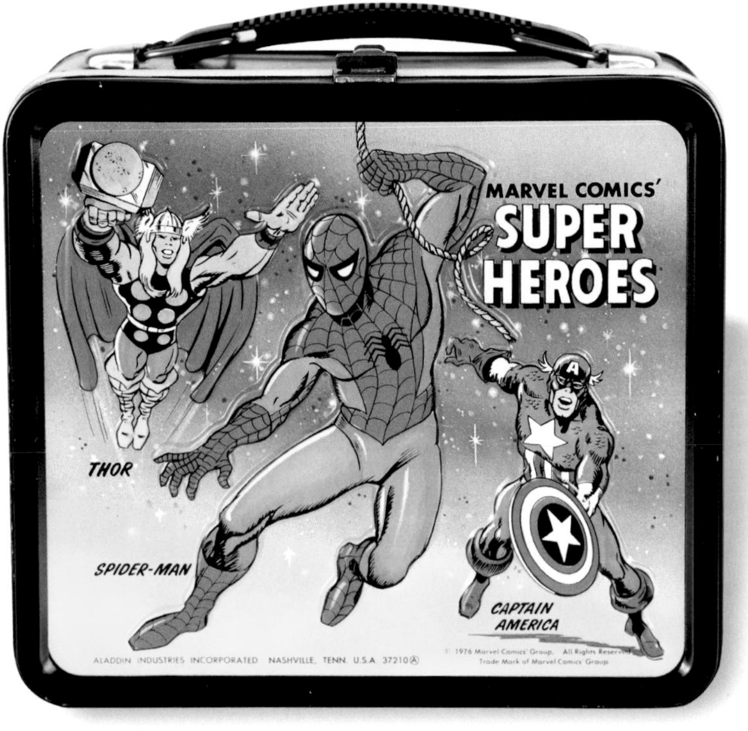
MARVEL COMICS'
SUPER HEROES
THOR
SPIDER-MAN
CAPTAIN AMERICA
ALADDIN INDUSTRIES INCORPORATED NASHVILLE, TENN. U.S.A. 37210

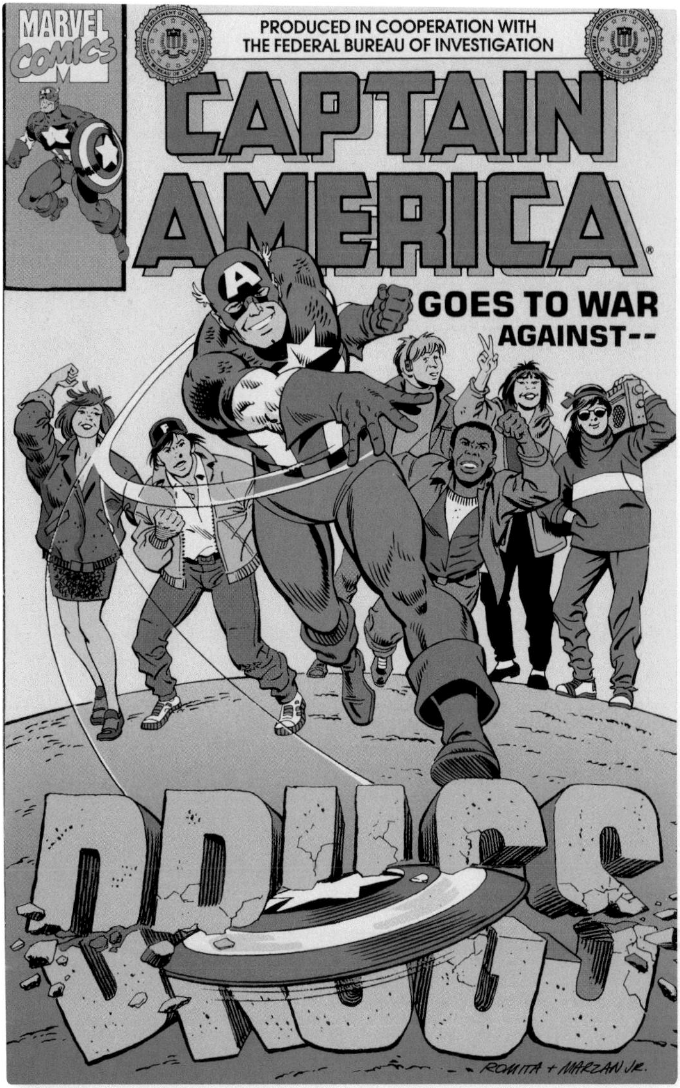
MARVEL COMICS
PRODUCED IN COOPERATION WITH
THE FEDERAL BUREAU OF INVESTIGATION
CAPTAIN AMERICA®
GOES TO WAR
AGAINST--
DRUGS
ROMITA + MARZAN JR.

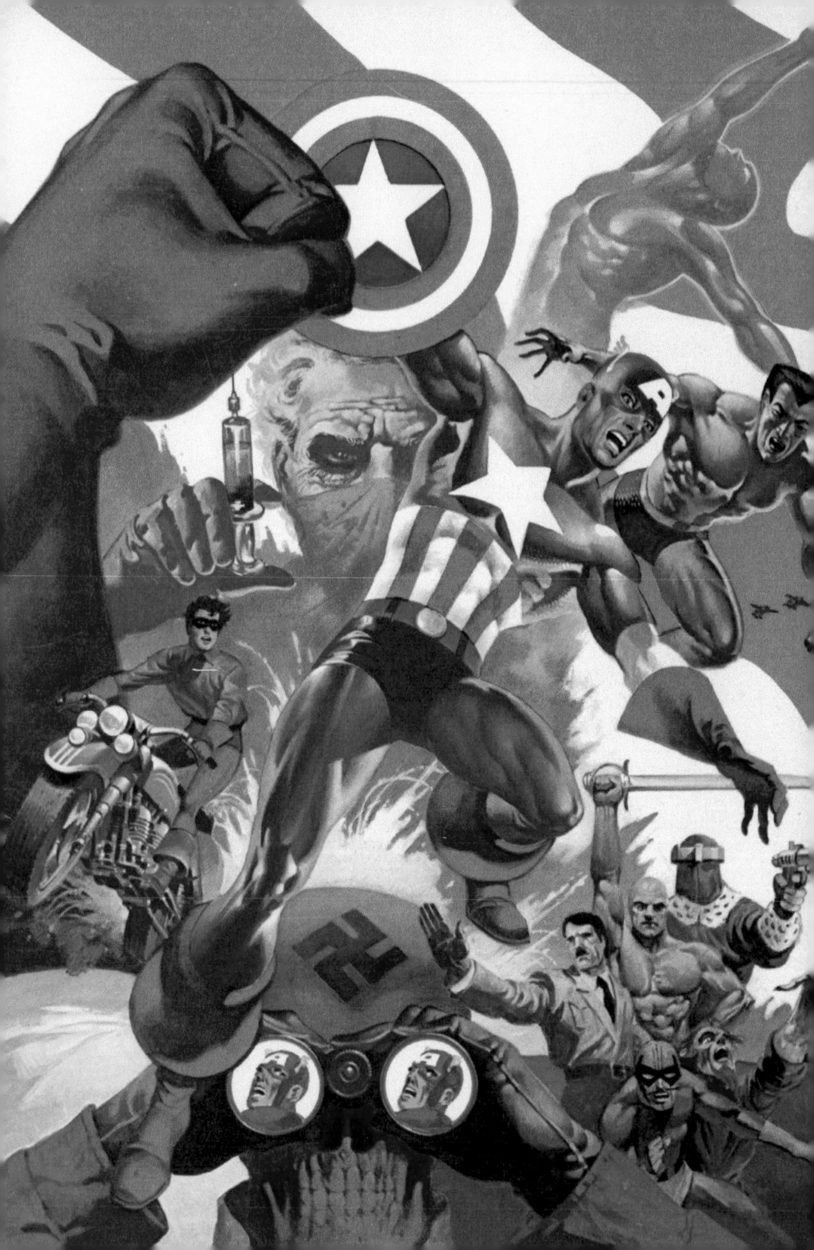

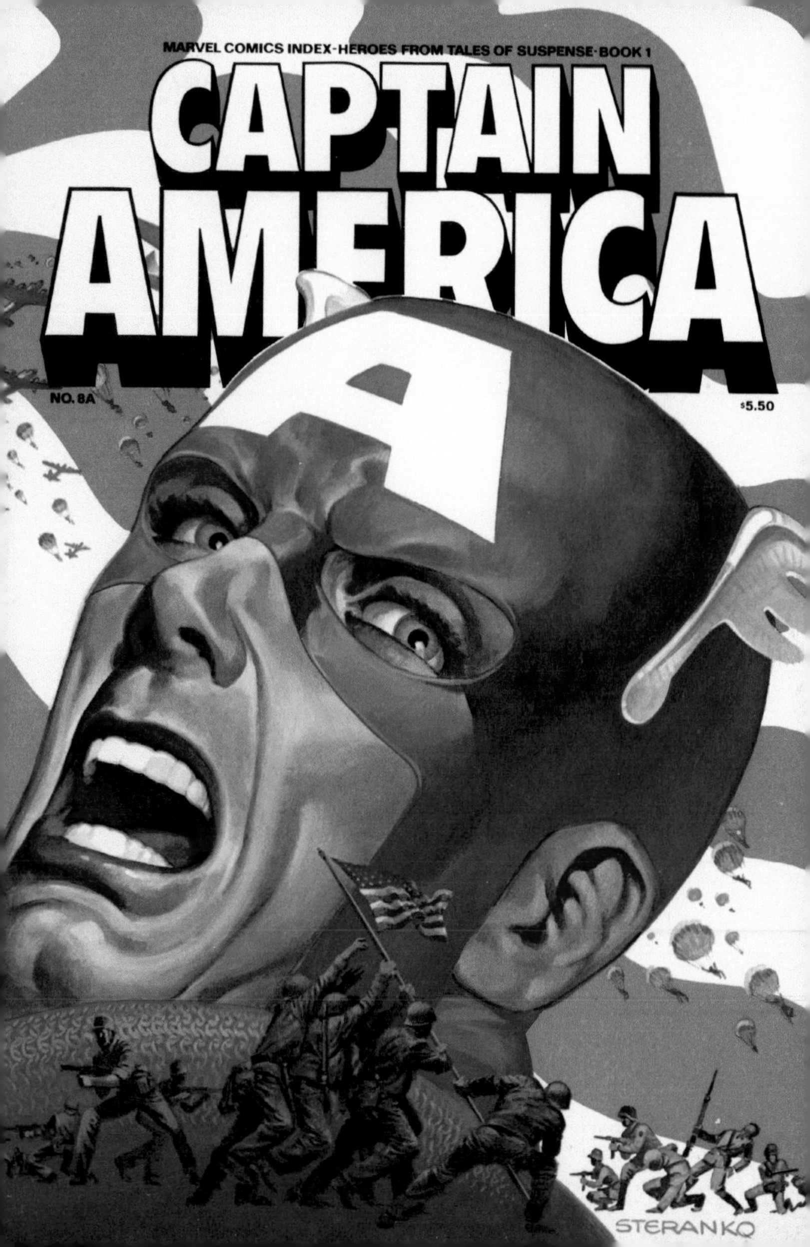
MARVEL COMICS INDEX-HEROES FROM TALES OF SUSPENSE·BOOK 1
CAPTAIN AMERICA
NO. 8A
$5.50
STERANKO

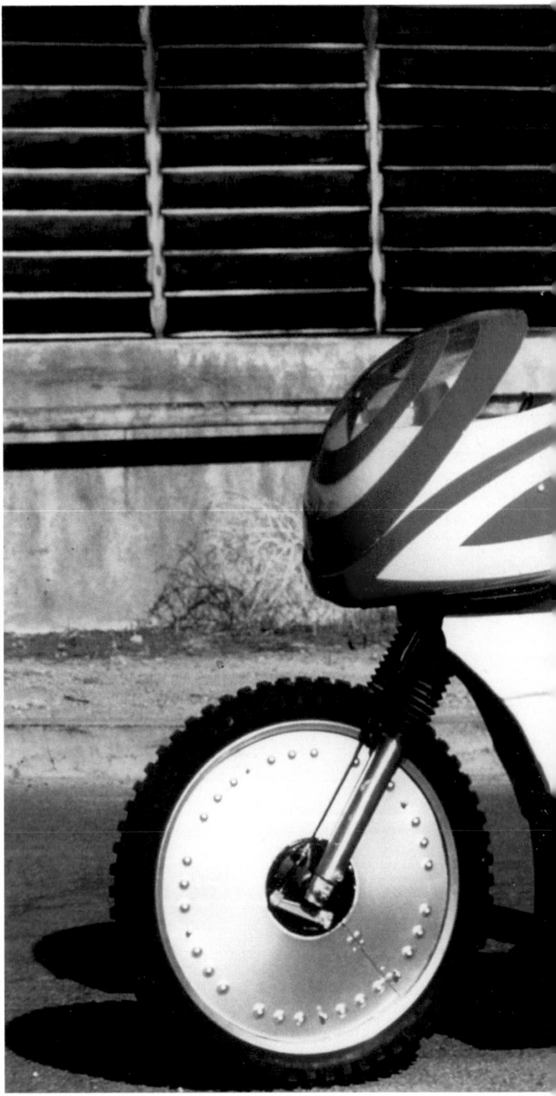

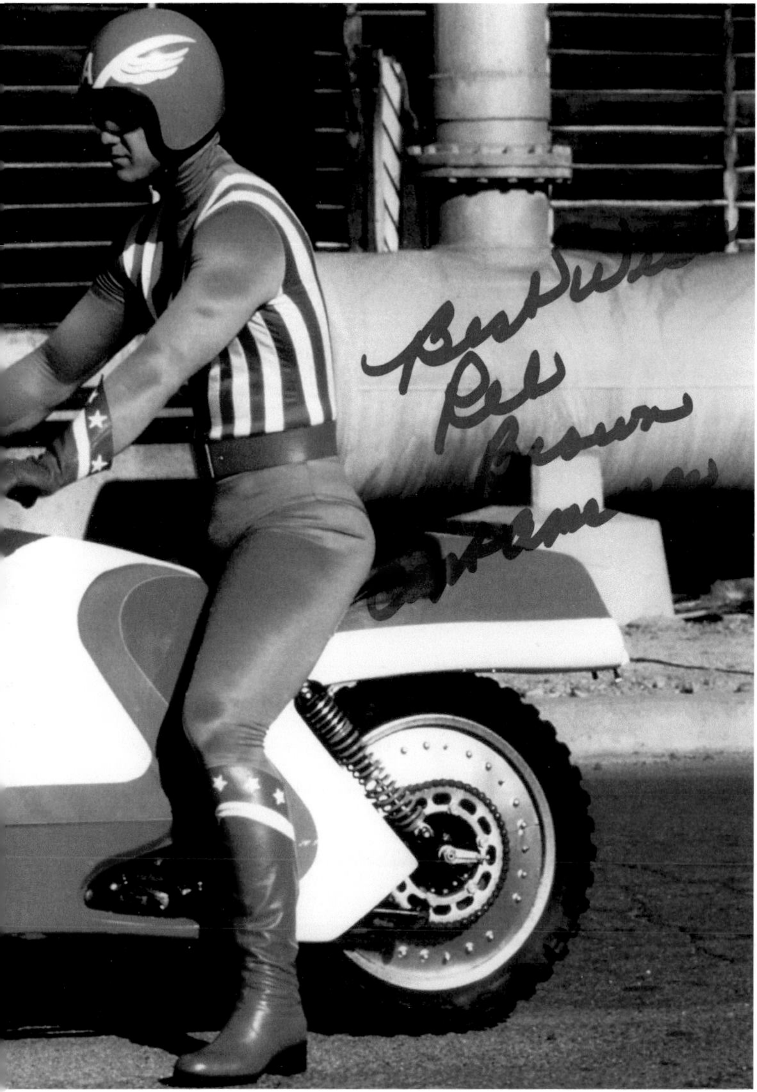

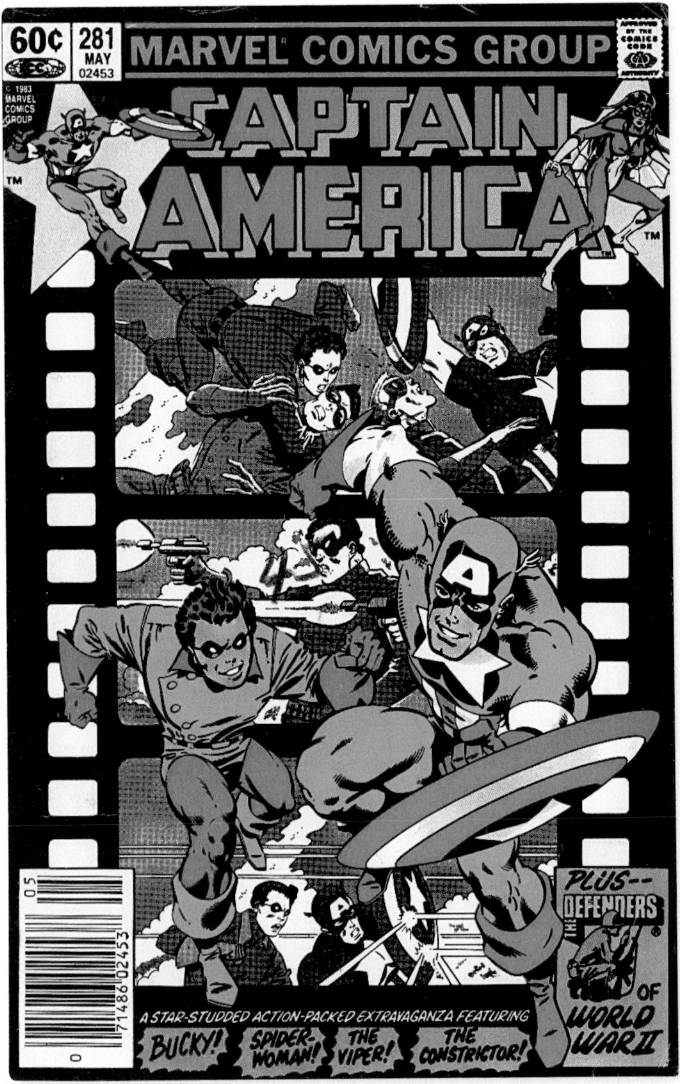
60¢
281
MAY
02453
MARVEL COMICS GROUP
© 1983 MARVEL COMICS GROUP
CAPTAIN AMERICA
PLUS--
THE DEFENDERS
OF WORLD WAR II
A STAR-STUDDED ACTION-PACKED EXTRAVAGANZA FEATURING
BUCKY!
SPIDER-WOMAN!
THE VIPER!
THE CONSTRICTOR!

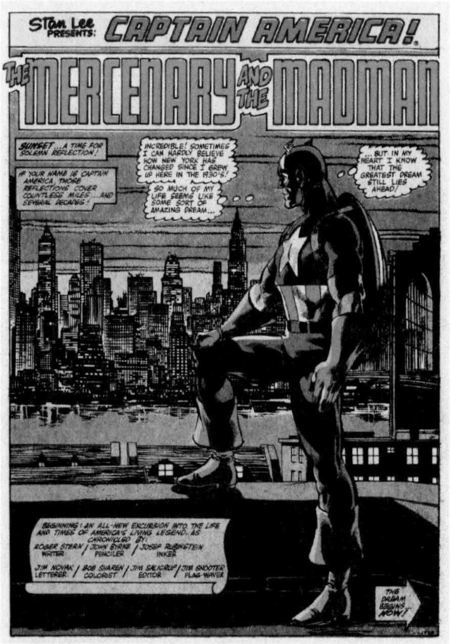
Stan Lee PRESENTS: CAPTAIN AMERICA!
THE MERCENARY AND THE MADMAN
SUNSET... A TIME FOR SOLEMN REFLECTION!
IF YOUR NAME IS CAPTAIN AMERICA, THOSE REFLECTIONS COVER COUNTLESS MILES... AND SEVERAL DECADES!
INCREDIBLE! SOMETIMES I CAN HARDLY BELIEVE HOW NEW YORK HAS CHANGED SINCE I GREW UP HERE IN THE 1930'S!
SO MUCH OF MY LIFE SEEMS LIKE SOME SORT OF AMAZING DREAM...
...BUT IN MY HEART I KNOW THAT THE GREATEST DREAM STILL LIES AHEAD!
BEGINNING: AN ALL-NEW EXCURSION INTO THE LIFE AND TIMES OF AMERICA'S LIVING LEGEND, AS CHRONICLED BY:
ROGER STERN / JOHN BYRNE / JOSEF RUBINSTEIN
WRITER / PENCILER / INKER
JIM NOVAK / BOB SHAREN / JIM SALICRUP / JIM SHOOTER
LETTERER / COLORIST / EDITOR / FLAG-WAVER
THE DREAM BEGINS NOW!

MIGHTY MARVEL MOVIES

Pages 144–45: *Publicity still,* Captain America *TV movie, CBS, 1979. Captain America* starred Reb Brown as a red-white-and-blue clad super hero that was quite different than the Marvel Comics version. With a high-tech motorcycle (and a see-through, disc-shaped windshield that detaches to become a redux version of the hero's trademark weapon) the show's makers (like all of Hollywood) approached the comic property with little interest in adapting the traditional contours of the enduring mythology or its proven iconography.

CAPTAIN AMERICA No. 281

Opposite: *Cover; pencils, Mike Zeck; inks, John Beatty; May 1983.* There have been many versions of Cap's sidekick, Bucky, over the years; this issue features the return of Jack Monroe.

CAPTAIN AMERICA No. 251

Above: *Interior, "The Mercenary and the Madman"; script, Roger Stern; pencils, John Byrne; inks, Joe Rubinstein; November 1980.*

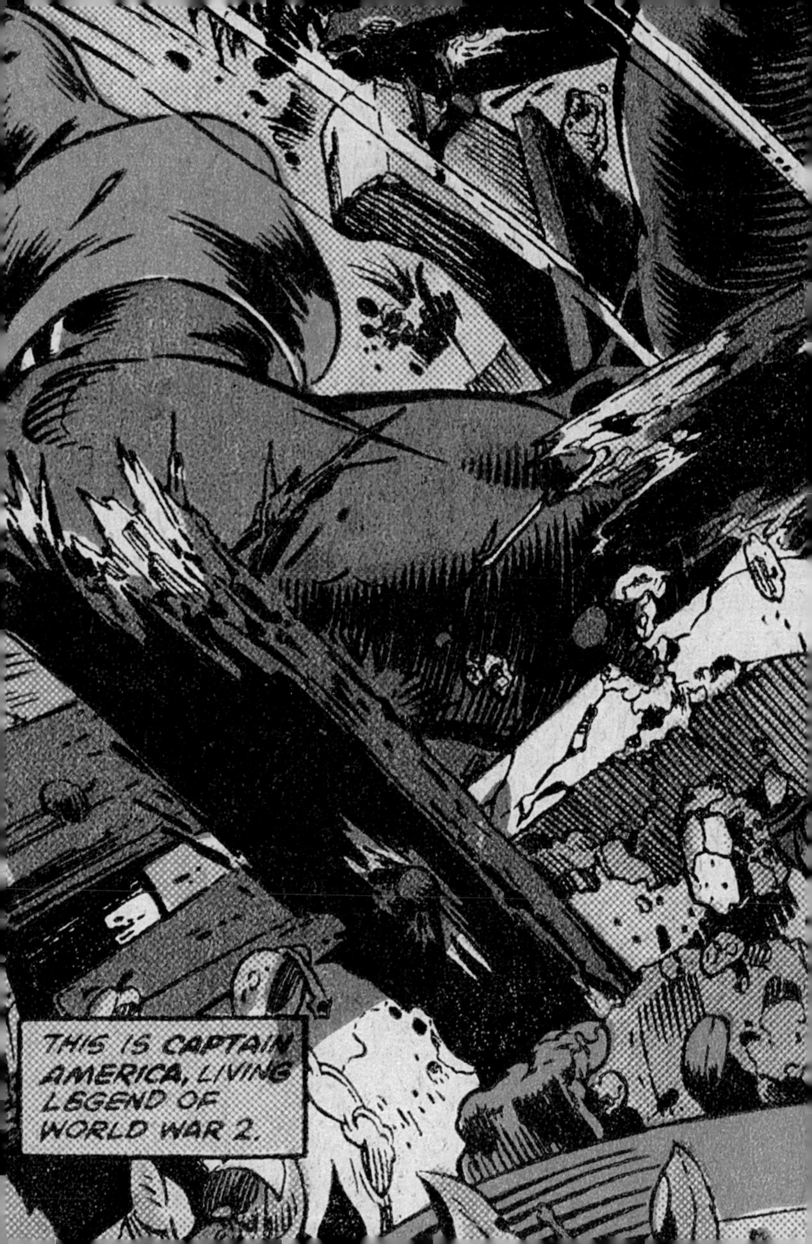
THIS IS CAPTAIN AMERICA, LIVING LEGEND OF WORLD WAR 2.

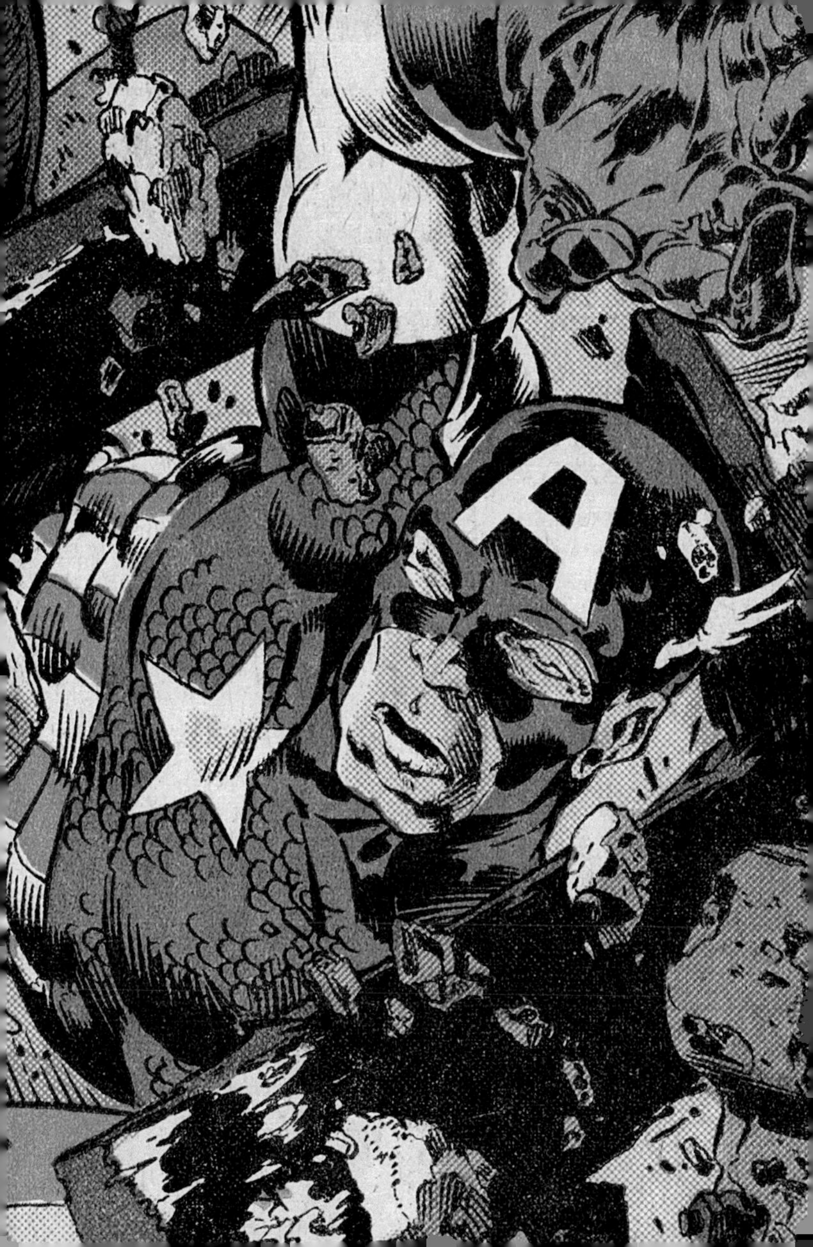

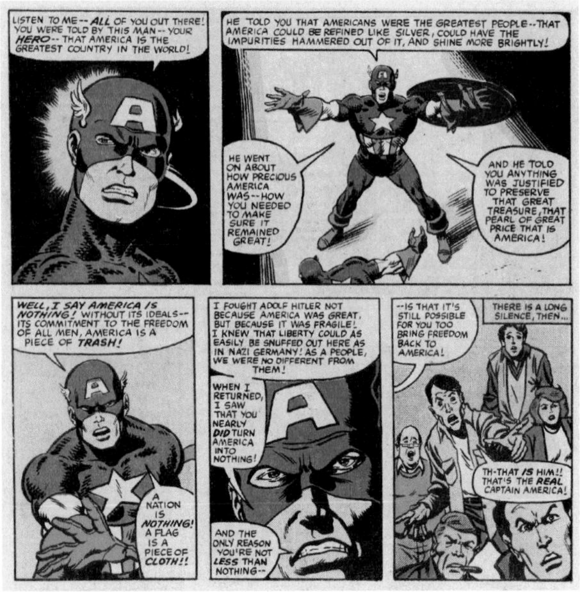
LISTEN TO ME-- ALL OF YOU OUT THERE! YOU WERE TOLD BY THIS MAN-- YOUR HERO-- THAT AMERICA IS THE GREATEST COUNTRY IN THE WORLD!
HE TOLD YOU THAT AMERICANS WERE THE GREATEST PEOPLE--THAT AMERICA COULD BE REFINED LIKE SILVER, COULD HAVE THE IMPURITIES HAMMERED OUT OF IT, AND SHINE MORE BRIGHTLY!
HE WENT ON ABOUT HOW PRECIOUS AMERICA WAS--HOW YOU NEEDED TO MAKE SURE IT REMAINED GREAT!
AND HE TOLD YOU ANYTHING WAS JUSTIFIED TO PRESERVE THAT GREAT TREASURE, THAT PEARL OF GREAT PRICE THAT IS AMERICA!
WELL, I SAY AMERICA IS NOTHING! WITHOUT ITS IDEALS-- ITS COMMITMENT TO THE FREEDOM OF ALL MEN, AMERICA IS A PIECE OF TRASH!
A NATION IS NOTHING! A FLAG IS A PIECE OF CLOTH!!
I FOUGHT ADOLF HITLER NOT BECAUSE AMERICA WAS GREAT, BUT BECAUSE IT WAS FRAGILE! I KNEW THAT LIBERTY COULD AS EASILY BE SNUFFED OUT HERE AS IN NAZI GERMANY! AS A PEOPLE, WE WERE NO DIFFERENT FROM THEM!
WHEN I RETURNED, I SAW THAT YOU NEARLY DID TURN AMERICA INTO NOTHING!
AND THE ONLY REASON YOU'RE NOT LESS THAN NOTHING--
--IS THAT IT'S STILL POSSIBLE FOR YOU TOO BRING FREEDOM BACK TO AMERICA!
THERE IS A LONG SILENCE, THEN...
TH-THAT IS HIM!! THAT'S THE REAL CAPTAIN AMERICA!

AVENGERS ANNUAL No. 10

Pages 148–49: *Interior, "By Friends — Betrayed!"; script, Chris Claremont; pencils, Michael Golden; inks, Armando Gil; 1981.* An uncommon sight: Cap is (temporarily) defeated. His assailant? The mutant Rogue, making her debut as a villain who absorbs Ms. Marvel's memories and power, using them to subdue Cap.

WHAT IF? No. 44

Above: *Interior, "What If Captain America Were Not Revived Until Today?"; script, Peter B. Gillis; pencils, Sal Buscema; inks, Dave Simons; April 1984.* In this out-of-continuity story, Captain America isn't freed from that block of ice until the mid-1980s — and he doesn't like what he sees. Though with Cap, there's always hope. Despite its noncanonical status, some of Cap's most rousing patriotic invective can be found within the pages of this issue.

CAPTAIN AMERICA No. 260

Opposite: *Cover; pencils and inks, Al Milgrom; August 1981.* In "Prison Reform!," which Milgrom also wrote, the hero is locked up at Rikers Island — to see if the prison's security is up to snuff. While inside, he helps a young prisoner change his ways.

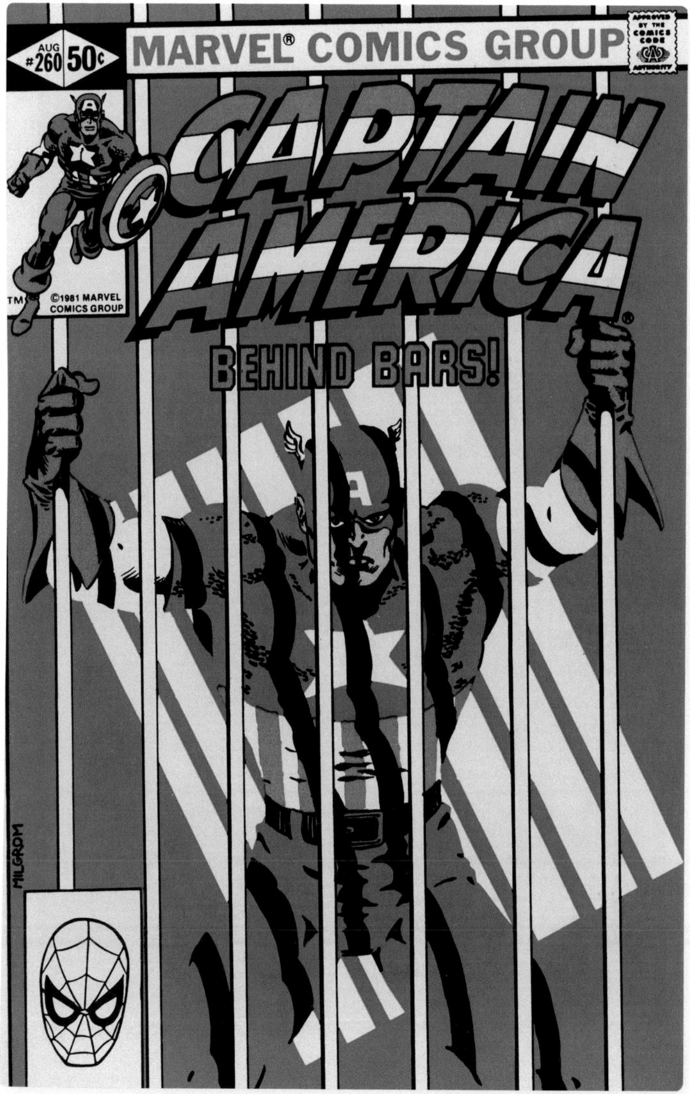
AUG
#260
50¢
MARVEL® COMICS GROUP
APPROVED BY THE COMICS CODE AUTHORITY
CAPTAIN AMERICA
TM
©1981 MARVEL COMICS GROUP
BEHIND BARS!
MILGROM

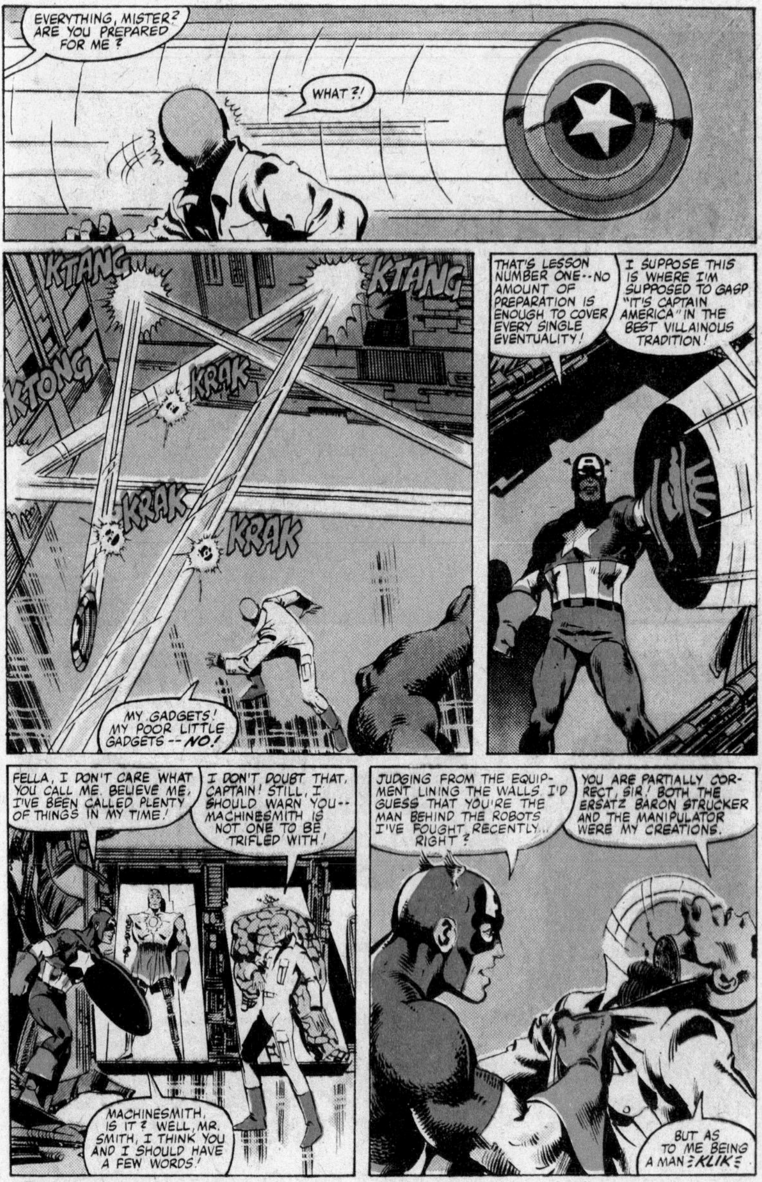
EVERYTHING, MISTER? ARE YOU PREPARED FOR ME?
WHAT?!
KTANG
KTANG
KTONG
KRAK
KRAK
KRAK
MY GADGETS! MY POOR LITTLE GADGETS -- NO!
THAT'S LESSON NUMBER ONE -- NO AMOUNT OF PREPARATION IS ENOUGH TO COVER EVERY SINGLE EVENTUALITY!
I SUPPOSE THIS IS WHERE I'M SUPPOSED TO GASP "IT'S CAPTAIN AMERICA" IN THE BEST VILLAINOUS TRADITION!
FELLA, I DON'T CARE WHAT YOU CALL ME. BELIEVE ME, I'VE BEEN CALLED PLENTY OF THINGS IN MY TIME!
I DON'T DOUBT THAT, CAPTAIN! STILL, I SHOULD WARN YOU-- MACHINESMITH IS NOT ONE TO BE TRIFLED WITH!
MACHINESMITH, IS IT? WELL, MR. SMITH, I THINK YOU AND I SHOULD HAVE A FEW WORDS!
JUDGING FROM THE EQUIPMENT LINING THE WALLS, I'D GUESS THAT YOU'RE THE MAN BEHIND THE ROBOTS I'VE FOUGHT RECENTLY... RIGHT?
YOU ARE PARTIALLY CORRECT, SIR! BOTH THE ERSATZ BARON STRUCKER AND THE MANIPULATOR WERE MY CREATIONS.
BUT AS TO ME BEING A MAN -KLIK-

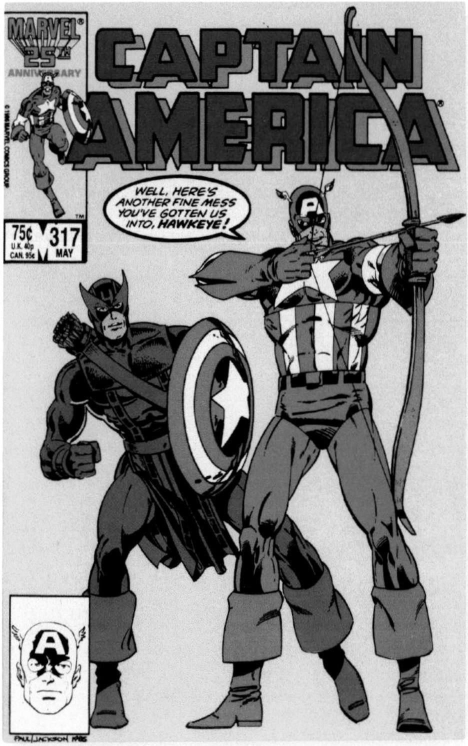
MARVEL 25th ANNIVERSARY
CAPTAIN AMERICA
WELL, HERE'S ANOTHER FINE MESS YOU'VE GOTTEN US INTO, HAWKEYE!
75¢ U.K. 40p CAN. 95¢
317 MAY

CAPTAIN AMERICA No. 249

Opposite: *Interior, "Death, Where Is Thy Sting?"; plot and script, Roger Stern; plot and pencils, John Byrne; inks, Joe Rubinstein; September 1980.* Cap gives a master class in villain intimidation, by hurling his shield and bouncing it off walls to make a perfect star, replicating the symbol on the shield itself.

CAPTAIN AMERICA No. 317

Above: *Cover; pencils, Paul Neary; inks, Jackson Guice; May 1986.*

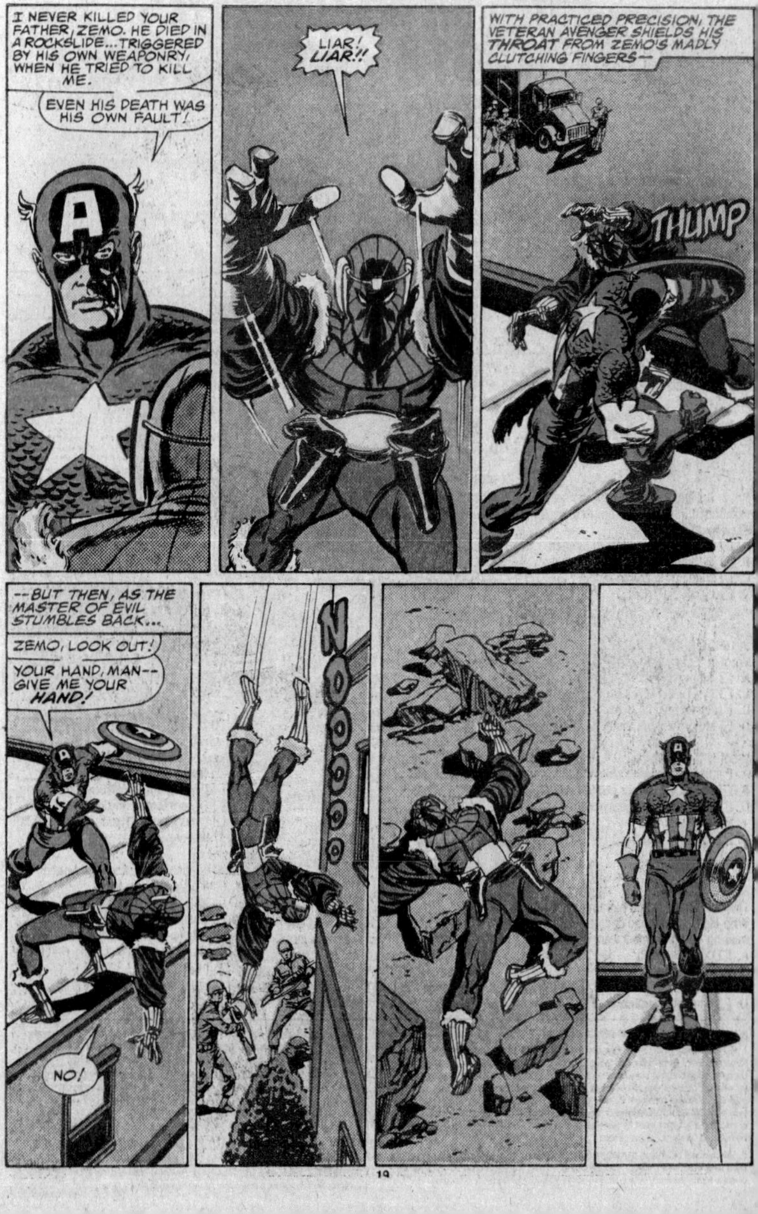

I NEVER KILLED YOUR FATHER, ZEMO. HE DIED IN A ROCKSLIDE... TRIGGERED BY HIS OWN WEAPONRY, WHEN HE TRIED TO KILL ME.
EVEN HIS DEATH WAS HIS OWN FAULT!
LIAR! LIAR!!
WITH PRACTICED PRECISION, THE VETERAN AVENGER SHIELDS HIS THROAT FROM ZEMO'S MADLY CLUTCHING FINGERS--
THUMP
--BUT THEN, AS THE MASTER OF EVIL STUMBLES BACK...
ZEMO, LOOK OUT!
YOUR HAND, MAN-- GIVE ME YOUR HAND!
NO!

THE AVENGERS No. 277

Opposite and below: *Interiors, "The Price of Victory"; script, Roger Stern; pencils, John Buscema; inks, Tom Palmer; March 1987.* In a high point of late '80s' Marvel, Roger Stern and John Buscema's Masters of Evil storyline wrapped up here, featuring a final showdown between Captain America and Baron Zemo.

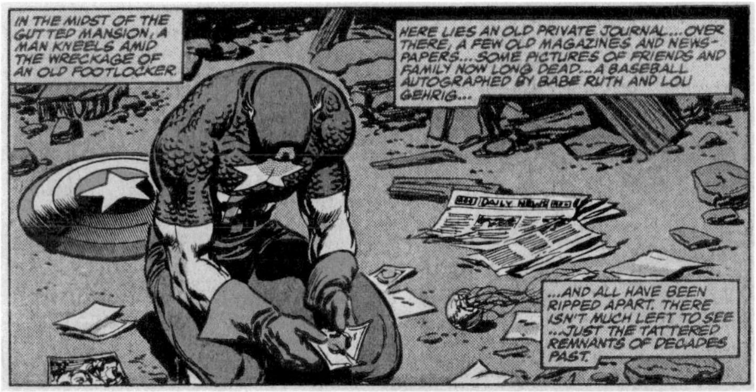
IN THE MIDST OF THE GUTTED MANSION, A MAN KNEELS AMID THE WRECKAGE OF AN OLD FOOTLOCKER.
HERE LIES AN OLD PRIVATE JOURNAL... OVER THERE, A FEW OLD MAGAZINES AND NEWS-PAPERS... SOME PICTURES OF FRIENDS AND FAMILY NOW LONG DEAD... A BASEBALL AUTOGRAPHED BY BABE RUTH AND LOU GEHRIG...
DAILY NEWS
...AND ALL HAVE BEEN RIPPED APART. THERE ISN'T MUCH LEFT TO SEE ...JUST THE TATTERED REMNANTS OF DECADES PAST.

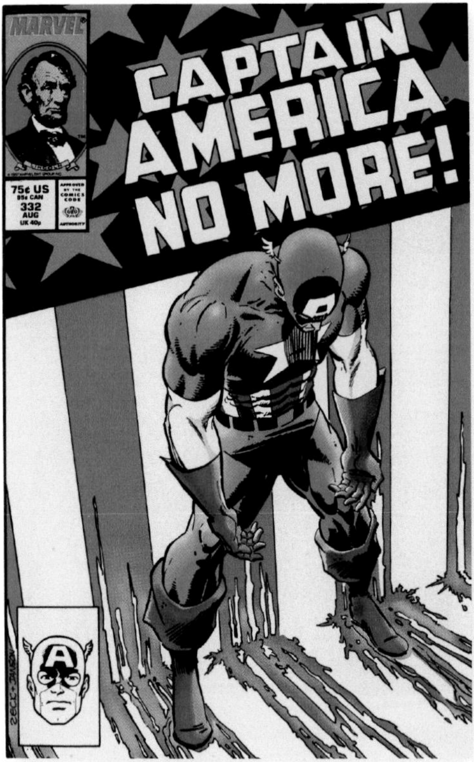
MARVEL
CAPTAIN AMERICA NO MORE!
75¢ US
332
AUG
UK 40p

CAPTAIN AMERICA No. 332

Above and opposite: *Cover; pencils, Mike Zeck; inks, Klaus Janson. Interiors, "The Choice"; script, Mark Gruenwald; pencils, Tom Morgan; inks, Bob McLeod; August 1987.* Beloved editor and writer Gruenwald continued the tradition of Lee and Englehart, allowing Cap to act as a barometer of the political climate. Cap sees himself as a champion of the people—and forced to work for the U.S. government, he realizes he has to walk away once again.

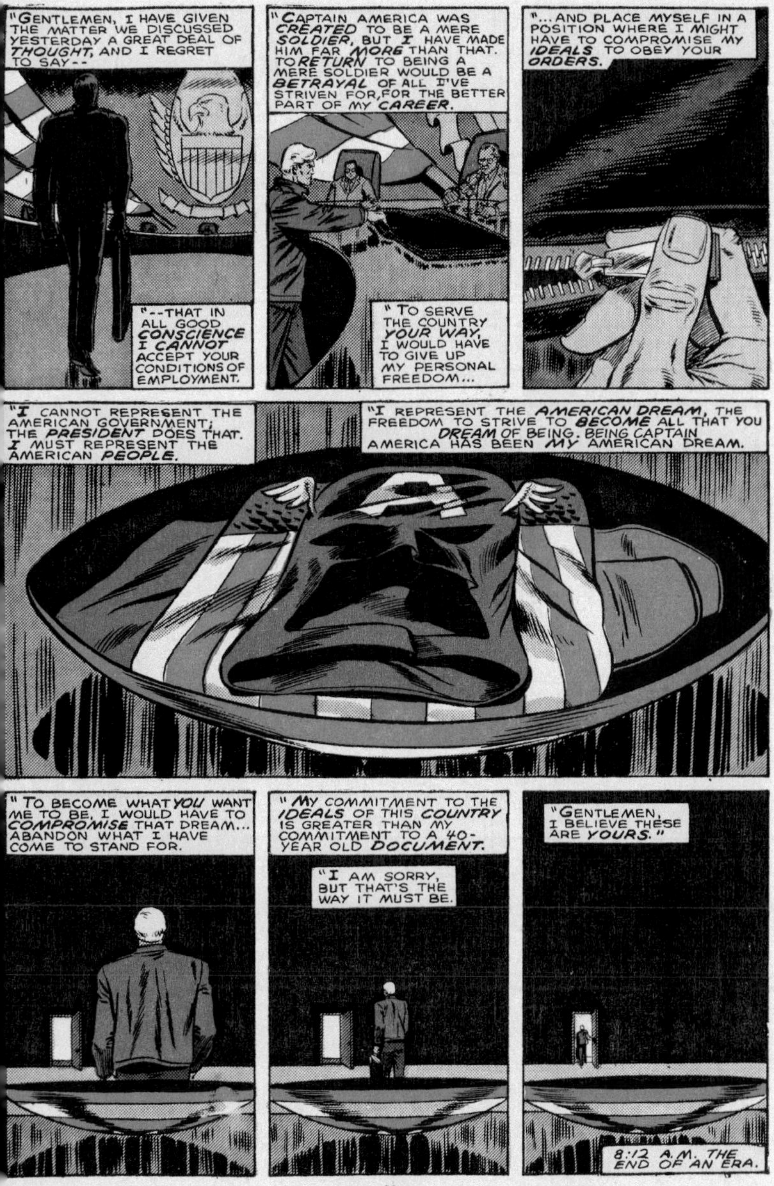
"GENTLEMEN, I HAVE GIVEN THE MATTER WE DISCUSSED YESTERDAY A GREAT DEAL OF THOUGHT, AND I REGRET TO SAY--
"--THAT IN ALL GOOD CONSCIENCE I CANNOT ACCEPT YOUR CONDITIONS OF EMPLOYMENT.
"CAPTAIN AMERICA WAS CREATED TO BE A MERE SOLDIER, BUT I HAVE MADE HIM FAR MORE THAN THAT. TO RETURN TO BEING A MERE SOLDIER WOULD BE A BETRAYAL OF ALL I'VE STRIVEN FOR, FOR THE BETTER PART OF MY CAREER.
"TO SERVE THE COUNTRY YOUR WAY, I WOULD HAVE TO GIVE UP MY PERSONAL FREEDOM...
"...AND PLACE MYSELF IN A POSITION WHERE I MIGHT HAVE TO COMPROMISE MY IDEALS TO OBEY YOUR ORDERS.
"I CANNOT REPRESENT THE AMERICAN GOVERNMENT; THE PRESIDENT DOES THAT. I MUST REPRESENT THE AMERICAN PEOPLE.
"I REPRESENT THE AMERICAN DREAM, THE FREEDOM TO STRIVE TO BECOME ALL THAT YOU DREAM OF BEING. BEING CAPTAIN AMERICA HAS BEEN MY AMERICAN DREAM.
"TO BECOME WHAT YOU WANT ME TO BE, I WOULD HAVE TO COMPROMISE THAT DREAM... ABANDON WHAT I HAVE COME TO STAND FOR.
"MY COMMITMENT TO THE IDEALS OF THIS COUNTRY IS GREATER THAN MY COMMITMENT TO A 40-YEAR OLD DOCUMENT.
"I AM SORRY, BUT THAT'S THE WAY IT MUST BE.
"GENTLEMEN, I BELIEVE THESE ARE YOURS."
8:12 A.M. THE END OF AN ERA.

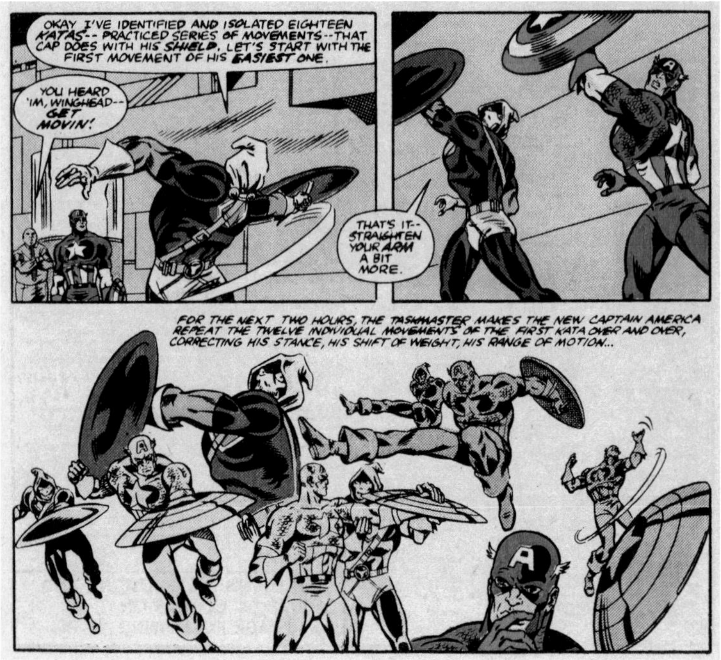
OKAY, I'VE IDENTIFIED AND ISOLATED EIGHTEEN KATAS-- PRACTICED SERIES OF MOVEMENTS--THAT CAP DOES WITH HIS SHIELD. LET'S START WITH THE FIRST MOVEMENT OF HIS EASIEST ONE.
YOU HEARD 'IM, WINGHEAD-- GET MOVIN'!
THAT'S IT-- STRAIGHTEN YOUR ARM A BIT MORE.
FOR THE NEXT TWO HOURS, THE TASKMASTER MAKES THE NEW CAPTAIN AMERICA REPEAT THE TWELVE INDIVIDUAL MOVEMENTS OF THE FIRST KATA OVER AND OVER, CORRECTING HIS STANCE, HIS SHIFT OF WEIGHT, HIS RANGE OF MOTION...

CAPTAIN AMERICA No. 334

Above: *Interior, "Basic Training"; script, Mark Gruenwald; pencils, Tom Morgan; inks, Dave Hunt; October 1987.* Cap's replacement was John Walker—the hero known as Super Patriot—who was trained by the Taskmaster. Walker's Bucky would be Lemar Hoskins.

CAPTAIN AMERICA No. 337

Opposite: *Cover; pencils, Mike Zeck; inks, Bob McLeod; January 1988.* Steve Rogers returns again, this time calling himself simply, "The Captain." This issue's cover is an homage to *Avengers* No. 4, from nearly 25 years earlier, when Captain America was defrosted into the Marvel Age.

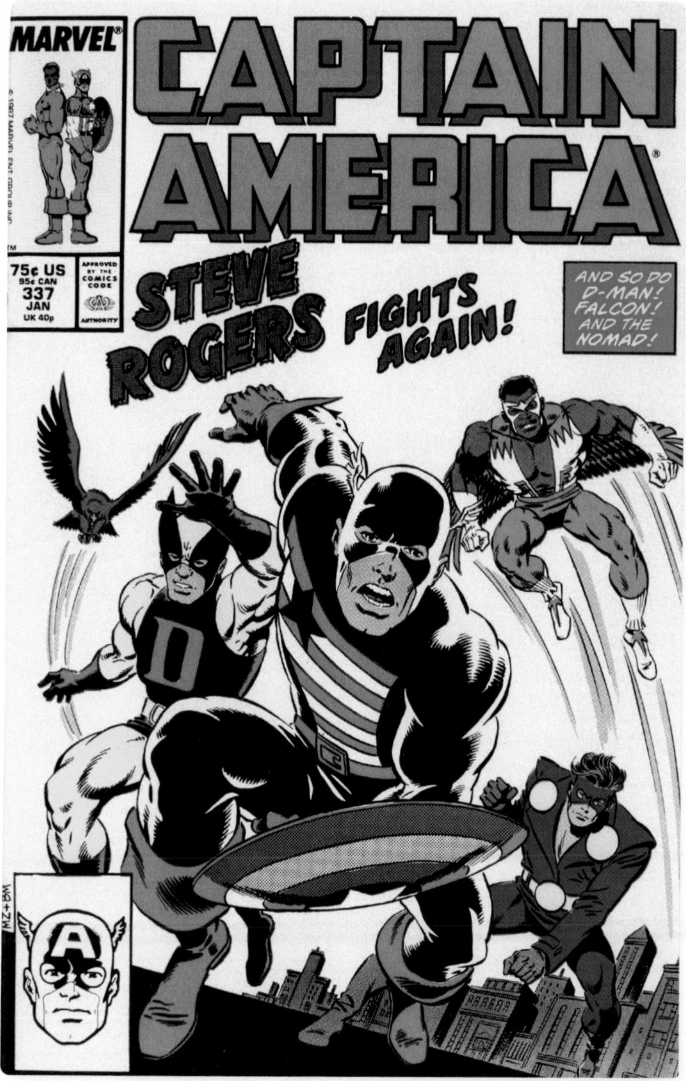
MARVEL
CAPTAIN AMERICA
75¢ US
95¢ CAN
337
JAN
UK 40p
APPROVED BY THE COMICS CODE AUTHORITY
STEVE ROGERS FIGHTS AGAIN!
AND SO DO D-MAN! FALCON! AND THE NOMAD!

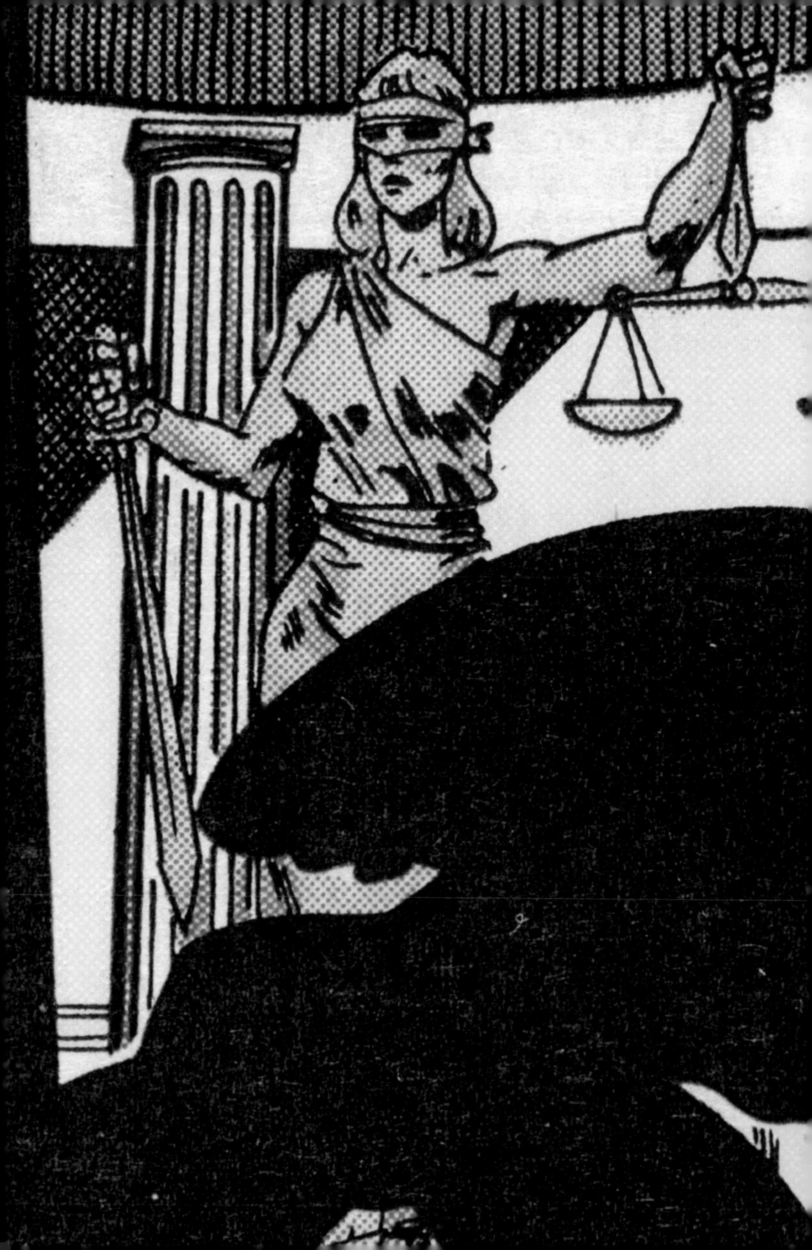

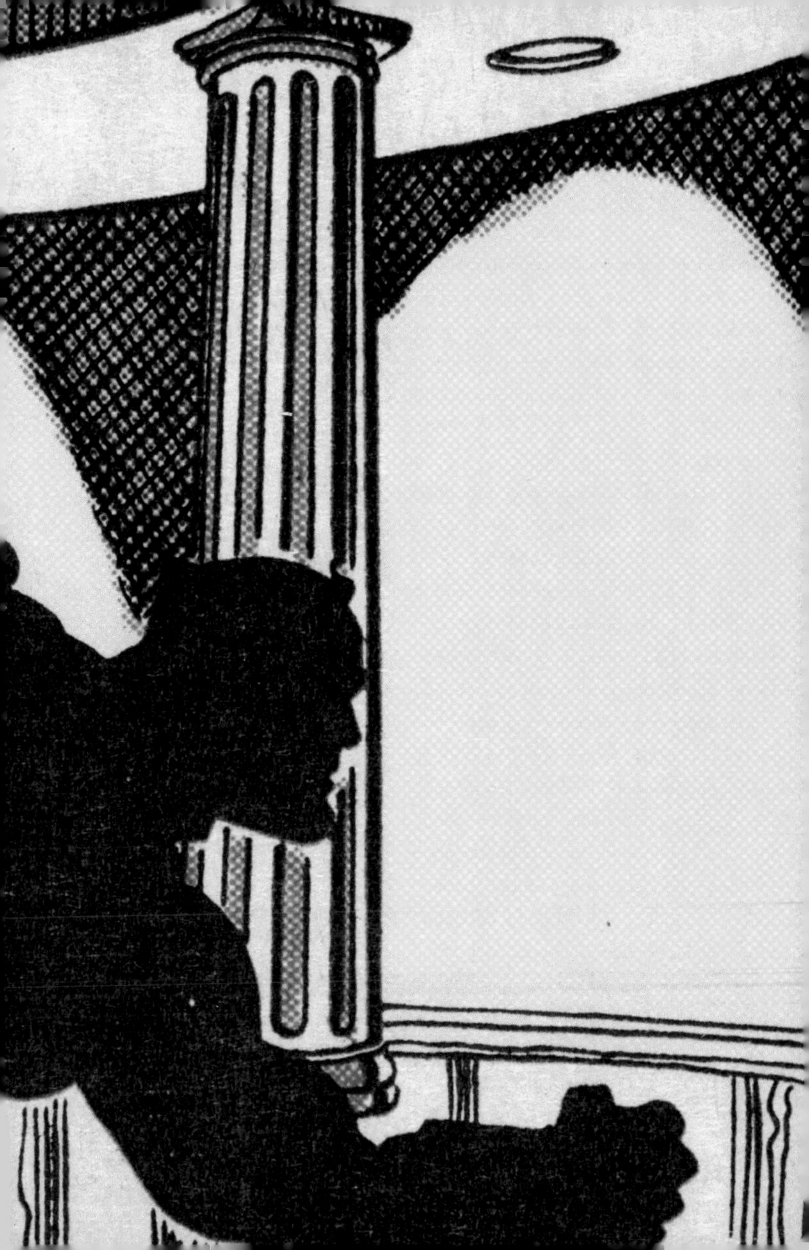

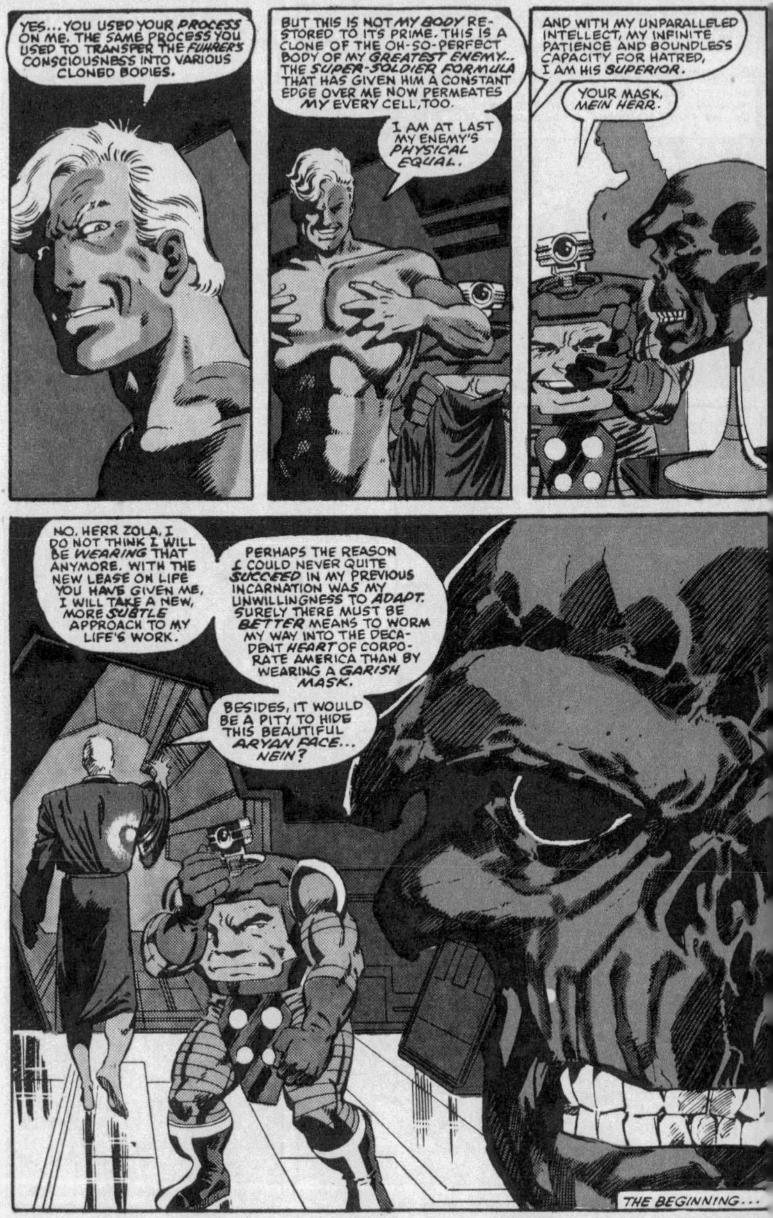
YES... YOU USED YOUR PROCESS ON ME. THE SAME PROCESS YOU USED TO TRANSPER THE FUHRER'S CONSCIOUSNESS INTO VARIOUS CLONED BODIES.
BUT THIS IS NOT MY BODY RESTORED TO ITS PRIME. THIS IS A CLONE OF THE OH-SO-PERFECT BODY OF MY GREATEST ENEMY... THE SUPER-SOLDIER FORMULA THAT HAS GIVEN HIM A CONSTANT EDGE OVER ME NOW PERMEATES MY EVERY CELL, TOO.
I AM AT LAST MY ENEMY'S PHYSICAL EQUAL.
AND WITH MY UNPARALLELED INTELLECT, MY INFINITE PATIENCE AND BOUNDLESS CAPACITY FOR HATRED, I AM HIS SUPERIOR.
YOUR MASK, MEIN HERR.
NO, HERR ZOLA, I DO NOT THINK I WILL BE WEARING THAT ANYMORE. WITH THE NEW LEASE ON LIFE YOU HAVE GIVEN ME, I WILL TAKE A NEW, MORE SUBTLE APPROACH TO MY LIFE'S WORK.
PERHAPS THE REASON I COULD NEVER QUITE SUCCEED IN MY PREVIOUS INCARNATION WAS MY UNWILLINGNESS TO ADAPT. SURELY THERE MUST BE BETTER MEANS TO WORM MY WAY INTO THE DECADENT HEART OF CORPORATE AMERICA THAN BY WEARING A GARISH MASK.
BESIDES, IT WOULD BE A PITY TO HIDE THIS BEAUTIFUL ARYAN FACE... NEIN?
THE BEGINNING...

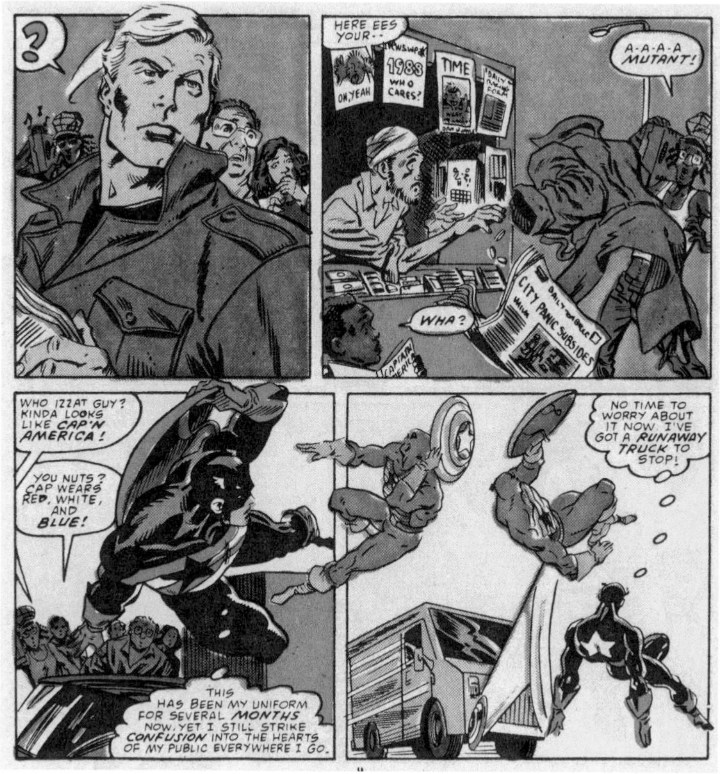
?
HERE EES YOUR--
A-A-A-A MUTANT!
OH, YEAH
1983 WHO CARES?
TIME
WHA?
CITY PANIC SUBSIDES
WHO IZZAT GUY? KINDA LOOKS LIKE CAP'N AMERICA!
YOU NUTS? CAP WEARS RED, WHITE, AND BLUE!
THIS HAS BEEN MY UNIFORM FOR SEVERAL MONTHS NOW, YET I STILL STRIKE CONFUSION INTO THE HEARTS OF MY PUBLIC EVERYWHERE I GO.
NO TIME TO WORRY ABOUT IT NOW. I'VE GOT A RUNAWAY TRUCK TO STOP!

CAPTAIN AMERICA No. 350

Pages 160–61, opposite, and above: *Interiors, "Seeing Red"; script, Mark Gruenwald; pencils, Kieron Dwyer; inks, Al Milgrom; February 1989.* Steve Rogers ditches "The Captain" to become Captain America again, after beating an insane John Walker in a fight.

MADRIPOOR, IN THE LATE-SUMMER OF 1941...

IN TIMES TO COME, HE'LL MAKE MOVES LIKE THIS WITHOUT A SECOND THOUGHT--

--FEAR BALANCED BY A COOL AWARENESS OF HIS OWN CAPABILITIES...

...AND A LIGHTNING-QUICK, UNCANNILY ACCURATE ASSESSMENT OF HIS FOES'.

BUT THAT'S THEN.

THIS IS NOW.

AND THE THOUGHT BUBBLING TREACHEROUSLY ACROSS THE BASE OF STEVE ROGERS' SKULL -- AS HE LAUNCHES HIMSELF INTO THE FACE OF WHAT FOR ANYONE ELSE WOULD BE CERTAIN DEATH--

--IS HOW HE COULD HAVE BEEN DUNCE ENOUGH TO WILLINGLY VOLUNTEER TO TAKE ON THE MANTLE OF THE STAR-SPANGLED SENTINEL OF LIBERTY:

CAPTAIN AMERICA!

THE UNCANNY X-MEN' Vol. 1, No. 268, Late September, 1990. (ISSN 0274-5372) Published by MARVEL COMICS. James E. Galton, President. Stan Lee, Publisher. Michael Hobson, Group Vice President Publishing. OFFICE OF PUBLICATION: 387 PARK AVENUE SOUTH, NEW YORK, N.Y. 10016. SECOND CLASS POSTAGE PAID AT NEW YORK, NY AND AT ADDITIONAL MAILING OFFICES. Published monthly. Copyright © 1990 by Marvel Entertainment Group, Inc. All rights reserved. Price $1.00 per copy in the U.S. and $1.25 in Canada. Subscription rate for 12 issues: U.S. $12.00; Canada $17.00, and foreign $24.00. Printed in the U.S.A. No similarity between any of the names, characters, persons, and/or institutions in this magazine with those of any living or dead person or institution is intended, and any such similarity which may exist is purely coincidental. This periodical may not be sold except by authorized dealers and is sold subject to the condition that it shall not be sold or distributed with any part of its cover or markings removed, nor in a mutilated condition. THE UNCANNY X-MEN (including all prominent characters featured in this issue and the distinctive likenesses thereof) are trademarks of MARVEL ENTERTAINMENT GROUP INC. POSTMASTER: SEND ADDRESS CHANGES TO THE UNCANNY X-MEN, c/o MARVEL COMICS, SUBSCRIPTION DEPT. 387 PARK AVENUE SOUTH, NEW YORK, N.Y. 10016.

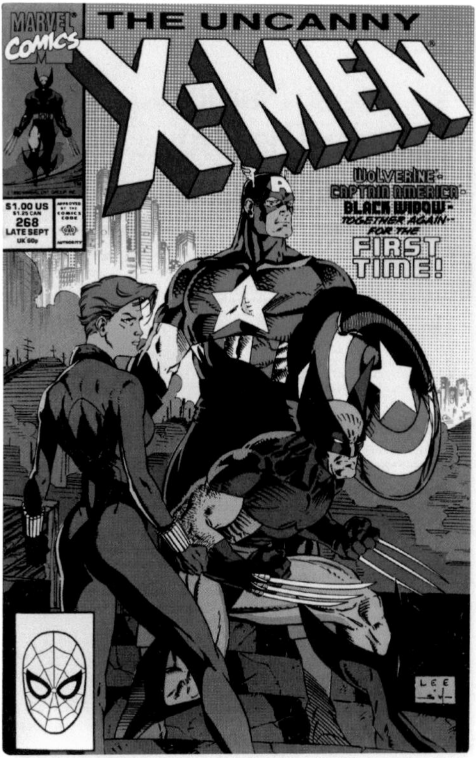
MARVEL COMICS
THE UNCANNY
X-MEN
$1.00 US
268
LATE SEPT
WOLVERINE
CAPTAIN AMERICA
BLACK WIDOW
TOGETHER AGAIN
FOR THE
FIRST
TIME!
LEE

UNCANNY X-MEN No. 268

Above and opposite: *Cover; pencils, Jim Lee; inks, Scott Williams. Interior, "Madripoor Knights"; script, Chris Claremont; pencils, Lee; inks, Williams; September 1990.* Just a year away from shattering records, becoming an A-list comics superstar, and selling more than eight million copies of *X-Men* No. 1, Jim Lee penciled a nine-issue run written by longtime X-scribe Chris Claremont — offering Cap fans a rare treat when Cap and Black Widow guest starred.

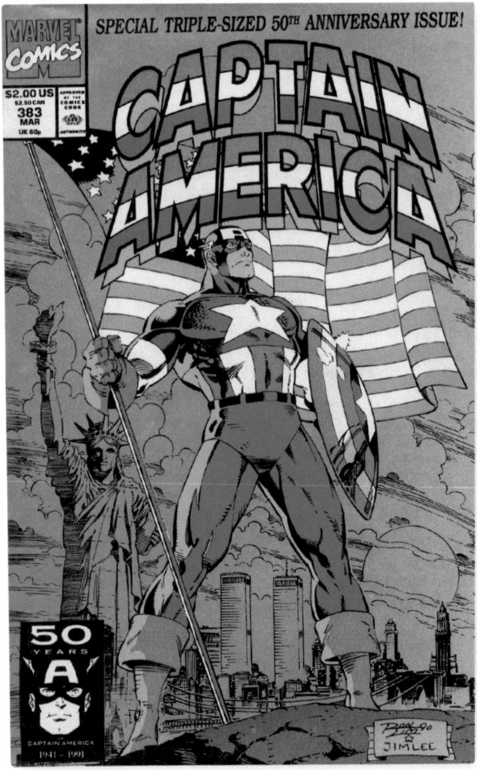
MARVEL COMICS
SPECIAL TRIPLE-SIZED 50TH ANNIVERSARY ISSUE!
CAPTAIN AMERICA
$2.00 US
$2.50 CAN
383
MAR
UK 60p
50
YEARS
A
CAPTAIN AMERICA
1941 – 1991
JIM LEE

CAPTAIN AMERICA No. 383

Above: *Cover; pencils, Ron Lim; inks, Jim Lee; March 1991.*

CAPTAIN AMERICA No. 450

Opposite: *Cover; pencils and inks, Ron Garney; April 1996.* Mark Waid and Ron Garney's rendition of Cap was popular with fans, and mostly free of '90s comics excesses, as seen in this striking cover made to look like a weekly news magazine.

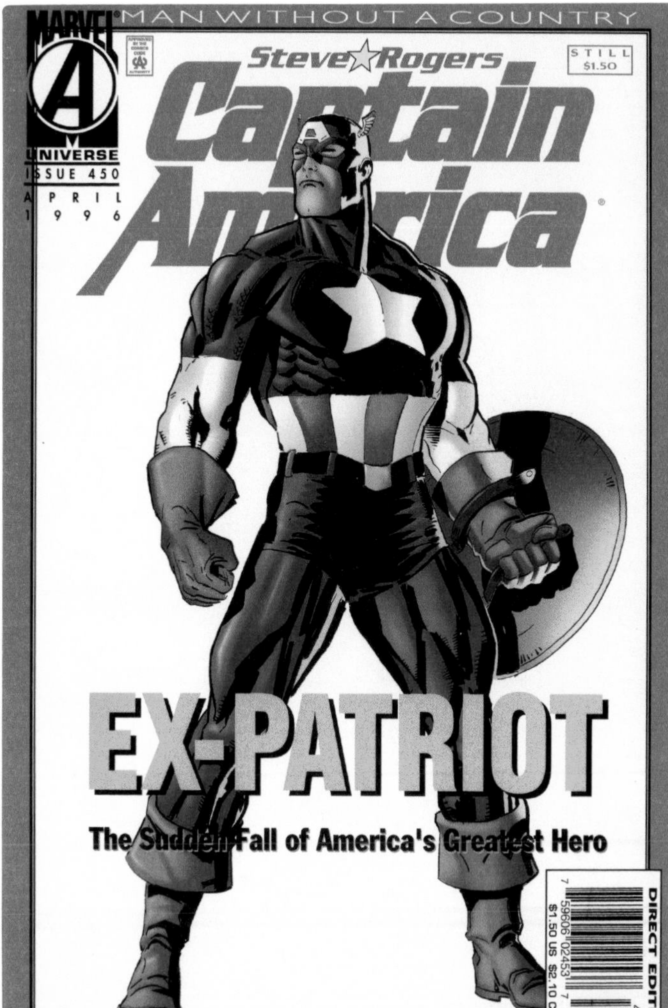
MARVEL
MAN WITHOUT A COUNTRY
UNIVERSE
ISSUE 450
APRIL 1996
Steve Rogers
Captain America
STILL $1.50
EX-PATRIOT
The Sudden Fall of America's Greatest Hero
DIRECT EDITION
$1.50 US $2.10 CAN
GARNEY
FEBRUARY 6, 1996 $1.50 US

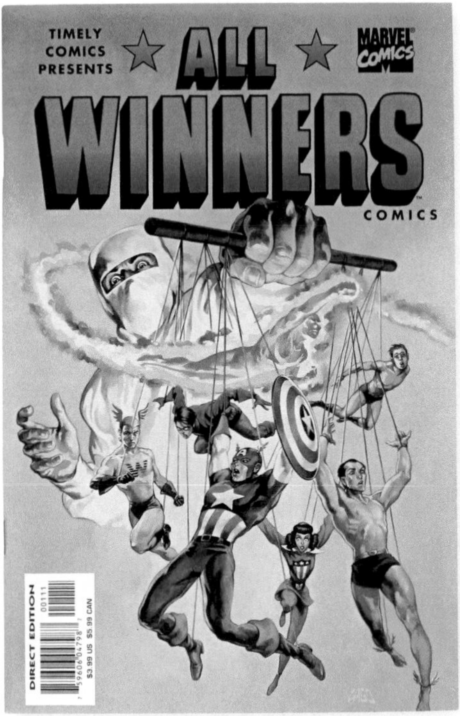
TIMELY COMICS PRESENTS
ALL WINNERS
COMICS
MARVEL COMICS
DIRECT EDITION
$3.99 US $5.99 CAN

TIMELY PRESENTS: ALL WINNERS

Above: *Cover; art, Ray Lago; December 1999.* This one-shot reprints *All-Winners* No. 19 from 1946 (with a cover that is an homage to the original), which features the All-Winners Squad, a team that includes Captain America, Human Torch, Sub-Mariner, Bucky, Whizzer, Toro, and Miss America.

CAPTAIN AMERICA No. 14

Opposite: *Cover; pencils and inks, John Cassaday; August 2003.*

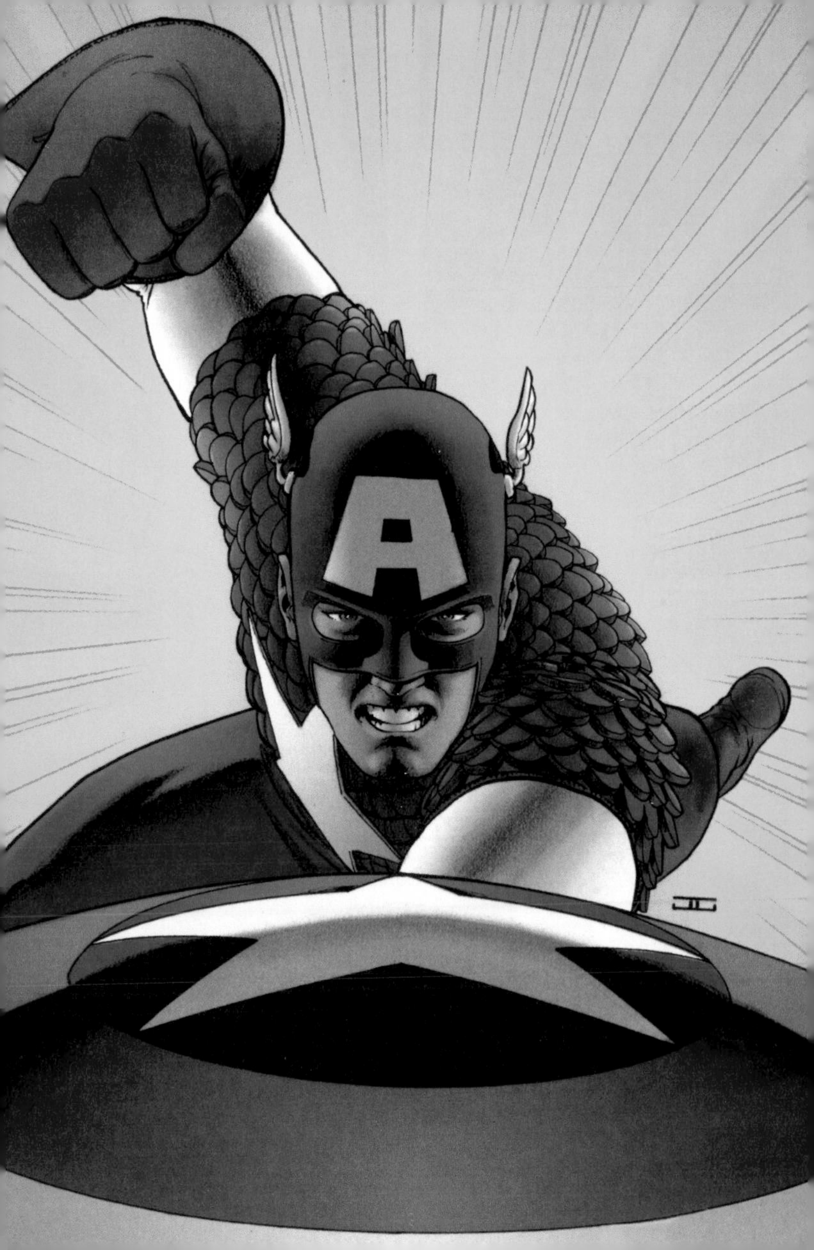

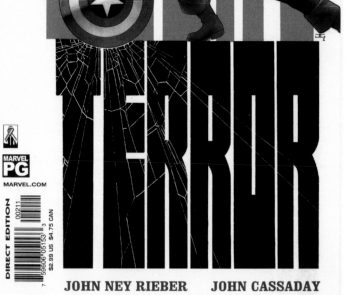

Captain America

FIGHT TERROR

JOHN NEY RIEBER   **JOHN CASSADAY**

x

MARVEL PG

MARVEL.COM

DIRECT EDITION

00211

$2.99 US $4.75 CAN

7 59606 05153 3

170

CAPTAIN AMERICA No. 2

Opposite: *Cover; pencils and inks, John Cassaday; July 2002.*

CAPTAIN AMERICA No. 5

Below: *Cover; pencils and inks, John Cassaday; October 2002.* John Cassaday took a two-year break from his acclaimed DC series *Planetary*, drawing the first story arc of the 2002 Marvel Knights relaunch of Captain America, which was heavily grounded in current American events in the aftermath of 9/11.

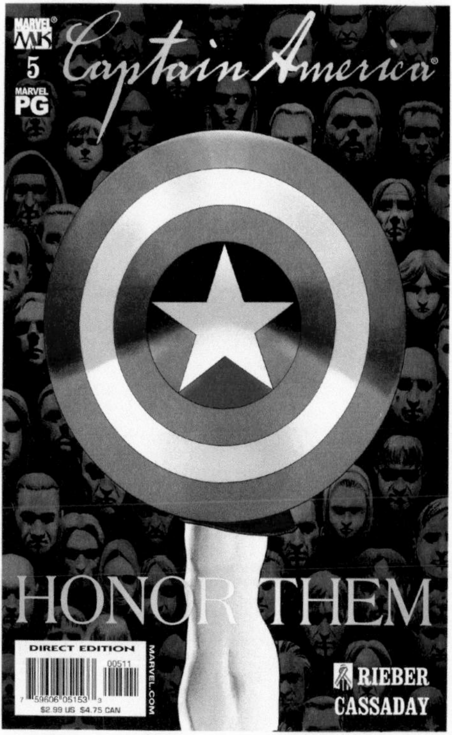
MARVEL MK
5
Captain America
MARVEL PG
HONOR THEM
DIRECT EDITION
$2.99 US $4.75 CAN
MARVEL.COM
RIEBER
CASSADAY

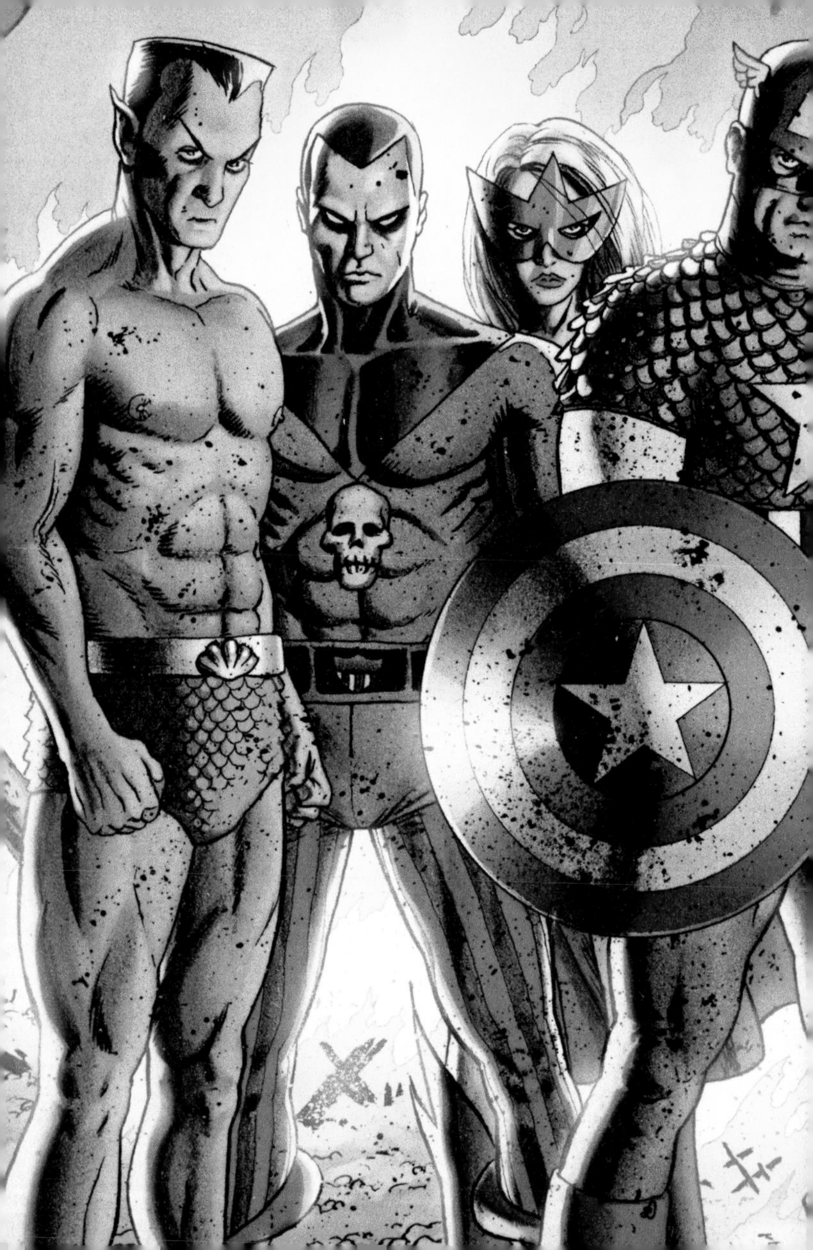

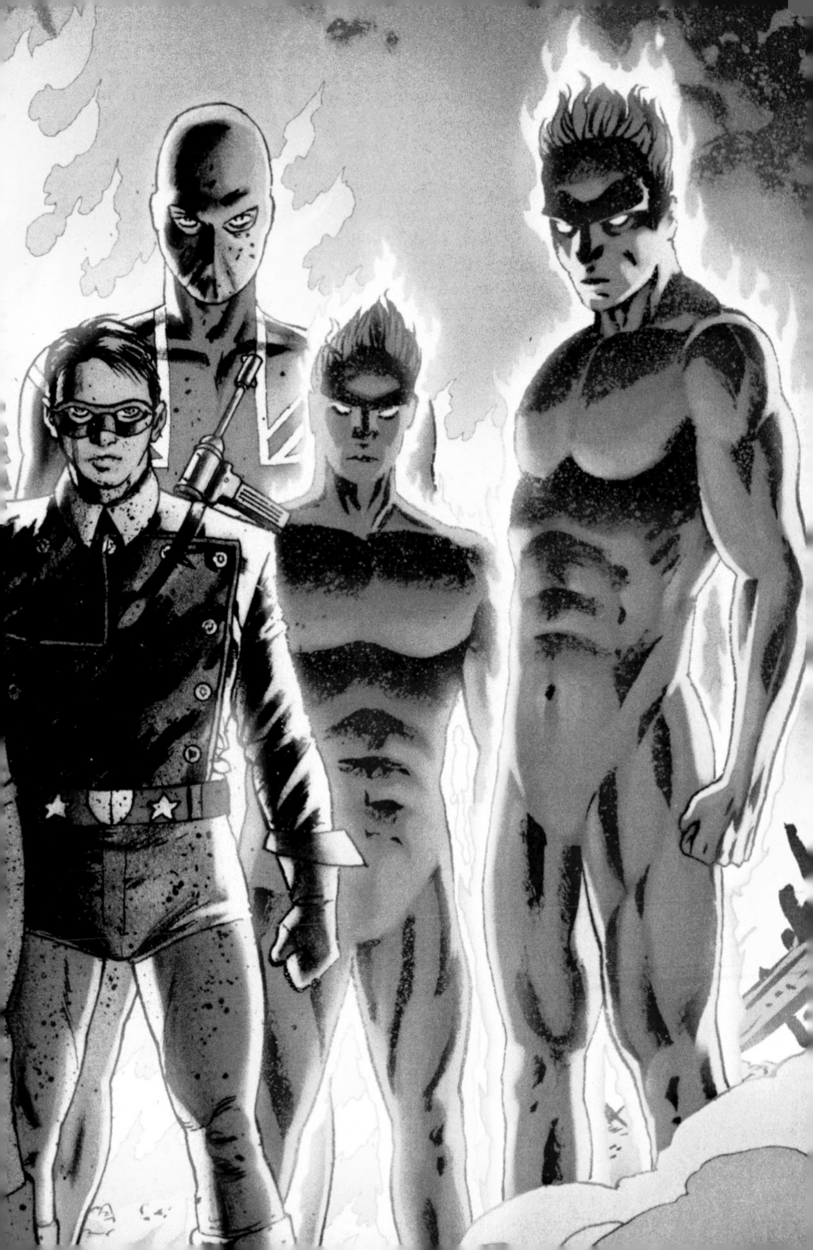

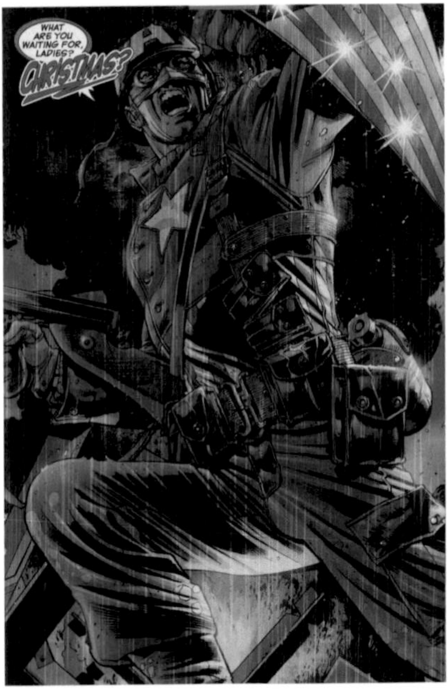
WHAT ARE YOU WAITING FOR, LADIES?
CHRISTMAS?

CAPTAIN AMERICA: REBORN No. 3

Pages 172–73: *Cover; art, John Cassaday; November 2009.* A look at the Captain America mythos circa 2009 shows Marvel's commitment to exploring the full breadth of its universe — with characters from its Golden, Silver, and Modern ages all sharing in the storylines.

ULTIMATES No. 1

Above: *Interior; script, Mark Millar; pencils, Bryan Hitch; inks, Andrew Currie; March 2002.* Millar and Hitch's *The Ultimates* was known for its cinematic visuals and dialogue, and the wide-screen aspect ratio of the series — and even some of the casting! — was an influence on the *Avengers* film.

CAPTAIN AMERICA: MAN OUT OF TIME No. 1

Opposite: *Interior, "Man Out of Time Part 1"; script, Mark Waid; pencils, Jorge Molina; inks, Karl Kesel; January 2011.* This mini-series chronicled Captain America's unthawing in *present-day* America, and the troubles Cap has adjusting as a "man out of time."

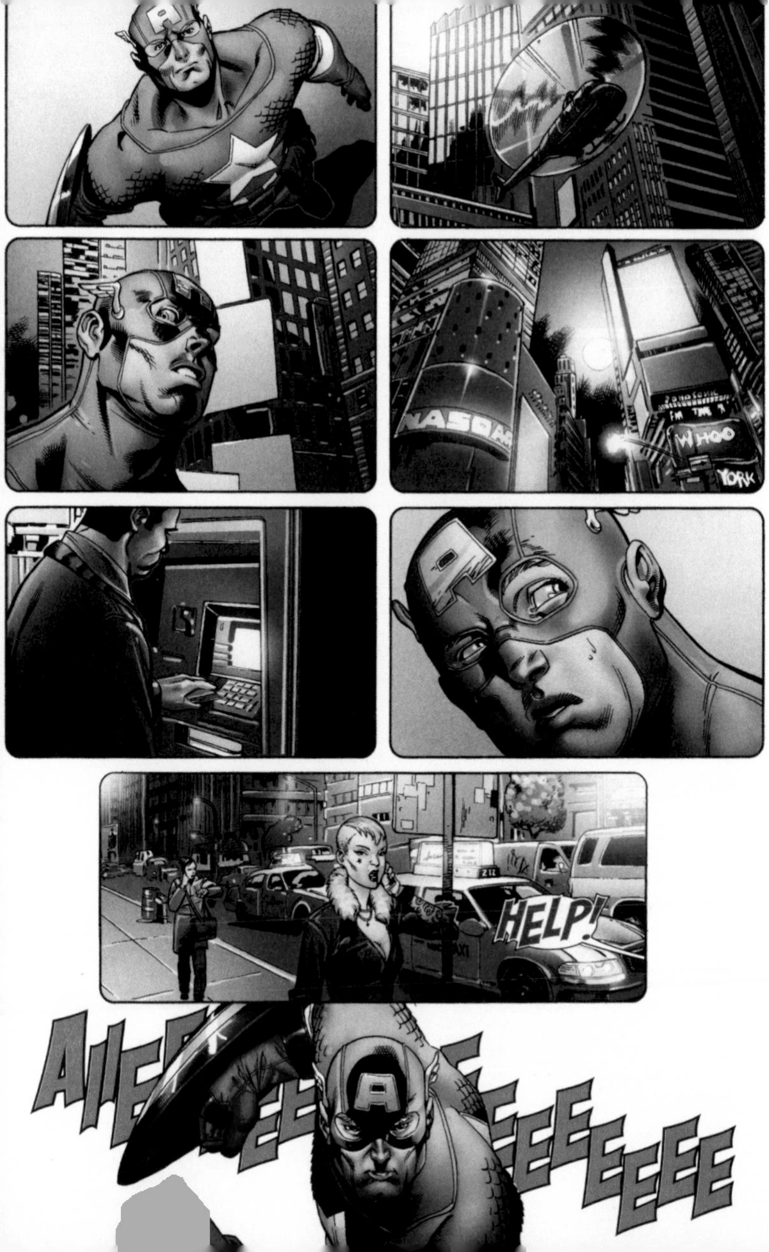
HELP!
AIEEEEEEEEEEEEEEE

CAPTAIN AMERICA No. 1

Below: *Interior, "Enemy: Chapter One—Dust"; script, John Ney Rieber; pencils and inks, John Cassaday; June 2002.*

ULTIMATES No. 12

Opposite: *Interior, "Persons of Mass Destruction"; script, Mark Millar; pencils, Bryan Hitch; inks, Paul Neary; November 2003.* "You think this A on my head stands for France?!" The line instantly became one of the best and most memorable one-liners in Cap's history.

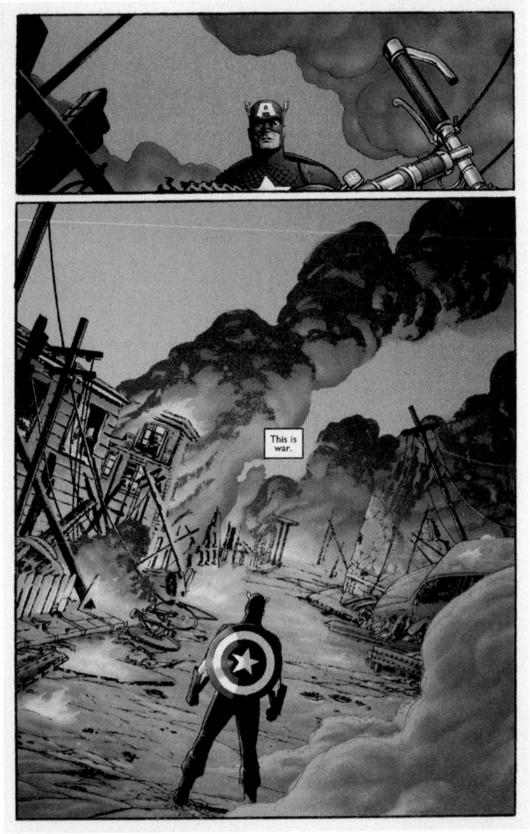
This is war.

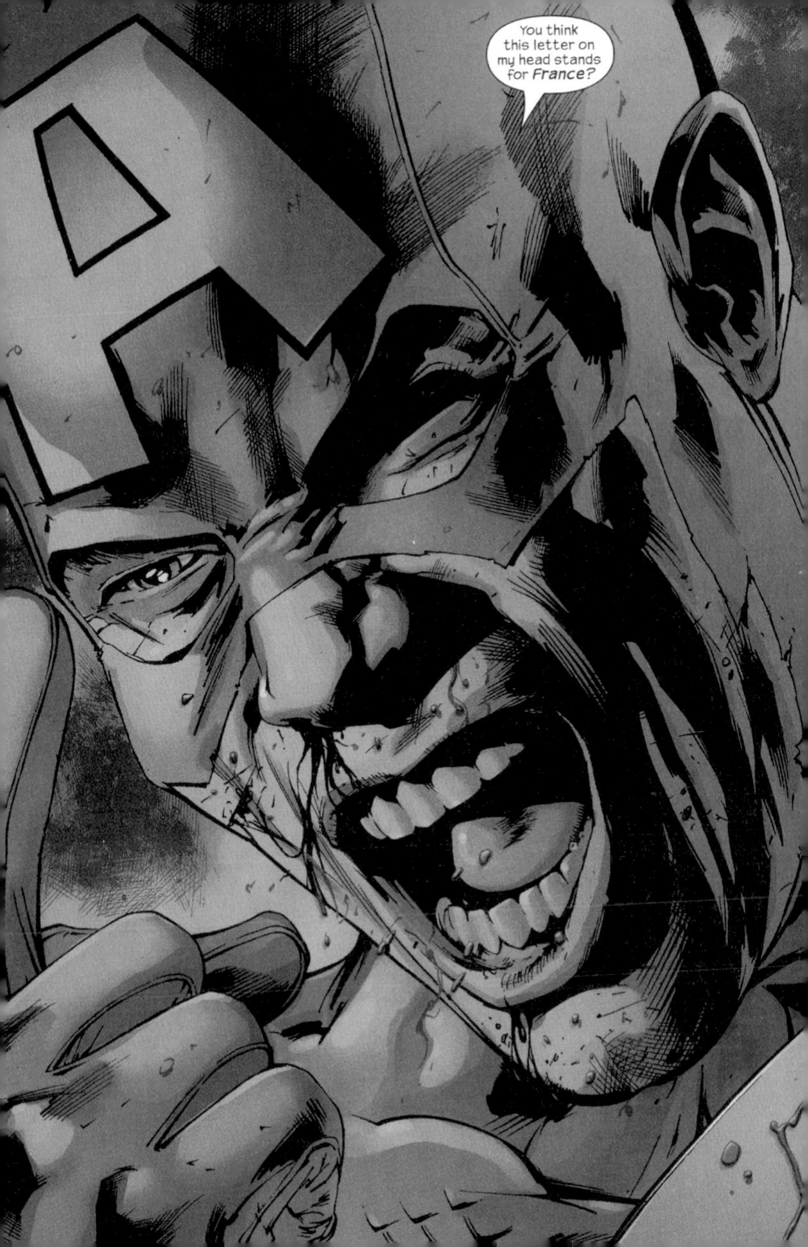
You think this letter on my head stands for France?

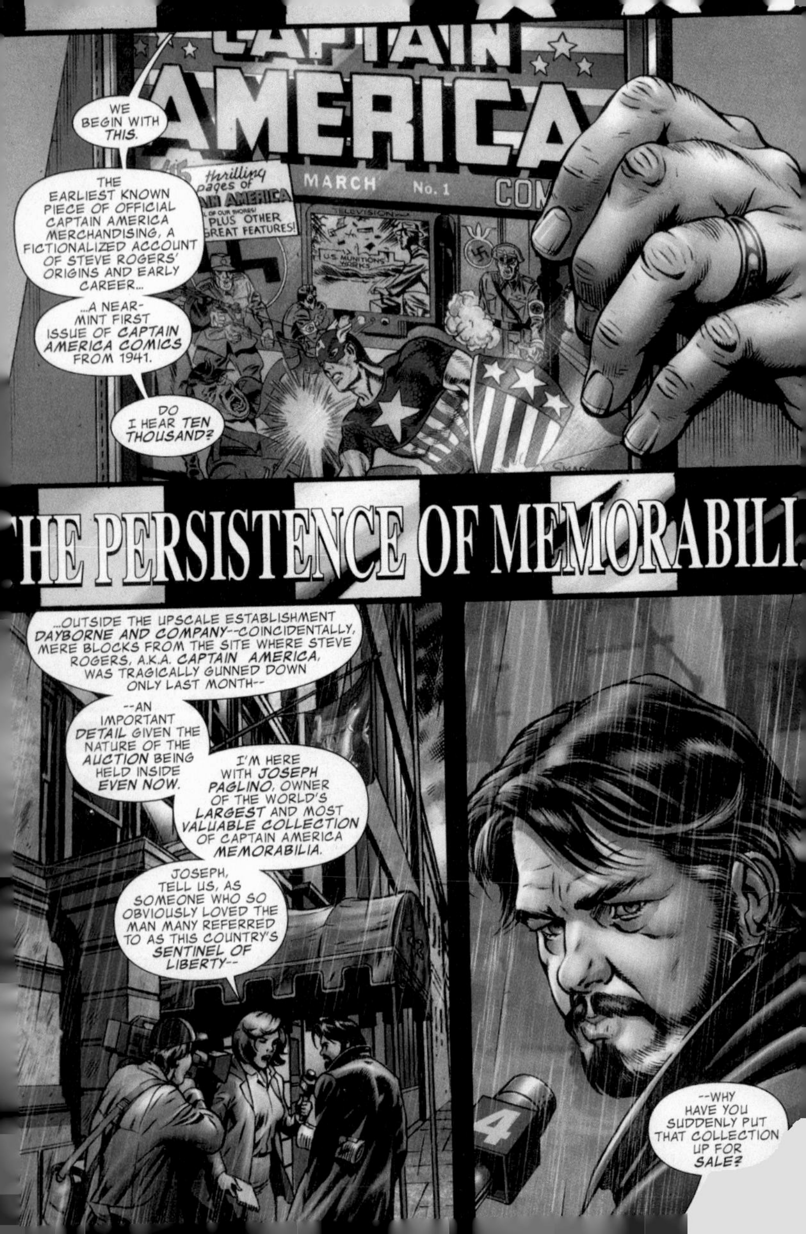

CAPTAIN AMERICA
WE BEGIN WITH THIS.
MARCH No. 1
PLUS OTHER GREAT FEATURES!
THE EARLIEST KNOWN PIECE OF OFFICIAL CAPTAIN AMERICA MERCHANDISING, A FICTIONALIZED ACCOUNT OF STEVE ROGERS' ORIGINS AND EARLY CAREER...
...A NEAR-MINT FIRST ISSUE OF CAPTAIN AMERICA COMICS FROM 1941.
DO I HEAR TEN THOUSAND?
HE PERSISTENCE OF MEMORABILI
...OUTSIDE THE UPSCALE ESTABLISHMENT DAYBORNE AND COMPANY--COINCIDENTALLY, MERE BLOCKS FROM THE SITE WHERE STEVE ROGERS, A.K.A. CAPTAIN AMERICA, WAS TRAGICALLY GUNNED DOWN ONLY LAST MONTH--
--AN IMPORTANT DETAIL GIVEN THE NATURE OF THE AUCTION BEING HELD INSIDE EVEN NOW.
I'M HERE WITH JOSEPH PAGLINO, OWNER OF THE WORLD'S LARGEST AND MOST VALUABLE COLLECTION OF CAPTAIN AMERICA MEMORABILIA.
JOSEPH, TELL US, AS SOMEONE WHO SO OBVIOUSLY LOVED THE MAN MANY REFERRED TO AS THIS COUNTRY'S SENTINEL OF LIBERTY--
4
--WHY HAVE YOU SUDDENLY PUT THAT COLLECTION UP FOR SALE?

MARVEL
2 of 5
KIRKMAN
PHILLIPS
CHUNG
MARVEL
ZOMBIES
DIRECT EDITION
RATED T+
$2.99 US $4.25 CAN

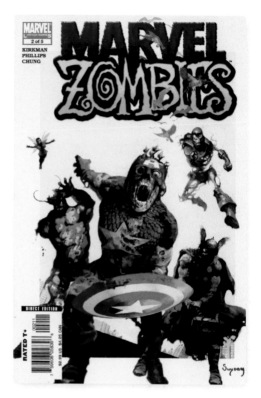

CAPTAIN AMERICA No. 600

Opposite: *Interior, "The Persistence of Memorabilia"; script, Mark Waid; pencils, Dale Eaglesham; August 2009.* The original run of *Captain America* ended with No. 454. After many reboots, the series' 2005 incarnation jumped from No. 50 back to 600, continuing with the series' original numbering. With its title a play on a Dalí painting, this short story begins with *Captain America Comics* No. 1 at auction.

MARVEL ZOMBIES No. 2

Above: *Cover; art, Arthur Suydam; March 2006.* As *The Walking Dead* was slowly gaining traction and readers, Robert Kirkman penned this miniseries in which the Marvel super heroes had been turned into zombies. The title is a reference to the long-time nickname for hardcore Marvel fans—"Marvel zombies."

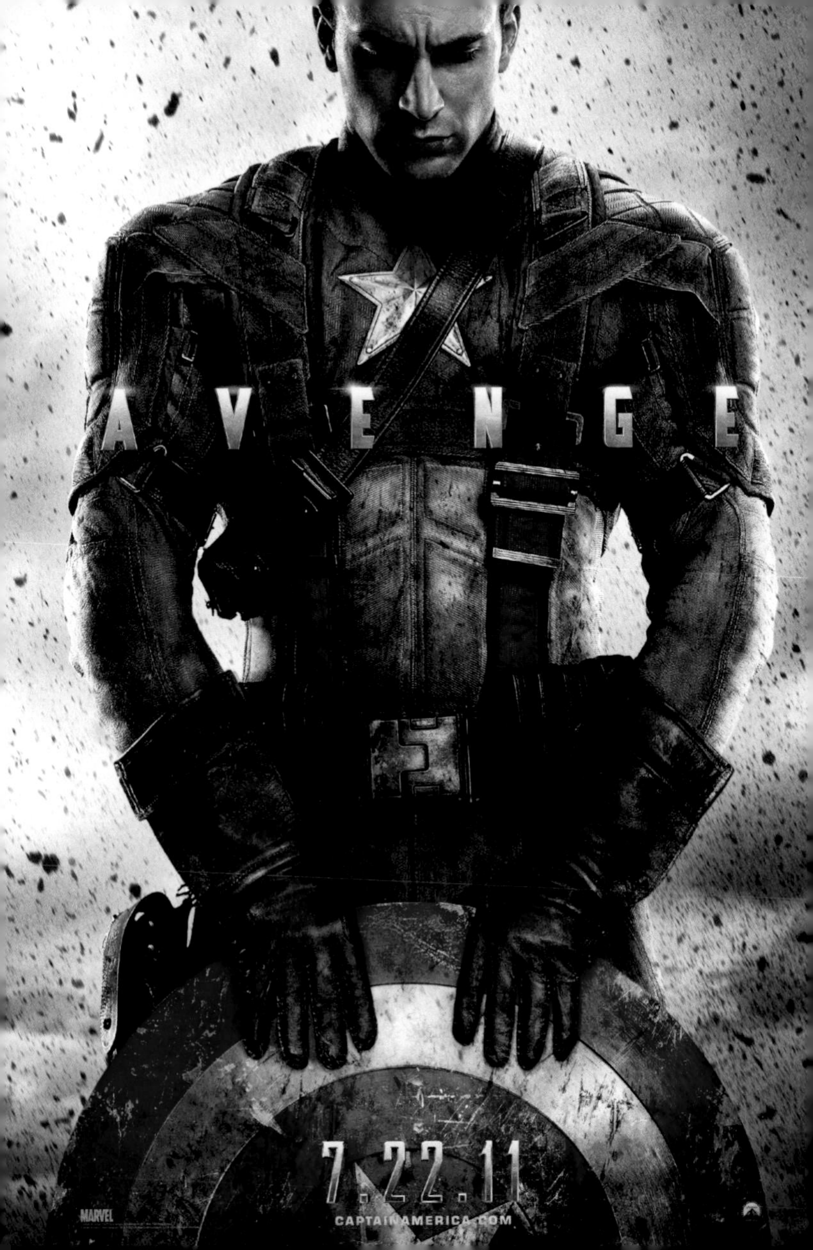
AVENGE
7.22.11
MARVEL
CAPTAINAMERICA.COM

CAPTAIN AMERICA: THE FIRST AVENGER

Opposite: *Poster, Captain America: The First Avenger; Paramount Pictures; 2011.* Chris Evans swaps Johnny Storm for Steve Rogers as Cap hits the big screen. The blockbuster movie, largely set during World War II, directly sets the stage for the big screen assembly of the Avengers, not least with its title.

CAP'S LAST SUPPER

Below: *Photograph, Joyce Dopkeen; Joe Simon in his home studio, Manhattan; 2007.* The great Joe Simon shows off a Marvelous take on Michelangelo's iconic *Last Supper*, with Cap fittingly in the prime seat. "I look back, I say, 'Who did this stuff? Who was that guy?'" Simon recalled in 2008. His eight-decade career in comics was "just a lovely way for a tailor's son to make a living." The beloved Captain America artist remained a presence at conventions until his death in 2011 at age 98.

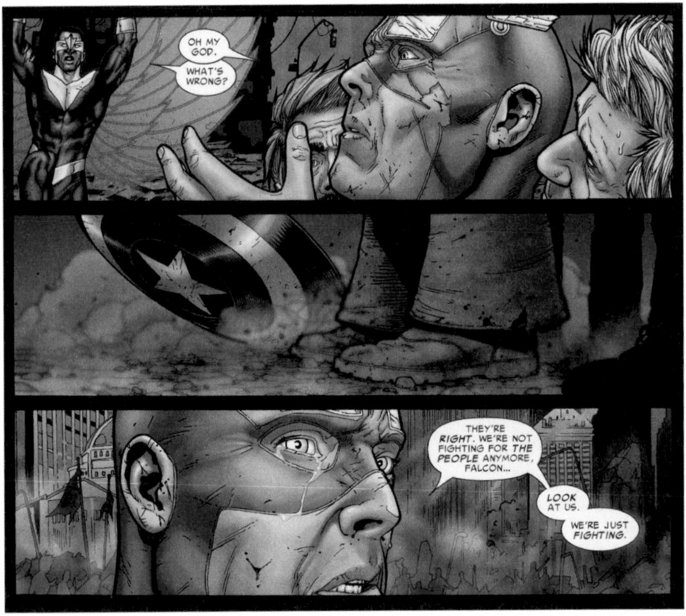
OH MY GOD.
WHAT'S WRONG?
THEY'RE RIGHT. WE'RE NOT FIGHTING FOR THE PEOPLE ANYMORE, FALCON...
LOOK AT US.
WE'RE JUST FIGHTING.

CIVIL WAR No. 7

Above: *Interior; script, Mark Millar; pencils, Steve McNiven; inks, John Dell, Tim Townsend, and Dexter Vines; January 2007.* Mark Millar asked Marveldom the question "Whose side are you on?" as teammates and old friends Iron Man and Captain America went to war over the forced registration of super humans. A sales blockbuster, *Civil War* showed how strongly fans hunger to see heroes ditch their villains and just go at it, mano a super mano.

CAPTAIN AMERICA No. 25

Opposite: *Interior, "The Death of the Dream: Part One"; script, Ed Brubaker; art, Steve Epting; April 2007.* The hoo-ha over the death of Steve Rogers reflected an increasing trend for spoilers (the archenemy of the comic book fan) not only on dedicated comic news websites, but also in mainstream media, as savvy publishers realized that headlines boost sales. ABC's Bryan Robinson said "You're not crazy if you think Captain America's struggle parallels the debates over the Iraq War, the Patriot Act, the Bush domestic surveillance program and other controversial programs in the post-9/11 world."

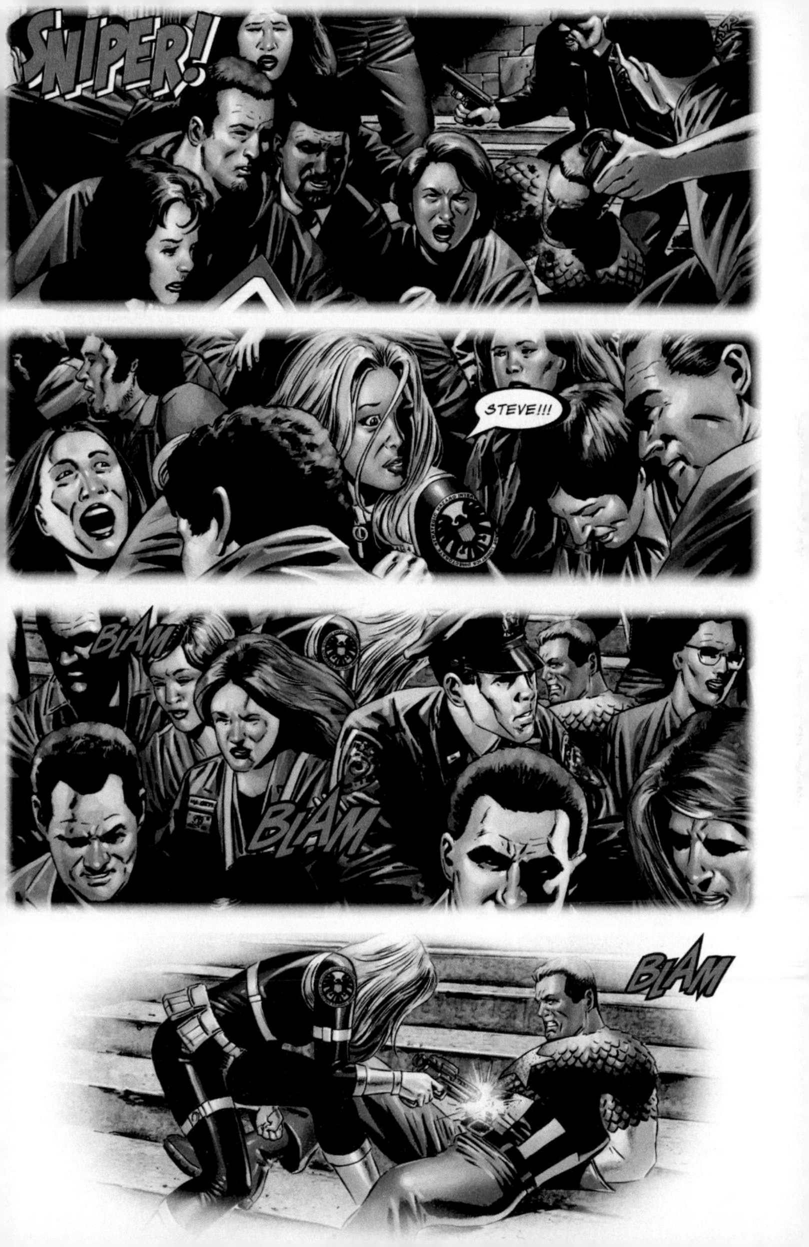
SNIPER!
STEVE!!!
BLAM
BLAM
BLAM

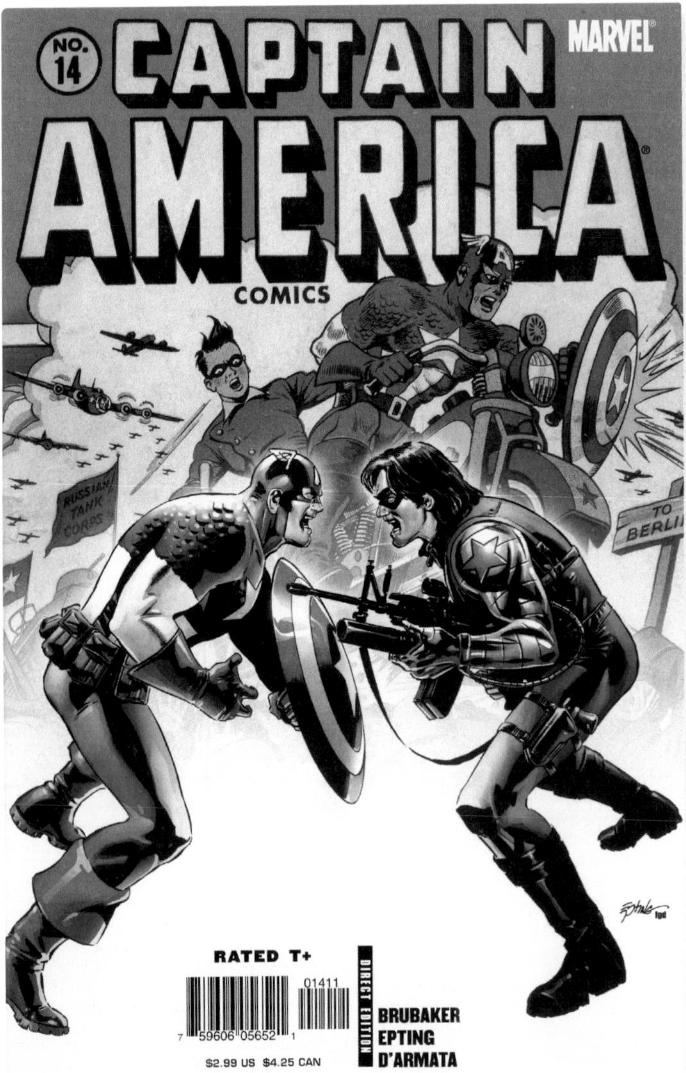

NO. 14
CAPTAIN AMERICA
COMICS
MARVEL
RUSSIAN TANK CORPS
TO BERLI
RATED T+
DIRECT EDITION
BRUBAKER
EPTING
D'ARMATA
$2.99 US $4.25 CAN

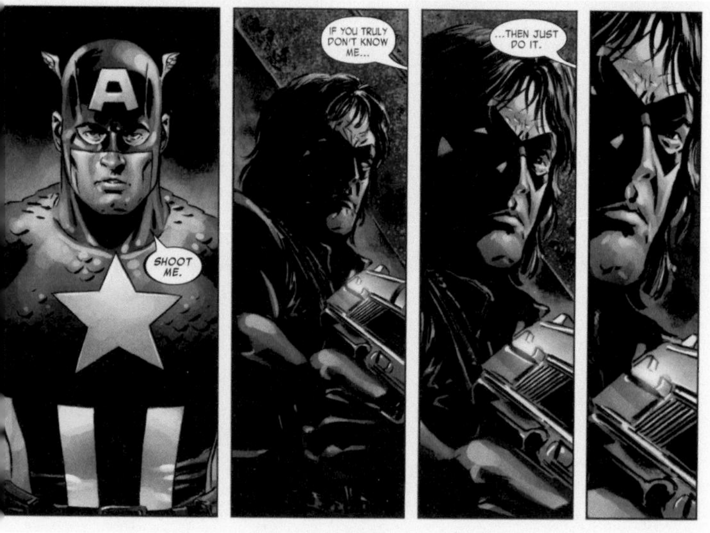
SHOOT ME.
IF YOU TRULY DON'T KNOW ME...
...THEN JUST DO IT.

CAPTAIN AMERICA No. 14

Opposite: *Cover; pencils and inks, Steve Epting and Alex Schomburg; April 2006.*

CAPTAIN AMERICA No. 11

Above: *Interior, "The Winter Soldier, Part 3"; script, Ed Brubaker; pencils and inks, Steve Epting; November 2005.* Ed Brubaker wrote both the 2005 and 2011 relaunches of *Captain America*, giving him an eight-year run as the character's main writer. Brubaker reintroduced the original Bucky—long presumed dead—as the Winter Soldier, a Russian assassin who inspired the Russo brothers' 2014 movie sequel, *Captain America: The Winter Soldier*.

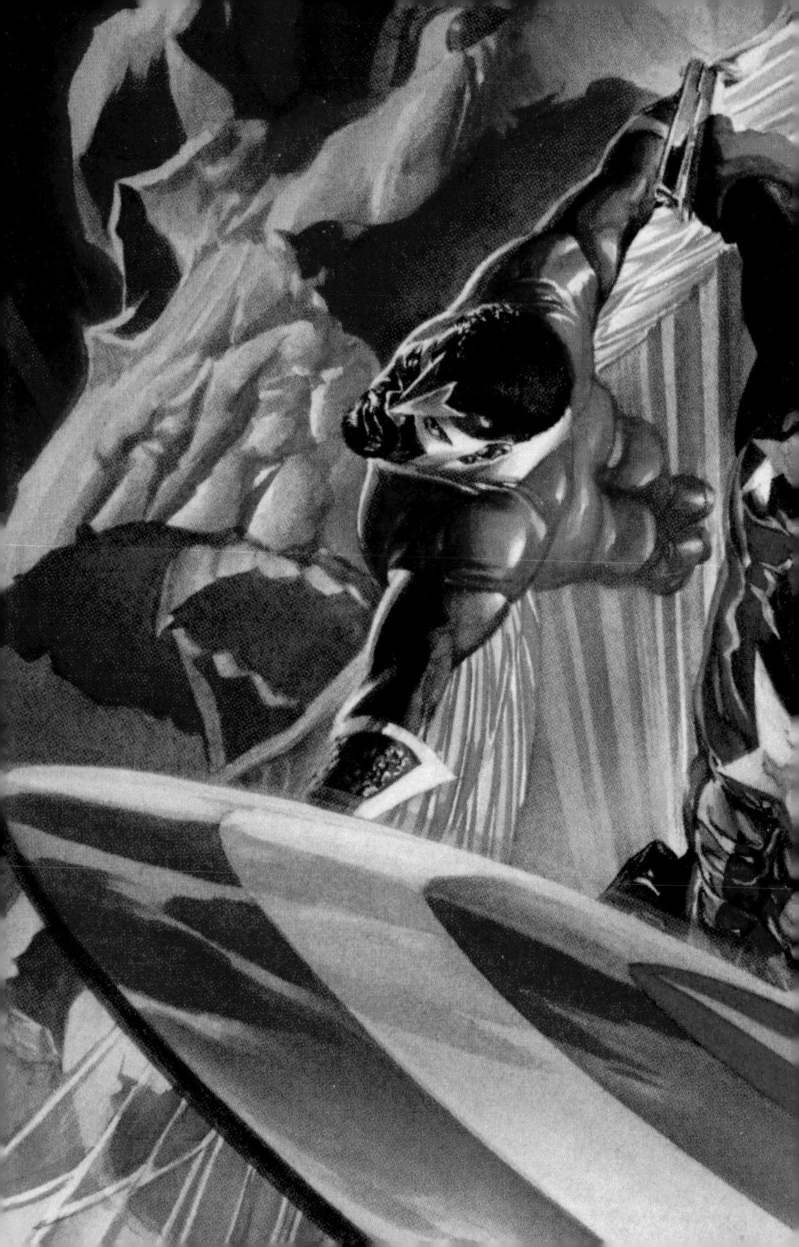

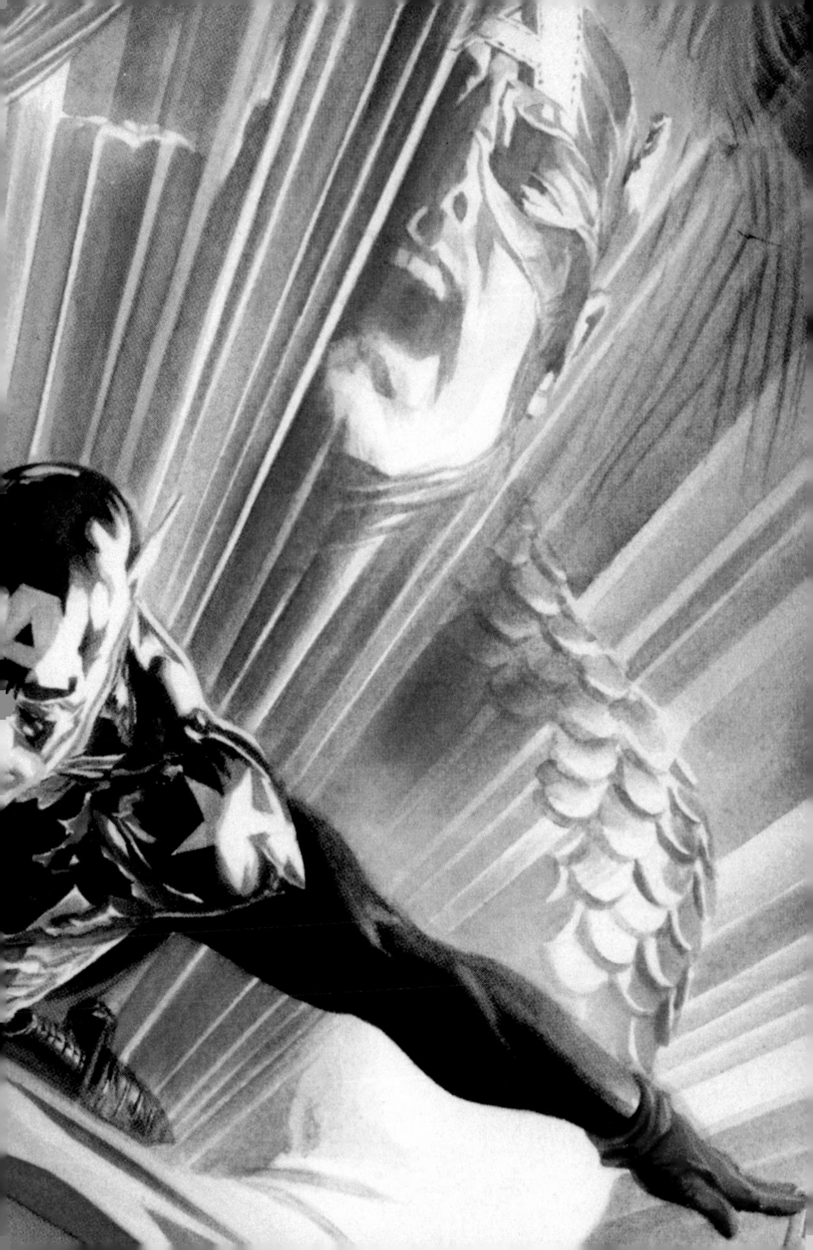

CAPTAIN AMERICA No. 600

Pages 186–87: *Cover; art, Alex Ross; August 2009.*

CAPTAIN AMERICA No. 22

Opposite: *Cover; art, Alex Ross; September 2014.* The painter Alex Ross is known for his majestic, heroic, yet realistic artwork — in the tradition of beloved American illustrator Norman Rockwell — that comic book fans have continually revered since Ross rose to prominence in the early '90s.

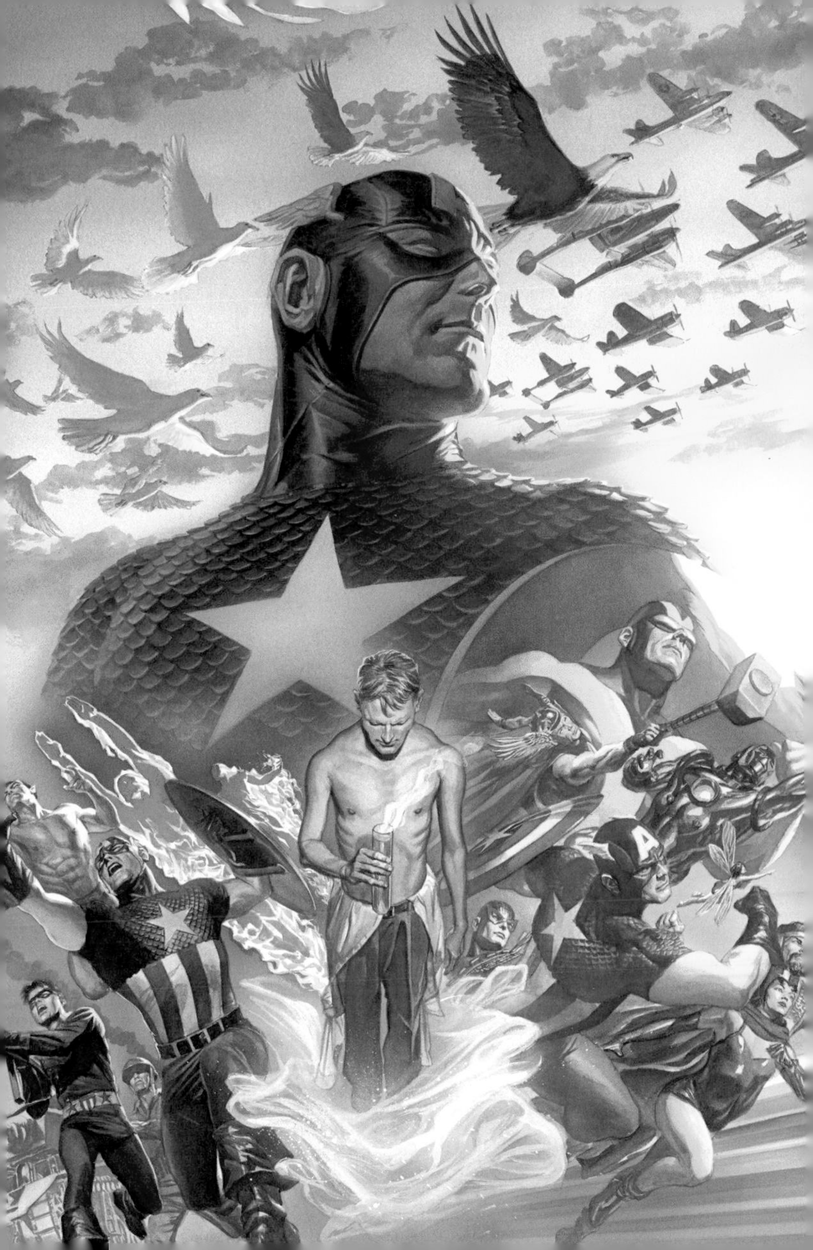

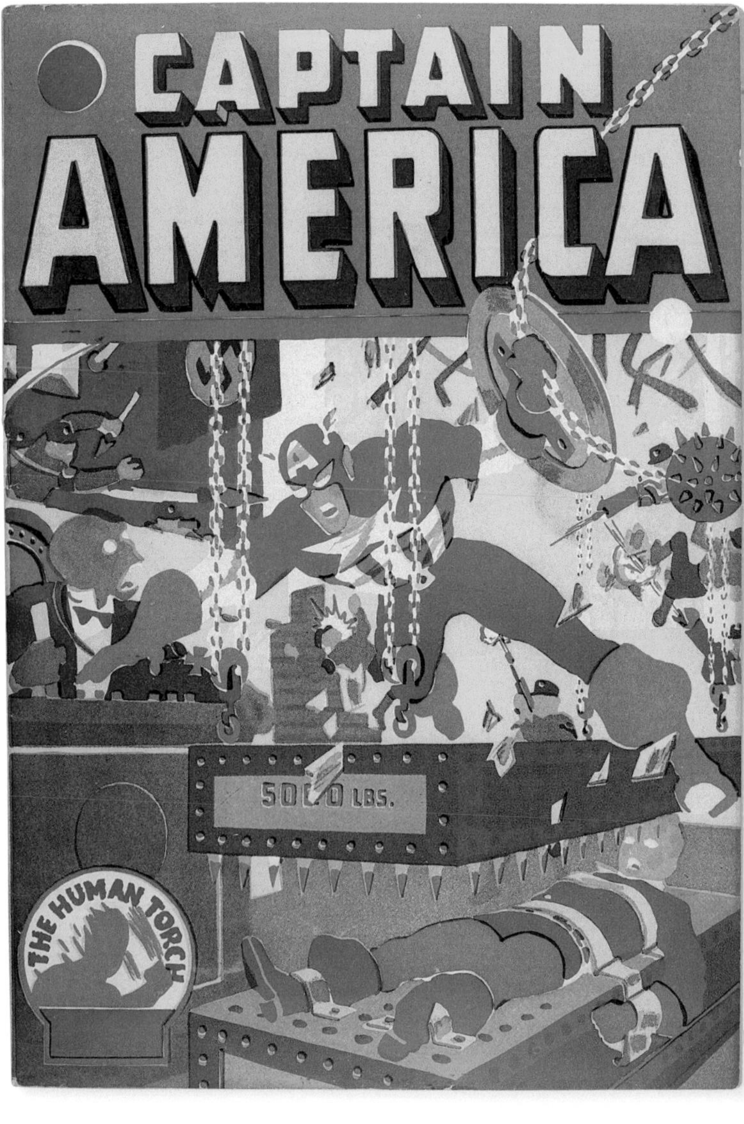
CAPTAIN
AMERICA
5000 LBS.
THE HUMAN TORCH

THE AVENGERS No. 16

Front cover: *Cover; pencils, Jack Kirby; inks, Sol Brodsky; May 1965.*

ALL-WINNERS COMICS No. 1

Pages 4–5: *Cover; art, Alex Schomburg; Summer 1941.*

CAPTAIN AMERICA COMICS No. 28

Opposite: *Cover; pencils and inks, Alex Schomburg; July 1943.*

CAPTAIN AMERICA No. 22

Back cover: *Cover; art, Alex Ross; September 2014.*

© 2017 MARVEL
marvel.com

TASCHEN GMBH
Hohenzollernring 53, D-50672 Köln
taschen.com

Editor/art director: Josh Baker, Oakland
Design/layout: Nemuel DePaula, Los Angeles
Editorial coordination: Jascha Kempe,
  Cologne; Nina Wiener, New York
Production: Stefan Klatte, Cologne
German translation: Reinhard Schweizer,
  Freiburg
French translation: Éric Andret, Paris
Editorial consultants: Nick Caputo,
  Maurene Goo, Blake Hennon, Barry Pearl,
  Rhett Thomas, Michael J. Vassallo,
  Scott Bryan Wilson
Special consultant to Roy Thomas:
  Danny Fingeroth

CREDITS

The majority of the comics included in this volume were photographed from the collections of Bob Bretall, Nick Caputo, Marvel, Barry Pearl, Michael J. Vassallo, and Warren Reece's Chamber of Fantasy. Also: Jesse and Sylvia Storob, John Chruscinski, Glen David Gold, Andrew Farago, Hake's, Robin Kirby, Colin Stutz, and images from the archives of TwoMorrows Publishing. Courtesy David Armstrong: 100. Joyce Dopeken/The New York Times/Laif TBC: 181. Courtesy Ivan Briggs: 49. *Captain America* No. 66, Edwin and Terry Murray Comic Book Collection, David M. Rubenstein Rare Book & Manuscript Library, Duke University: 60, 61. 1941 photo courtesy Jason Goodman: 36. Photo courtesy of Heritage Auctions, ha.com: 26, 28, 42, 44–45, 46, 47, 48, 74, 78, 80, 83, 103, 107, 112, 113, 119, 123, 126, 134, 135, 190. Courtesy Stan Lee/POW! Entertainment: 39. Courtesy David Mandel: 75. From the Collection of MetropolisComics.com: 50, 59. National Cartoonist Society: 77. Courtesy of the Patterson Family Trust: 94–95. © picture-alliance/AP/Schwarz: 138. Courtesy of the Richard Synchef Archive: 114. Courtesy Tellshiar: 96, 97, 137. Topps ® Krazy Little Comics used courtesy of The Topps Company, Inc.: 87. © MARVEL/Stan Lee Collection, American Heritage Center, University of Wyoming: 131.

EACH AND EVERY TASCHEN BOOK PLANTS A SEED!
TASCHEN is a carbon neutral publisher. Each year, we offset our annual carbon emissions with carbon credits at the Instituto Terra, a reforestation program in Minas Gerais, Brazil, founded by Lélia and Sebastião Salgado. To find out more about this ecological partnership, please check: *www.taschen.com/zerocarbon*
Inspiration: unlimited. Carbon footprint: zero.

To stay informed about TASCHEN and our upcoming titles, please subscribe to our free magazine at *www.taschen.com/magazine*, follow us on Twitter, Instagram, and Facebook, or e-mail your questions to *contact@taschen.com*.

Printed in Italy
ISBN 978-3-8365-6783-1